CU00674901

On a Faraway Day...

A New View of Genesis in Ancient Mesopotamia

Alan P. Dickin

On a Faraway Day...

A New View of Genesis in Ancient Mesopotamia

Alan P. Dickin

Copyright © 2002
All Rights Reserved

PUBLISHED BY:
BRENTWOOD CHRISTIAN PRESS
4000 BEALLWOOD AVENUE
COLUMBUS, GEORGIA 31904

On a faraway day, indeed on a faraway day,
On a faraway night, indeed on a faraway night,
In a faraway time, indeed in a faraway time...

School tablet, 2500 B.C.
Translation: R. D. Biggs

PREFACE

What was it like to be Abraham? Many people think of him as a nomadic tent-dweller who lived in the very remote past... if in fact he actually existed. But the present author argues that Abraham was not so different from many people living today. He was a member of a cosmopolitan society who broke away from an affluent lifestyle and became a refugee in another country... one man trying to obey his God amongst a mass of humanity with different religions. He lived about 4000 years ago, but he could look into a past that stretched back so far, some of its events must have seemed more like stories... a time when all peoples spoke one language... a great flood that destroyed all of the known world... and ultimately, a man and woman who had tasted immortality, only to have it slip from their grasp...

What was it like to be Adam? To many people this is an impossible question, since Adam is separated from us by events so cataclysmic that life was completely different... a man who experienced the perfection of God's revelation before the Fall. But the author believes that Adam *can* be comprehended by people living today. Anyone who has experienced a moment of sublime revelation, only to slip back into their human shortcomings, knows something of the experience of Adam...

But in order to understand Adam and Abraham better, we need to look at them in the context of the society in which they lived... ancient Mesopotamia. Hence, this book aims to achieve a new understanding of the book of Genesis in the context of ancient Mesopotamian history, where God first revealed himself to a man... *On a Faraway Day...*

ACKNOWLEDGEMENTS

The author is very grateful to friends and family who read earlier draft manuscripts of this work and made comments for its improvement. In particular to Malcolm Horsnell for a very careful reading which resulted in many technical improvements, and to Fred and Dorice Dickin for patient proofreading. Also, thanks to the staff at Brentwood Christian Press for their excellent layout of the text and figures.

The author has made every effort to give due credit to the originators of ideas and theories presented in this book. Any omissions or errors which come to light after printing will be posted on the web site of this book: 'onafarawayday.com'.

All scripture references in this book are from the New International Version of the Bible, copyright by the New York International Bible Society. The author also acknowledges numerous scholars for their original translations of other ancient sources, as cited in the list of references.

Finally, the author acknowledges Morning Star publications for use of an extract from *The Final Quest* by Rick Joyner (Morning Star Fellowship Church, PO Box 19409, Charlotte NC 28919-9409. Phone:1-800-542-0278, www.morningstarministries.org)

CONTENTS

CHAPTER 1

THE VIEW FROM HERE

What is the origin of the Universe? Who is God? Where did Mankind come from? These are questions that have always fascinated people, and never more than at the present day, as we enter the New Millennium. People have searched to the ends of the earth and translated ancient texts in strange languages in search of these truths, yet the most widely distributed book in the world, the Bible, claims to answer these questions in the book of Genesis. It speaks of the creation of the world, the first man, and his experience of God, but unfortunately no book in the world has been interpreted in so many different and conflicting ways.

1.1 The Problem

If the Bible is the inspired word of God, as Christians claim, why did God allow Genesis to be written in a way that could lead to such confusion? In order to answer this question we have to take our eyes off the problem and take a long view of history. The fact is that controversy over the meaning of Genesis began only 200 years ago when amateur scientists first started to notice geological evidence for the great antiquity of the earth. A Scottish physician, James Hutton (Fig. 1.1) summarised this evidence in a now-classic quote (Hutton, 1795):

No vestige of a beginning, no prospect of an end...

More recent geological investigations have now revealed some faint vestiges of the earth's beginning, but it is only in the past one hundred years that radioactive dating of rocks has been developed, and only in the past thirty years that these dating methods have attained high degrees of precision and accuracy. Similarly, it is only in the past one hundred years that the architecture and literature of ancient Mesopotamia have been unearthed and translated, providing an essential backdrop to the Genesis narrative. Indeed, it is only within the last thirty years or so that scholarly understanding of the world's oldest written languages has reached some degree of maturity.

Fig. 1.1
Portrait of James Hutton,
geological pioneer.

The fact that these advances in scientific and literary understanding are so recent should give us hope that the problem of correctly interpreting Genesis can be solved in the near future. However, before we can do this, we have to understand something of the history of the problem.

For the past century the interpretation of Genesis has been strongly polarised between two conflicting theologies that I will call Fundamentalism and Liberalism. Both of these viewpoints grew over a period of time, but were also given particular shape by a few prominent authors who laid out their doctrinal principles. We will now examine some of these principles.

1.2 Liberal Theology and the Documentary Hypothesis

Liberal theologians regard much of the Old Testament as 'story' rather than 'history'. Therefore, many of the characters in the Bible, particularly in Genesis, are not regarded as real people. For example, Alt (1966), argued that the patriarchs Abraham, Isaac and Jacob were not part of a single family but from unrelated tribes whose descendants merged over time and created a composite history. A recent commentator (Sauer, 1996) summarised this position as follows:

Today, the conventional wisdom- or at least the view of many mainstream scholars- is that the patriarchal stories do not have a setting in a particular archaeological period, that there is no patriarchal period as such.

This view of the non-historicity of Genesis was largely pioneered by Wellhausen (Fig. 1.2), who argued that major portions of the Old Testament were composed around 600 BC, during the exile of the Israelites in Babylon. In a classic book, Wellhausen (1883) suggested that the 'history' of Israel was composed during the Babylonian exile in order to provide a religious focus for the nation, to replace the temple of Jerusalem that had been destroyed by the Babylonians. Hence he argued that the history of the world and mankind in Genesis were projected backwards from the exile in order to justify the religious establishment at the time of writing.

Fig. 1.2
Portrait of Julius Wellhausen,
influential German theologian.

Wellhausen's 'Development Hypothesis' was largely founded on the earlier 'Documentary Hypothesis', which is the cornerstone of much scholarly interpretation of Genesis. This theory says that Genesis consists of two or more documents that were cut and pasted together by an editor without significantly changing the content of the original documents. The Documentary Hypothesis recognises these source documents on the basis of their use of two different Hebrew words for God, *Elohim* and *Yahweh*, translated in most English versions of the Bible as 'God' and 'LORD' respectively. However, two more sources were ultimately invoked, making a total of four: the Yahwist (J), Elohist (E), Deuteronomist (D), and Priestly (P). Hence the acronym 'JEDP' by which this model is commonly identified.

In some parts of Genesis the Documentary Hypothesis makes good sense: for example in the Creation Story of Chapter 1, Elohim is used thirty times and Yahweh not at all, so this section could be said to be Elohist in its origin (although it is actually called the 'Priestly' source). However, in other parts of Genesis, for example the Flood Story of Chapters 6 to 9, Elohim and Yahweh appear to be used more-or-less

9

interchangeably, and in intimate juxtaposition. This has led, under the Documentary Hypothesis, to the idea that the Flood Story was made from two separate documents minutely interleaved by the editor of Genesis.

This model can be tested by comparing the biblical Flood Story with ancient Mesopotamian flood stories. The remarkable parallels between these documents suggest a common source, but the biblical version, when considered as a single unit, has more parallels with the Mesopotamian versions than either of the two hypothetical text sources claimed by the Documentary Hypothesis (section 20.1). This suggests the Flood Story was derived from a Mesopotamian source as a single unit, and not from the two sources proposed by the Documentary Hypothesis.

Of course, the resemblances between the biblical and Mesopotamian Flood stories do not prove that Noah or the other biblical Patriarchs existed. However, such 'proof' may never be obtained, any more than the existence of God can be proved. The 17th century French philosopher, Descartes, attempted to prove the existence of God on a rational basis, but his contemporary, Pascal, called him *'Descartes, useless and uncertain'* (*Pensées*, # 887) because the certainty that Descartes claimed to give, based on rational argument, did not meet human need (Byrne, 1997, p. 78-87). Instead, Pascal argued that our reasoning should be based on the foundation of a belief in God. Although such belief is based on faith and personal experience rather than rational argument, it is nevertheless reasonable. A similar approach can be taken to the existence of the biblical Patriarchs by saying 'supposing that the Patriarchs did exist, what would this mean for our understanding of the Bible and our interpretation of ancient history?' If the resulting reconstruction works as a piece of history and as an explanation of religious experience, this supports its truthfulness.

1.3 Fundamentalism and Creationism

Fundamentalists believe in a literal interpretation of the whole Bible, and nowhere is the literal interpretation more hotly defended than the first chapter of Genesis, describing the story of creation in six days. This belief in a literal interpretation of the creation narrative has been labelled 'Creationism', and was laid out by Whitcomb and Morris (Fig. 1.3) in their classic book *'The Genesis Flood'* (Whitcomb and Morris, 1961)[1]. These authors insisted that since the Bible is the Written Word of God, Genesis Ch 1 must represent a scientifically accurate record of the creation of the whole universe in six days of 24 hours each. Similarly, they insisted that the Great Flood described in Genesis Ch 6 must have been of worldwide extent. But do Creationists really adhere to a strictly literal interpretation of the creation narrative? To test their approach, we must closely examine the creation narrative of Genesis Ch 1.

Fig. 1.3 Whitcomb and Morris, authors of the Creationist classic 'The Genesis Flood'.

According to Genesis 1:2, the earth was originally a watery chaos. After the creation of light on the First Day, God's creative words on the Second Day are described as follows[2] (Gen 1:6-8):

> God said "Let there be an expanse between the waters to separate water from water." So God made the expanse and separated the water under the expanse from the water above it. And it was so. God called the expanse "sky".

This text shows that the author of Genesis understood the sky as separating some waters 'below the sky' (forming the seas) from other waters located 'above the sky' (which give rise to rain). In between these two bodies of water, the 'expanse of the sky', in which the birds fly (Gen 1:20) was conceived of as the interior of a rigid dome (Seeley, 2001), resembling a planetarium (Fig. 1.4).

11

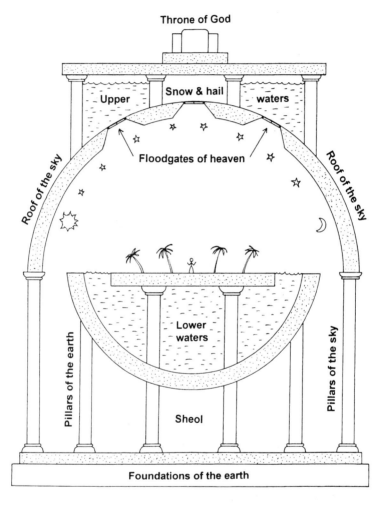

Fig. 1.4 A visualisation of the Heavens and the Earth, as described in Genesis, Job, Psalms and Isaiah.

Moving now to the Fifth Day, God's creative acts are described as follows (Gen 1:16-17):

> *God made two great lights- the greater light to govern the day and the lesser light to govern the night. He also made the stars. God set them in the expanse of the sky to give light on the earth...*

The language used in this text is quite precise; it is quite clear that God set the sun, moon and stars IN the expanse of the sky, and hence below the 'upper waters'. However, in *The Genesis Flood*, Whitcomb and Morris (1961) presented a very different interpretation of these verses, in which the sun, moon and stars were no longer *set in* the sky, but only their *light* appeared in the sky:

> *Mention is made in Genesis 1:7 of a division of the waters covering the earth at the time of creation, into two portions, separated by an expanse of atmosphere in which birds were to fly (Genesis 1:20) and in which the light from the sun, moon and stars was to be refracted and diffused to give light on the earth (Genesis 1:17).*

Why didn't Whitcomb and Morris accept the literal meaning of verse 1:17, that the sun, moon and stars were set *in* the sky? In other cases where the interpretation of Genesis is in doubt, they turn to other biblical texts for clarification. However, concerning the location of the stars *in* the sky, the Bible holds a consistent position. For example, in describing the manner of his second coming, Jesus (Mark 13:24-25) quotes Isaiah 13:10 and 34:4 as follows:

> *The sun will be darkened, and the moon will not give its light; the stars will fall from the sky, and the heavenly bodies will be shaken.*

The original text of Isaiah 34:4b gives more detail:

> *All the starry host will fall like withered leaves from the vine, like shrivelled figs from the fig-tree.*

This description of the stars falling from the sky makes it clear that Jesus is understanding Isaiah 34:4 and Genesis 1:17 to mean that the stars are literally objects *in* the sky, from where they can fall to earth. We should also note that the phrase 'all the starry host' (Isaiah 34:4b) rules out the possibility that the Bible is talking about a few meteor showers; it is referring to the constellations that we see above us on every clear night.

So the witness of the Bible should lead a Creationist to deny that the stars are distant suns in the depths of space, and to affirm that they are set *in* the sky. The only evidence against this view is observational scientific evidence. So we can see that Creationists do believe scientific evidence over and above the Bible when they feel compelled to by the strength of this scientific evidence, when a literal interpretation of the Bible would lead them to a position that is apparently untenable in the 21st century AD. Creationism then is actually a deception, because its proponents believe that they follow a strictly literal interpretation of Genesis, whereas in fact they follow an interpretation partially based on scientific evidence which denies the literal interpretation of Genesis.

God could have revealed the Creation from the perspective of 2000 AD, but this would have been meaningless to mankind 6000 years BC. So, of course God revealed his creation from the point of view that mankind could at least begin to understand at the time; standing on the ground and looking up at the vault of the heavens. As such, Genesis Chapter 1 is neither a literal account nor a non-literal account, but a 'cosmology of sight experience' (Flanders *et al.*, 1988), because it explains the origin of the heavens and the earth that ancient man could see and experience.

A study of history shows that God has allowed certain things to be said in the Bible that could easily be misinterpreted by legalists. For example, Psalm 104:5 states that *'He set the earth on its foundations; it can never be moved'*, a verse which caused the Roman Catholic Church to reject for hundreds of years the scientific arguments that the earth orbits the sun. Similarly, in the New Testament, Paul's admonition *'women should remain silent in the churches'* (1st Corinthians 14:34) has caused many Church denominations to prohibit for hundreds of years the speaking ministry of women. Most believers now understand that these verses must be interpreted in the context of the time when they were written, and that a legalistic interpretation is actually not in accord with God's will.

1.4 The search for a New Way

Despite the fact that Liberalism and Fundamentalism are totally opposed to one another, they have had a similar influence on how many people approach Genesis: both have tended to 'mythologise' Genesis and make it less accessible to the reader. Liberalism has done this by claiming that none of the events described in Genesis really happened. Therefore, it is claimed, the only thing we can really learn from Genesis is the mind-set of the Israelite authors, who lived around the time of the Babylonian exile, about 600 BC. Ironically, Fundamentalism has also mythologised Genesis by claiming that all of the events described are to be taken literally. Since a modern reader knows that the Earth floats in space, he can only accept a true literal reading of Genesis Ch 1 by 'disconnecting' his mind so that he keeps Genesis in one box and his everyday life in a different box. Many Creationists have attempted to rationalize this process by arguing that the Flood separated the history of the world into 'pre-Flood' and 'post-Flood' periods, when even physical laws were different. Hence, if we were to follow this approach, we could never understand the mind of Adam.

The objective of the present book is to de-mythologise Genesis by putting it back into its historical context. As the quest for spiritual enlightenment has grown, both in the Church and in the non-Christian world, the writer believes that God wants to help us gain a right understanding of Genesis that will allow us to rise above the one-dimensional tug-of-war between Liberalism and Fundamentalism. Therefore, the goal of this study is a fresh understanding of Genesis in the context of the archaeological, scientific and written evidence that we have about the dawn of human history.

However, we can only understand Genesis the way God intended when we realise that it is a spiritual as well as a physical book (e.g. Bloesch, 1978, p. 74). Thus, we read in the New Testament letter to the Hebrews (11:6) that:

> *Without faith it is impossible to please God, because anyone who comes to him must believe that he exists and that he rewards those who earnestly seek him.*

Therefore, we can express our quest to understand the origin of mankind in similar terms:

> *Without faith it is impossible to understand Genesis, because anyone who comes to it must believe that God exists, and that he reveals the truth to those who earnestly seek it.*

The present book is written in the hope that a belief in God, coupled with a careful examination of the biblical and archaeological evidence, can give the reader an impression of what it was like to receive God's first revelation to mankind: *'On a faraway day...'*

CHAPTER 2

THE CONTEXT OF REVELATION

2.1 Personal revelation

Most people know that the book of Genesis (*origins* in Greek) describes the story of Creation, the Garden of Eden, the Flood, the Tower of Babel, and the history of the Patriarchs, but its underlying message is harder to discern. This message can only be understood from the perspective of the whole Bible, which is concerned with a series of 'Covenants' or 'Agreements' between God and Man, which culminate in the New Covenant or 'New Testament'. In this context, Genesis is a description of a series of initiatives taken by God to reveal himself to mankind, each involving a personal encounter and an impartation of knowledge (Bloesch, 1994, p. 49). It runs counter to the humanistic view that sees Man refining his concept of God over time, or even inventing gods for himself over time.

The truth is that, far from refining his concept of God, mankind is continually confusing the revelation that God has already given. So, in the Old Testament, we see God repeatedly calling out a man (or occasionally a woman) from his existing situation, giving him a new revelation, and making a new covenant with him, only to have that revelation later compromised and in need of further renewal.

Because biblical revelation always begins with individuals, it follows that there must have been an individual who received God's first supernatural revelation. According to his descendants who wrote the Bible, this first individual was simply 'the man', who we refer to as 'Adam'. Therefore, it will be one of the aims of this book to persuade the reader that the biblical Patriarchs, including Adam, were all real people, who lived in real human cultures. If the readers find this hard to believe, they will need to temporarily suspend their disbelief while the author tries to make his case.

When the Bible describes God's revelation to mankind, this revelation always has a historical context. In the case of the birth of Jesus, this context is described in the Gospels: Jesus was born in Bethlehem of Judah at the time of the census of Caesar Augustus, during the governorship of Quirinius and the reign of King Herod, and his birth was marked by the appearance of a new 'star' in the sky (Luke 2:1-2; Matthew 2:1-2). Unfortunately, despite all of these markers, there is uncertainty as to the precise date of Jesus' birth relative to our modern calendar, which was set up by monks several hundred years later. However, this uncertainty is caused by an incomplete understanding of the different viewpoints of the two Gospel writers (e.g. Smith, 2000), and not by a lack of contextual references in their accounts.

God's revelations to Adam and Abram[3] are also recorded in their spatial and temporal context in Genesis. However, since these revelations occurred thousands of years before Jesus' birth, it should not surprise us that there is uncertainty in the interpretation of the contextual information.

2.2 The geographical context

In many ways, the land between the Tigris and Euphrates rivers is the cradle of human civilisation. In Greek, the expression *'land between the rivers'* gives us the word Mesopotamia, the most accurate geographical description of this region, which lies within present-day Iraq (Fig. 2.1). Similarly, from the perspective of Israel, Mesopotamia is referred to as the 'Land beyond the River' (Joshua 24:3), meaning the region beyond the Euphrates.

Genesis provides strong evidence that God's revelations to both Adam and Abram took place in Mesopotamia. In addition there is good evidence for a Mesopotamian context for God's covenant with Noah, based on the description of the settling of Mesopotamia immediately after the Flood (Gen 10:32 and 11:2). This biblical evidence for a Mesopotamian context is also supported by the remarkable similarities between the biblical and Mesopotamian stories of the Flood, which will be examined in detail at a later point. In the meantime, we will briefly review what Genesis has to say about the geographical context in which its account is set.

This context begins with the location of the Garden of Eden. Many people probably don't believe there ever was a physical 'Garden of Eden'. However, the reader will need to agree that man's first encounter with God must have occurred in a physical place. This place is described as follows (Gen 2:8):

Fig. 2.1 Map of the Middle East showing the location of Mesopotamia and its rivers relative to modern political boundaries.

Now the LORD God planted a garden in the east, in Eden; and there he put the man he had formed.

The location of this garden can be estimated from the rivers that watered it, as follows (Gen 2:10):

A river watering the garden flowed from Eden, and from there it divided; it had four headstreams.

These headstreams are named as the Pishon, Gihon, Tigris and Euphrates. At the present day, the latter two rivers rise in fairly close proximity in Eastern Turkey, run down either side of the Mesopotamian plain, and join at Qurna, some 170 km NW of the head of the Persian

18

Gulf (Fig 2.1). Some people have argued that Eden is located near the source of these rivers in Turkey. However, since they do not join at this point, this location does not fit the text. Therefore, the most probable location of Eden is where the rivers join at the southeast end of the Mesopotamian plain. This is consistent with the simplest derivation of the word Eden, from the ancient Sumerian word *edin* meaning 'plain'. However, we cannot precisely locate the ancient point of confluence between the rivers because sea-level rose until about 3000 BC and flooded the earlier course of the rivers (see section 8.3).

We should not assume that the writer is speaking of the direction of river flow when he says '*from there it divided*'. Instead, we should simply accept that the river flowed through the plain (Eden) and had four head-streams. Since no permanent rivers drain the Arabian desert, the two unknown head-streams Pishon and Gihon are generally assumed to flow from the mountains of Iran. An alternative proposed by Sauer (1996) is that these rivers drained the Arabian peninsular during a wetter climatic period before 3500 BC. However, the names of these rivers seem, in Hebrew, to approximate to the descriptive names 'Leaper' and 'Gusher', suggesting to several authors (e.g. Clifford, 1972, p. 101) that these are symbolic rather than real names. In this case they would have been included with the Tigris and Euphrates to make a total of four rivers. Four was the symbol of completeness in the ancient world, as indicated by the expression 'the four corners of the earth'.

Mid-way between the time of Adam and Abram, Genesis 11:2 describes the settling of the plain of Shinar (Mesopotamia) after Noah's Flood. Genesis 10:2 also names three famous cities of the plain amongst the first centres of Nimrod's kingdom: Babylon, Erech (called Uruk by its ancient inhabitants) and Akkad. All that remains of these once-great cities are mounds of decayed bricks set in a desert landscape. For example, Fig. 2.2 shows the ruined ziggurat of Uruk set against a totally flat horizon. Both Babylon and Uruk have been ruined since ancient times, and the location of Akkad has been wiped completely off the map, believed to be a judgement of God against the sinfulness of mankind.

The Mesopotamian episode of biblical history ends in another well-known city of the ancient world, 'Ur of the Chaldeans', from which Abram's departure is described in Genesis 11:31. The reference to the Chaldeans must be a later editorial comment, since the Chaldeans were not known until after 1000 BC. However, the significance of the reference to the Chaldeans is that they were a people from the south of

Fig. 2.2 The ruined ziggurat of Uruk (biblical Erech) as it appears today.

Mesopotamia, where the ancient city of Ur was one of the principal centres of Mesopotamian civilisation throughout the Third Millennium[4].

However, the city of Ur in southern Mesopotamia is not the only contender for identification as the biblical Ur. For example, Gordon (1958, 1987) objected to this identification on the grounds that the city of Ur is located to the west of the Euphrates, and hence not 'beyond the River' (Joshua 24:3). Instead, he proposed that the town of Urfa, only 30 km from Haran in SE Turkey, should be identified as biblical Ur (Fig. 2.3).

It is true that local tradition claims Urfa to be the site of Abram's birth. However, it is also claimed that sacred carp in a local pool date back to a miraculous intervention by God when Abram was captured by bandits and about to be burned alive (BAR Editorial, 2000, p. 19). Such traditions should not be believed. In contrast, Genesis 11:31 describes Abram's migration from Ur to Haran as follows:

> *Terah took his son Abram, his grandson Lot son of Haran, and his daughter-in-law Sarai, the wife of his son Abram, and together they set out from Ur of the Chaldeans to go to Canaan. But when they came to Haran, they settled there.*

This account shows that Urfa could not possibly be Abram's birthplace, since it would be ridiculous to speak of interrupting the migration to Canaan by settling in Haran if this was only 30 km from the starting point (Woolley, 1936, p. 60). On the other hand, Ur and Haran, despite being 900 km apart, were closely linked by the great trade route up the Euphrates river, and also shared a common veneration for the moon god. Therefore, it seems likely that Terah stopped in Haran because of his attachment to Mesopotamian culture and religion. Such an attachment is consistent with the reference in Joshua 24:2 that Terah 'lived beyond the River and worshipped other gods'.

Regarding the objection that Ur is not beyond the River, this is a misleading argument since Ur, like many of the other great cities of Mesopotamia, was built *on* the banks of the River Euphrates. Long after Abram's time the river changed its course to the east of the city, but even now the city cannot be approached from the west, since this is occupied by the Arabian desert. Therefore, Ur of the Chaldeans remains 'Beyond the River' in spirit even if not in geography. Hence, we can confidently conclude that Abram grew up in southern Mesopotamia and inherited its culture and traditions.

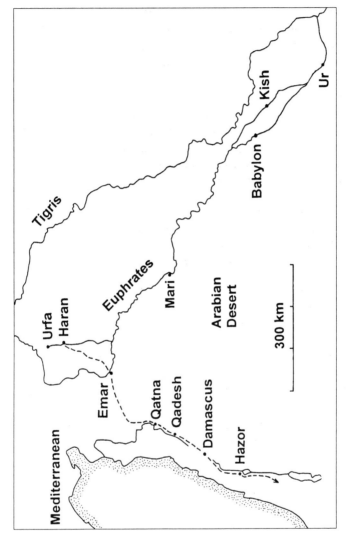

Fig. 2.3 Map of Mesopotamia to show the trade route up the Euphrates River from Ur to Haran, and the over-land trade route from Haran to Canaan.

22

2.3 The genealogical context

Between God's revelations to Adam and Abram, representing the beginning and end of the Mesopotamian period of Genesis, the Bible provides a chronological framework based on the genealogies of the Patriarchs. If these genealogies were intended to be chronologically accurate then we could use them to build up a continuous record of years. However, we must recognise that, by their very nature, genealogies are normally assembled after a long period of time has elapsed. During this period of time the essential relationships of a genealogy may be preserved, but details are often lost (e.g. Johnson, 1969; Wilson, 1977).

The chronology of Bishop Ussher, placing the creation at 4004 BC, was an attempt to calculate an absolute date for Creation based on the ages of the Patriarchs in the biblical genealogies. These imply a period of 1656 years from Adam's creation until the Flood, and 367 years between the Flood and Abram's departure from Haran (e.g. Wenham, 1987, p. 131, 250). However, there are many evidences that the genealogies of Genesis Ch 4-5 and 10-11 were meant to be schematic, rather than to record the exact passage of time, as even Fundamentalists have agreed. For example, Whitcomb and Morris (1970, appendix 2) commented on the genealogy of Shem as follows:

> *If the strict-chronology interpretation of Genesis 11 is correct, all the postdiluvian patriarchs, including Noah, would still have been living when Abram was fifty years old; three of those who were born before the earth was divided (Shem, Shelah, and Eber) would have actually outlived Abram; and Eber, the father of Peleg, not only would have outlived Abram, but would have lived for two years after Jacob arrived in Mesopotamia to work for Laban! On the face of it, such a situation would seem astonishing, if not almost incredible.* (their punctuation)

One reason why biblical genealogies cannot give simple chronological information is 'generational skipping'. For example, there are several examples in the Bible where father-son relationships are implied, but where we know from other biblical texts that a more distant ancestor-descendant relationship actually existed. Often, the reason for this process of generational skipping is to make a theologically important point.

23

An example of this process comes from the royal line of descent of the kings of Judah. This line of descent, as recorded in 2nd Kings Ch 8-15 and 2nd Chronicles Ch 21-27, is shown in the first column of Table 2.1. But in the first chapter of his gospel, Matthew gives a 'shortened' genealogy in which Joram (ie Jehoram) is said to be the father of Uzziah, and Josiah the father of Jeconiah (second column in Table 2.1). These omissions might seem inconsequential, but Matthew uses his shortened genealogy to make a special point (Matt 1:17):

Thus there were fourteen generations in all from Abraham to David, fourteen from David to the exile to Babylon, and fourteen from the exile to the Christ.

Table 2.1 Alternative genealogies of the Kings of Judah

2nd Kings 2nd Chronicles		Matt Ch 1
David		David
Solomon	1	Solomon
Rehoboam	2	Rehoboam
Abijah	3	Abijah
Asa	4	Asa
Jehoshaphat	5	Jehoshaphat
Jehoram	6	Joram (=Jehoram)
Ahaziah			
Joash			
Amaziah			
Uzziah	7	Uzziah
Jotham	8	Jotham
Ahaz	9	Ahaz
Hezekiah	10	Hezekiah
Manasseh	11	Manasseh
Amon	12	Amon
Josiah	13	Josiah
Jehoiakim			
Jehoiachin	14	Jeconiah (=Jehoachin)

By quoting the numbers of generations in each segment of the genealogy, Matthew makes it clear that he takes Jehoram literally as the father of Uzziah, rather than his great-great-grandfather, and Josiah as literally the father of Jeconiah rather than his grandfather. So how does he justify this interpretation against the evidence from Kings and Chronicles? It seems impossible that Matthew did not know that he was 'mis-quoting' the genealogy, so we must infer that he felt entitled to do so in order to make his genealogy fit the 2 x 7 (twice perfect) numerical pattern, and thus to demonstrate the divine plan behind Jesus' ancestral lineage. This practice might seems strange to the modern scientific mind but we must accept it as evidence of how genealogies were treated by biblical authors. In fact, we should assume that this text (Matthew 1:17) is in the Bible partly to illuminate the correct treatment of biblical genealogies as theological rather than chronological statements.

A second example of the schematic nature of biblical genealogies comes directly from the list of Shem's descendants (Genesis Ch 11). In this case the genealogy given in Luke Ch 3 agrees with the Greek 'Septuagint' translation of Genesis Ch 11. This is the genealogy shown in column 2 of Table 2.2. However, the Hebrew ('Masoretic') text of Genesis omits Cainan, whose name is shown in brackets in Table 2.2. The important point here is that the inclusion of Cainan makes the list of Shem's descendants match the list of Adam's descendants, with a linear genealogy of ten generations leading to a triple branch (Table 2.2). The Masoretic text probably represents the original form of the genealogy, which would also have ten generations if Noah was included at its head, although this would involve an overlap of two generations between columns 1 and 2. The Septuagint translation, which is quoted in Luke 3:36, can be regarded as an 'improved version' that brings perfect symmetry to these two genealogies by 'generational insertion'.

Table 2.2 Genealogies of the Patriarchs

Ch 5:3-32	Ch 11:10-26
Adam	Shem
Seth	Arphaxad
Enosh	(Cainan)
Kenan	Shelah
Mahalalel	Eber
Jared	Peleg
Enoch	Reu
Methuselah	Serug
Lamech	Nahor
Noah	Terah
Shem, Ham, Japheth	Abram, Nahor, Haran

These examples do not invalidate the biblical genealogies or other genealogies as historical documents, but they show that ancient genealogies are not the kind of historical documents that modern observers are very familiar with. They were not intended to be used simplistically to determine chronologies, but were intended to demonstrate relationships and express connections between those patriarchs who were the recipients of God's special revelations (Adam, Noah and Abram). Therefore, if we want to construct scientific chronologies we must turn to other sources of evidence, which may be other historical documents, or scientific dating methods. These other lines of evidence will be discussed below.

2.4 The significance of the Flood

If Adam and Abram mark the beginning and the end of the Mesopotamian period of Genesis then the Great Flood represents its crucial turning point, a turning point emphasised by the expressions *'Before the Flood'* and *'After the Flood'* used in both biblical and Mesopotamian literature. The Flood, even more than the Creation itself, also represents the critical test of our approach to the interpretation of Genesis. For this reason, the attempt to place the Flood in its historical context is one of the main aims of this book, and a subject to which we must repeatedly return as we examine different facets of the problem.

Belief in a Universal (worldwide) Flood is a central tenet of the Fundamentalist interpretation of Genesis, and the evidence for this belief must be carefully examined and tested. When these views are combined with a belief that all of creation occurred in six literal days they lead to the viewpoint which has been called 'Flood Geology'. This involves the belief that Noah's flood covered the whole globe and deposited all the fossil-bearing sedimentary rocks. In this view, fossils represent the bodies of animals that were alive before the Flood and whose remains were sorted out by hydrodynamic processes so that the smallest creatures are represented in the lower strata, while progressively more 'advanced' creatures are preserved in successively higher layers. This view was expounded in detail in the classic book *'The Genesis Flood'* by Whitcomb and Morris (1961). While much has been published since that time by organisations such as the Creation Research Centre, *The Genesis Flood* remains as an authoritative source regarding the Flood Geology model.

One of the fundamental assumptions of Whitcomb and Morris was a break in knowledge and understanding between the recent past, representing the history of mankind, and the geological past, which represents the history of the earth. To look at this in another way, they argued that there was a philosophical barrier between the repeatable experiments that scientists could perform in a laboratory, and the non-repeatable history of the Earth.

Several authors, including Whitcomb and Morris (e.g. preface to the 6th edition, p. 197) have tried to use this non-repeatability of history to argue that the study of Earth History is somehow unscientific, and must therefore be based on a kind of atheist 'faith'. If we take this argument to its logical conclusion then we can say that all our perceptions are based on faith: "I think I see the sun in the sky, but it could be a figment of my imagination". Kantian philosophers love to tie themselves in knots with this kind of argument, but the Bible knows nothing of philosophical double-talk; instead it talks of destroying the wisdom of the wise (1st Cor 1:19). Therefore, I will argue that a common sense approach to historical observations can bridge the gap between the present and the past, giving us a meaningful context within which to interpret the biblical stories of Creation and Flood.

CHAPTER 3

THE RADIOCARBON FLOOD

A common sense approach to Earth History is now possible in a way that was impossible 40 years ago when *The Genesis Flood* was written. In those days of the late 1950s and early 1960s, radioactive dating was in its infancy. In particular, there was a serious 'dating gap' between the historical period (back to 3000 BC) and the much more distant Geological Past. However, this situation has changed over the past 40 years with the huge flood of radiocarbon (C-14) dates that have become available. In order for the reader to understand the reliability of this method, it is necessary to give a brief explanation of how it works. A more detailed explanation is given in my specialist book on isotope dating (Dickin, 1995).

Carbon-14 is a natural radioactive isotope which is formed in small quantities in the earth's atmosphere when cosmic rays from distant stars hit air molecules. The C-14 atoms are incorporated into atmospheric carbon dioxide (CO_2), which is absorbed by plants during photosynthesis. While plants are alive, they all contain the same proportion of radioactive to normal carbon as the atmosphere. However, when a plant dies, it stops absorbing fresh atmospheric carbon dioxide, and the small amount of C-14 in its tissues gradually decays away.

Radioactive decay occurs in the nucleus of the atom, and each atom of the radioactive isotope has an equal probability of decaying. We cannot predict when each individual atom will decay, but in a large sample of atoms we can be certain that half of them will decay within a fixed period of time that we call the half-life. After another half-life, half of the remaining atoms decay, and so on as the radioactive atoms gradually disappear (Fig. 3.1).

Since we know the C-14 half-life (5730 yrs), we can use C-14 to date dead plant material, such as wood, paper and fabric, simply by measuring the proportion of radioactive C-14 relative to the total

28

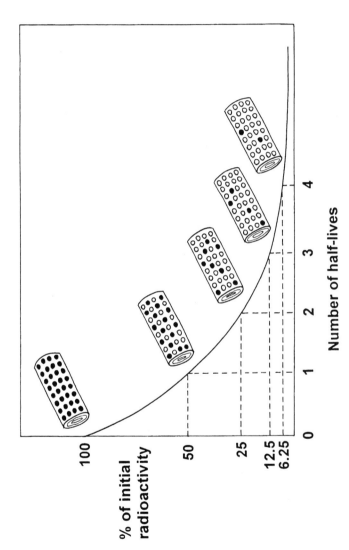

Fig. 3.1 Schematic illustration of the radioactive decay of C-14 atoms in a sample of wood.

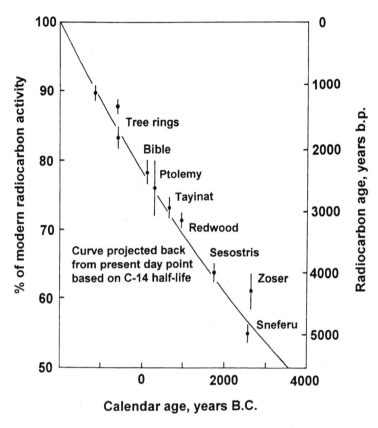

Fig. 3.2 Agreement between a theoretical curve of radiocarbon decay and radiocarbon dates on artifacts of known age. Vertical bars represent estimated analytical errors. Modified after Libby (1952).

amount of carbon in a sample. The way in which the C-14 content decays with time is shown in Fig. 3.2, which shows an early test of radiocarbon ages on artifacts of known historical age. The maximum range of the method is about 60,000 yrs, after which the radiocarbon has effectively disappeared. However, it is most reliable below 30,000 yrs.

Radiocarbon is the most important radioactive dating method in archaeology for several reasons. Its dating range is ideally suited to material a few thousand years old; it is suitable for dating a variety of artifacts; and perhaps most importantly, it has been very accurately tested and calibrated against the method of tree ring dating called 'dendrochronology'.

3.1 Dendrochronology

In most species of tree growing in mid latitudes the changing seasons of the year give rise to very reliable annual growth rings. By counting these growth rings we can tell the age of a tree with great certainty. Although every year gives rise to a growth ring, they are not all of the same width. In some years the amount of sunshine and rain produces a good growing year with a wider ring, whereas other years with bad weather produce narrow rings. If we take a group of trees growing fairly close together, which have experienced the same weather conditions, they will show the same patterns of wide and narrow rings in successive years.

Amongst a group of living trees, we can obviously tell the age of each tree by counting back the rings from the bark layer on the outside. However, using the varying width of annual rings it is also possible to date a piece of dead timber by comparing the banding signature with living trees, provided the dead timber has an overlapping age range with the living trees (Fig 3.3). The match between the two sections can then be independently tested by measuring the *relative* radiocarbon ages of a series of rings in the two samples. Irrespective of any uncertainty in the *absolute* radiocarbon ages of the specimens, an agreement between the relative radiocarbon signatures of the two specimens (within the limits of experimental uncertainty of the measurements) is a conclusive confirmation of the match-up of growth rings (Fig. 3.3).

The oldest living trees are from the species called Bristlecone Pine (*Pinus longaeva*), a stunted conifer which grows in the High Sierra of California. The oldest individual is a staggering 4800 years old, but several other individuals have ages above 4000 years. Because of the

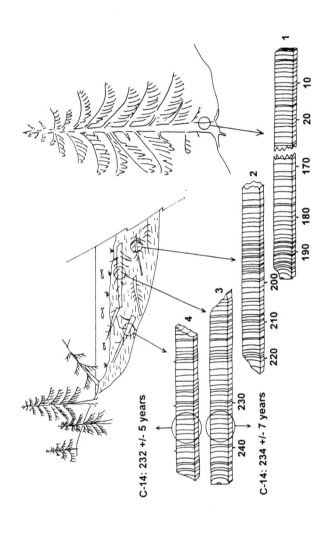

Fig. 3.3 Use of growth ring signatures to construct a dendrochronological series from a living tree and preserved older timber from a bog. The match between logs 3 and 4 is confirmed by the agreement of radiocarbon ages (within limits of experimental uncertainty).

great age of these trees we can get an excellent match-up between the banding signatures of living trees and of dead logs, allowing us to construct an overlapping series of ring sequences which stretches back thousands of years. To use this method in practice there must be conditions which allow the preservation of dead logs for thousands of years. In the case of the Bristlecone Pine, preservation of dead wood can occur on the ground in the near-desert conditions of growth. The dendrochronological time-scale that results from this work can be used to calibrate radiocarbon dates going back thousands of years. Before this calibration is applied, the raw data from a radiocarbon analysis yield what is called a 'convention age'. This is reported in years before the present (b.p.) and cannot be used for archaeological dating. However, after the dendrochronology calibration is applied the result is a true historical age which is usually quoted in years AD or BC.

Other types of tree from temperate latitudes around the world have also been used to set up calibration time-scales to provide independent testing of the Bristlecone Pine calibration. For example, the long-lived European Oak is very useful for calibration because it forms fairly large trees whose dead wood often falls into bogs where the lack of oxygen prevents decay. For most types of tree, sets of five or ten rings are usually combined together to make a sample large enough for radiocarbon analysis; however, the immense size of the Giant Redwood allows radiocarbon dates to be measured on individual rings from this tree.

In order to prepare a tree ring sample for dating it goes though a very rigorous chemical cleaning procedure to make sure that only wood cellulose deposited during the original growing season of the ring is dated for radiocarbon. The method has been verified by many different laboratories using different species of tree on different continents and now comprises an extremely reliable continuous chronology reaching back to 9700 years BC (Hughen *et al.*, 1998). This chronology is the most reliable dating tool ever invented. It is as reliable as the theory that the earth orbits the sun.

3.2 Coral chronology

The reliability of the radiocarbon dating method, back to 9700 BC, rests on calibration by dendrochronology, as described above. This calibration range covers the whole of the so-called Holocene period, the period of man's rise to modern civilisation. Unfortunately, dendrochronology has not yet reached further back into the past, due to the effects of the last ice age, which inhibited tree growth at mid latitudes. Until a few years ago, this caused a 'dating gap' between the radiocarbon method and the isotopic methods used for dating older rocks. However, this dating gap has now been eliminated by the development of the uranium-thorium (U-Th) method for dating corals.

The uranium-thorium method relies on the radioactive isotopes in a chain of decay reactions running from uranium to lead (Pb). The parent of this chain, U-238, is a very long-lived isotope, but the species which are intermediate between uranium and lead have much shorter half-lives. The U-Th method relies on the decay of one of these intermediate isotopes (U-234) to another (Th-230). For a more detailed description of the method, see Dickin (1995).

Because coral reefs rely on photosynthetic algae for their main supply of energy, they show annual growth bands similar to trees. Hence, it has been possible to test the U-Th dating method back to 1000 years by dating annual growth bands in living corals (Figure 3.4). It has also been tested back to 9000 years BC by analysing the same coral samples by uranium-thorium and radiocarbon. By showing that these different dating methods yield ages consistent with each other and with dendrochronology, we provide powerful evidence for the constancy of radioactive half-lives through Earth History. Apart from this experimental evidence, there is another very good reason for believing that radioactive half-lives are constant. This is because radioactivity is a fundamental property of atomic nuclei, controlled by the laws of nuclear physics. There is no evidence that these fundamental laws have changed since the origin of the Universe.

3.3 Banded sediments

Some sediments can show annual bands analogous to tree rings or coral bands. These bands are called varves, and are usually caused by a change in the type of minerals being deposited at different times of the year. Sediment varves are not as reproducible as tree rings. For example, if sediment from the bottom is stirred up by strong winds and then redeposited, it may be possible for more than one varve layer to be deposited in a year. Hence, in the past the method has gotten a reputation for unreliability as an absolute dating method. However, the solution to the problem of lower reliability (relative to tree rings) is the calibration of a complete section by radiocarbon dating. Two excellent examples of varved sediment cores have recently been verified by radiocarbon calibration, and therefore merit examination as records of past sediment deposition. The results will be relevant to the question of the age and extent of the biblical Flood.

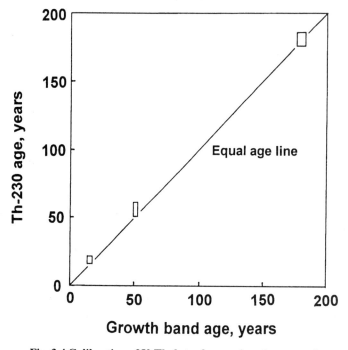

Fig. 3.4 Calibration of U-Th dates for coral against growth bands, showing a one-to-one correlation. (After Edwards et al., 1988).

The first example comes from Lake Suigetsu, near the coast in Central Japan (Kitagawa and van der Plicht, 1998). This is a small freshwater lake 3 km across with a water depth of 34m, but it contains a 75m-deep thickness of sediment at its bottom. The sediments show annual varves about 1mm thick, formed by variation from a winter season of dark clay deposition to a spring season of white diatom deposition (diatoms are algae with a skeleton made of silica). The sediments were cored, and the most clearly banded section from 10 m to 30m depth showed 29,100 varves. From within this section, 250 samples of wind-blown plant debris and insect wings were dated by radiocarbon, allowing this section to be anchored to the tree ring calibration curve. The radiocarbon results were in excellent agreement with the counting of varve layers, demonstrating that regular annual sediment deposition was occurring from 7000 to 36,000 BC.

The second example of a calibrated varve section is formed by marine sediments in the Cariaco basin of the Caribbean sea (Hughen *et al.*, 1998). The dated points in this sediment core showed exceptionally good agreement with the tree ring calibration curve and with dated coral samples in the range from 7000 to 12,000 BC (Fig. 3.5).

3.4 Significance for the age and extent of the Flood

Taken together, the evidence cited above shows conclusively that a flood of global extent did not occur in the recent past. Back to 7000 BC there is a continuous record of Bristlecone pine logs lying on the ground in the Sierra Nevada mountains that has obviously not been disturbed by a global flood. Furthermore there are numerous lakes whose sediment records can be traced back to this period based on the counting of annual varves. For example, Lake Van, near the sources of the Tigris and Euphrates in southeast Turkey, has a continuous record of annual varves reaching back from the present day to 13,000 BC (section 8.1). Beyond this range, the Lake Suigetsu calibrated varve record extends the period of undisturbed sediment deposition back to 36,000 BC. Hence, it must be concluded that the observational evidence rules out the possibility of a global flood within the past 38,000 years. On the other hand, if we push the date of Noah's flood back beyond 36,000 BC then we do such violence to the interpretation of Genesis that it is absurd. Therefore, we must conclude that there was no global flood, and that interpretations of Genesis which call for such a flood are misguided. This raises the question of what the Genesis account of the Flood does mean, which we will now examine.

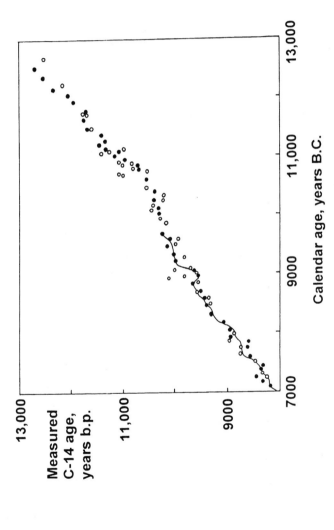

Fig. 3.5 Calibration points for the Cariaco basin varve section (•), showing excellent agreement with the dendrochronology calibration line (solid line) and U-Th dates on corals (o). Modified after Hughen et al. (1998).

CHAPTER 4

THE BIBLICAL FLOOD

4.1 The Flood as a chiasmus

The story of Noah's Flood in Genesis Ch 6 - 8 is a beautifully crafted narrative that has a symmetrical structure. Symmetrical or *'chiastic'* narratives are used widely in the Bible to give stories a memorable structure for oral recitation and to emphasise a central turning point in the story, usually marking the intervention of God in the situation. The story of the Flood lends itself very naturally to the construction of a chiasmus because of the rise and fall of the floodwaters; however, several commentators have suggested that the inherently symmetrical structure of the central story was enhanced by emphasising the symmetry of other events that happened immediately before and after the flood. In particular, Wenham (1978; 1987) emphasised the symmetrical structure of the days of the flood mentioned in the narrative:

  7 days of waiting for the flood (7:4)
    7 days of waiting for the flood (7:10)
      40 days of the flood increasing (7:17)
        150 days of the water flooding (7:24)
          God remembered Noah (8:1)
        150 days of the water going down (8:3)
      40 days of Noah waiting (8:6)
    7 more days waiting (8:10)
  7 more days waiting (8:12)

Many scholars have attributed the repetition of some of the events surrounding the Flood, and apparent contradictions over its duration, to the combination of more than one source document to make the Flood Story in Genesis. Thus, according to the Documentary Hypothesis, a Yahwist source (J) and a Priestly source (P) have been interleaved to make the complete Genesis account (Fig. 4.1).

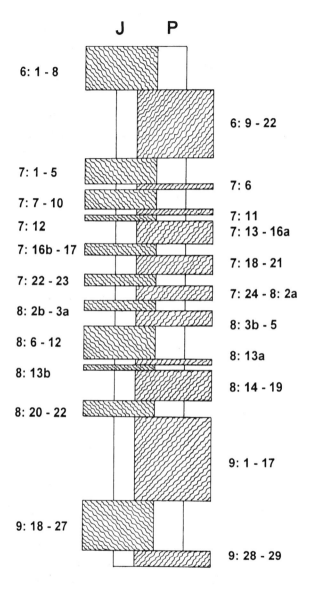

J P

6: 1 - 8

6: 9 - 22

7: 1 - 5

7: 6

7: 7 - 10

7: 11

7: 12

7: 13 - 16a

7: 16b - 17

7: 18 - 21

7: 22 - 23

7: 24 - 8: 2a

8: 2b - 3a

8: 3b - 5

8: 6 - 12

8: 13a

8: 13b

8: 14 - 19

8: 20 - 22

9: 1 - 17

9: 18 - 27

9: 28 - 29

Fig. 4.1 Application of the Documentary Hypothesis to the Flood
Story, showing proposed interleaving of the sources J and P.
After Blenkinsopp (1985).

However, Wenham argued that numbers describing the duration of the Flood had been utilised to create perfect symmetry for the chiasmus, even though the actual events described were not exactly symmetrical. Therefore, the apparent inconsistencies and repetitions identified by scholars are actually part of the artistry of a single account. For example, there were only seven days of waiting for the flood, but they are described in prospect (7:4) and in retrospect (7:10), thus artificially creating two sets of seven days. Similarly, at the end of the flood there are two periods of seven days mentioned, but a total of three weeks appears to have elapsed between four incidents when a bird was sent out:

8:7	Raven sent out
8:8	Dove sent out and returns
8:10	Dove sent out after 'seven more days'
8:12	Dove sent out again after 'seven more days'

The second time that the dove was sent out (Gen 8:10) was after *'seven more days'*. This implies that the first time the dove was sent out was also after seven days, but this period is only indirectly implied. By this device, three 7-day periods are indicated, but only two are actually described, thus preserving the symmetry of the narrative. This symmetrical structure of days can also be compared with a time-line based on days and months of the year:

17th day, 2nd month (year 600):	Flood begins
17th day, 7th month:	Ark rests on mountains of Ararat
1st day, 10th month:	Tops of mountains visible
1st day, 1st month (year 601):	Water had dried up
27th day, 2nd month:	Earth completely dry

The first two dates make it plain that the flood lasted a total of 5 months (=150 days) from its beginning until the Ark grounded. This period clearly overlaps with the 40 day period in which the Flood was increasing on the earth. However, the matching 40 day period before Noah sent out the raven is not clearly related to any other event. Because it appears to conflict with the 150 day duration of the Flood, it is assigned to a separate source by the Documentary Hypothesis. However, it was more likely inserted by the writer of the rest of the account to preserve the symmetry of the narrative.

The conclusion that one must draw from these observations is that the Flood Story is a very carefully crafted piece of writing. It has an elegant chiastic structure, yet in the construction of the chiasmus the story of events was not so distorted that it cannot be recovered from the narrative. These features show that the Flood Story as we have it is a single coherent narrative. If it had been constructed from more than one earlier source (as maintained in the Documentary Hypothesis) then these sources would need to have been significantly edited to produce the finely polished work in the Bible. This possibility is rendered very unlikely by a comparison between the biblical Flood Story and Mesopotamian parallels, to be undertaken later (section 20.3). In the meantime, we will examine the evidence that the biblical account provides for the nature of the Flood as a historical event.

4.2 The rise of the Flood

Genesis makes some crucial statements about the extent of the floodwaters and their source. The way in which we interpret these statements will not only influence our view of the Flood itself, but also our interpretation of Genesis as a whole. In Genesis 7:11 and 17-20, the sources of the waters and their rise on the earth are described as follows. Following many other commentators (e.g. Whitcomb and Morris, 1961), the reading in the footnote is taken for verse 20:

In the six hundredth year of Noah's life, on the seventeenth day of the second month- on that day all the springs of the great deep burst forth, and the floodgates of the heavens were opened.

For forty days the flood kept coming on the earth, and as the waters increased they lifted the ark high above the earth. The waters rose and increased greatly on the earth, and the ark floated on the surface of the water. They rose greatly on the earth and all the high mountains under the entire heavens were covered. The waters rose more than 15 cubits (7m), and the mountains were covered.

In their book *The Genesis Flood*, Whitcomb and Morris regarded the description of the flooding of the mountains in Gen 7:19-20 as a literal account, and hence as definitive evidence for a Global Flood (Whitcomb and Morris, 1961, p. 1-2). They also regarded the bursting of the *'springs of the great deep'* (Gen 7:11) as a literal release of vast quantities of water from immense subterranean reservoirs (Whitcomb and Morris, 1961, p. 122). However, they regarded the opening of the *'floodgates of heaven'* (Gen 7:11) as a metaphorical description of the source of the flood rains.

Because Whitcomb and Morris interpreted the first two statements literally, but the 'floodgates of heaven' non-literally, it is crucial to examine the latter case to see if their interpretation is consistent. Doubtless their metaphorical interpretation of the Floodgates was based on the well-known biblical text in Malachi 3:10, where God promises blessings if his people will bring their tithes and offerings to the temple storehouse:

> *"Bring the whole tithe into the storehouse, that there may be food in my house. Test me in this," says the LORD Almighty, "and see if I will not throw open the floodgates of heaven and pour out so much blessing that you will not have room enough for it."*

In this text the opening of the Floodgates is clearly used as a metaphor for the release of blessing, which has led to the popular conception that the Floodgates were a purely metaphorical concept in ancient times. However, in the metaphor, the objects released are a rain of *blessings* rather than a rain of *water*, so it is the *rain* that is metaphorical, not the Floodgates. By focussing on the role of the Floodgates to withhold or release a rain of blessing, this text is strengthening rather than weakening the tangible nature of the floodgates in the Genesis account.

The ancient view of the tangible nature of the Floodgates is confirmed by other biblical texts which show that the writers conceived of the sky as a rigid dome holding back the 'upper waters' of the cosmos. For example, in Job 37:18, Elihu asks Job:

> *"Can you join him* (God) *in spreading out the skies, hard as a mirror of cast bronze?"*

Similarly, the word used in the Genesis creation narrative to describe the expanse of the sky (pronounced *raqia*) is derived from a Hebrew root associated with hammering out metallic sheets (Seely, 1991). This sense is also found in ancient Sumerian, where the word for tin (an ingredient of bronze) is 'metal of heaven' (Kramer, 1963, p. 113). Thus, the original account of the creation of the sky (Gen 1:6-8) could be most accurately conveyed as follows, where the underlined words are modified from the more general word 'expanse' in the NIV translation:

And God said, "Let there be a <u>rigid dome</u> between the waters to separate water from water." So God made the <u>dome</u> and separated the water under the <u>dome</u> from the water above it. And it was so. God called the <u>dome</u> "sky". And there was evening, and there was morning- the second day.

In summary then, the biblical view is that the 'waters above the sky' were held back by a rigid floor that also formed the roof of the sky (Seely, 1992). Above this floor, the rain and snow were kept in storehouses or cisterns (Job 38:22, 37), from which they were released through openings that are sometimes called gates and sometimes windows.

How then did Whitcomb and Morris justify mixing literal interpretations of the 'mountains' and the 'fountains of the deep' with a metaphorical interpretation of the Floodgates? From their off-hand dismissal of the Floodgates in *The Genesis Flood*, it appears that Whitcomb and Morris were so conditioned by a Twentieth Century world-view that it never occurred to them to take the Floodgates literally. For example, they are not mentioned in the index to *The Genesis Flood*. However, it is precisely this type of world-view assumption that is so dangerous when interpreting the Bible. By glossing over their metaphorical interpretation of the Floodgates, Whitcomb and Morris gave the erroneous impression that they were following a completely literal view of the Genesis text. As a result, they built their whole theology of Flood Geology on a flawed foundation.

4.3 The flooding of the mountains

The southern Mesopotamian plain, deduced above to be the location of the Flood, is one of the flattest places on Earth. Based on evidence from recent topographic maps, the plain slopes less than 40m along its length of over 500 km from Baghdad to the Persian Gulf (Fig. 4.2). Within the Mesopotamian plain, the Tigris and (especially) the Euphrates form a network of meandering channels which have often changed their locations. This is because the plain is technically a delta. Over a period of hundreds of years the rivers deposit silt in their beds and on their banks, until eventually they build up to a higher level than the surrounding plain. Finally, after a catastrophic flood, the river breaks its banks, escapes from its elevated bed, and forms a new channel in a different location.

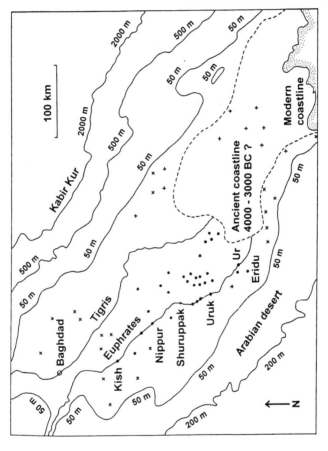

Fig. 4.2 Topography of Mesopotamia and surrounding regions. Contours in m, based on the 1:1,000,000 World Map. Spot heights: + = between sea-level and 20 m; x = between 21 and 50 m. Locations of ancient cities are shown, some of which are named. Coastline after Butzer (1995).

On the SW side of the plain, going towards Arabia, the ground rises only 200 m over a distance of 100 km (Fig. 4.2). However, because of the curvature of the Earth, topography less than 200 m high is invisible from 50 km away. So, apart from nearby sand dunes, the ground to the SW appears totally flat. On the NE side of the plain, the first high ground is the Kabir Kuh of western Iran, whose nearest high point has an elevation of 2800 m. This mountain peak is visible within a distance of about 130 km on the Mesopotamian plain. However, this would only apply during periods of exceptional visibility. At such times a viewer located near the River Tigris would see a perfectly flat plain, with distant mountains, standing like little 'cardboard cutouts' along a segment of the panorama to the northeast. However, all of the ancient settlements on the plain are near the old course of the Euphrates river, from which the Kabir Kuh are not visible.

Because no natural mountains are visible from the SW part of the plain, Molony (1936) suggested that Noah saw the flood-waters rising, not over natural mountains, but over certain 'high mounds' that had been raised by human endeavour. To illustrate the great distances over which such artificial mountains can be seen on the flat plain of Mesopotamia, we can consider the following description (Woolley, 1954, p. 11), of features more than 20 km distant that were visible from the ruined ziggurat of Ur:

> To the south-west the flat line of the horizon is broken by a grey upstanding pinnacle, the ruins of the staged tower of Eridu which the Sumerians believed to be the oldest city upon earth...

These artificial mountains were used for the worship of idols by means of ritual prostitution, as is well attested in later Mesopotamian literature (section 11.2). As the focus of the ritual practices that provoked God's wrath, it would be understandable that these artificial mountains were the focus of Noah's attention as he watched the Flood of God's retribution rise. Evidence in support of this interpretation comes from the ancient Sumerian word for the most sacred place in a temple interior, which is called the *du-ku(g)*. This is usually translated 'high place' and has the meaning of a 'holy mound' (Wilson, 1994, p. 19; 1996, p. 42). Similarly, the ziggurats on which these temples were built were regarded as sacred mountains. For example, the temple at Nippur was called the *E-kur* or *'House of the Mountain'*, and temples in other Sumerian cities were referred to in similar ways (Wilson, 1996, p. 22, 129).

45

Fig. 4.3 Drawing of the impression from a Third Millennium cylinder seal, showing the sun god rising from behind an artificial mountain. The divine status of this god and four other standing gods is indicated by their many-horned head-dresses. Height ca. 3 cm. British Museum.

46

The concept of the ziggurat of Babylon as a 'cosmic mountain' is echoed several times in the Bible. Apart from the allusion in the Tower of Babel story, to be discussed later, it also appears in Isaiah and Jeremiah, as discussed by Hamlin (1954). In Isaiah 14:13, a prophecy against the king of Babylon describes his ambitions as follows:

You said in your heart, "I will ascend to heaven;
I will raise my throne above the stars of God;
I will sit enthroned on the mount of assembly,
On the utmost heights of the sacred mountain."

Similarly, in Jeremiah Ch 51, two allusions to Babylon as a mountain are made as God speaks through Jeremiah (v 25 and 53):

"I am against you, O destroying mountain,
you who destroy the whole earth"

"Even if Babylon reaches the sky and fortifies her lofty stronghold,
I will send destroyers against her"

An invading army might destroy the sacred mountain in order to demonstrate that the city's gods were overthrown, reducing it to a hill of ruins. Thus Tiglath-Pileser III, king of Assyria, described how he reduced Samaria to look like the *'hills of ruined cities over which the Flood had swept'* (Pritchard, 1954, p. 283).

Obviously there are no surviving records of the nature of the sacred mountains from before the Flood, since only Noah escaped its destruction. However, there are pictorial records of 'sacred mountains' in later Mesopotamian art. Some of the best examples are seen on 'cylinder seals', which are small cylinders of carved stone, designed to be rolled over soft clay to leave a permanent impression. An example of such an artifact from ca. 2300 BC (Fig. 4.3) shows a mythological scene in which the sun god rises over an artificial mountain. He is identified by the rays coming from his shoulders, and by the serrated knife which he uses to cut a hole in the earth as he rises each morning.

We can infer that the tendency to build temple mountains before the Flood was most probably very similar to that after the Flood, because God specifically remarks that human nature did not change as a result of the Flood (Gen 8:21). Nevertheless, one way in which architecture did change over the millennia was the increasing tendency to use 'burned brick' rather than sun dried brick to build important monuments. It was this use of baked bricks that has allowed ziggurats from later Sumerian civilisation to survive partially intact up to the present day (section 9.1). However, if the temple mountains built before the Flood were made only of sun-dried bricks, we can expect that the Flood would indeed have had a devastating effect on them, reducing them to 'mountains of mud'.

4.4 The ebb of the Flood

The turning point of the Flood came when 'God remembered Noah' (Gen 8:1). The next three verses then describe the abating of the Flood:

> God remembered Noah... and he sent a wind over the earth and the waters receded. Now the springs of the deep and the flood-gates of the heavens had been closed, and the rain had stopped falling from the sky. The water receded steadily from the earth... and on the 17th day of the 7th month the ark came to rest on the mountains of Ararat.

The locality which is generally recognised today as 'Mount Ararat' is an extinct volcano in northeast Turkey called Agri Dagi (Fig. 4.4). With a height of 5123 m, and lying at the border of Turkey, Armenia and Iran, Agri Dagi is the highest mountain in a region that has a long association with the Flood tradition. For example, Josephus, the first century AD Jewish historian, records the tradition as follows (Antiquities, I.3.v):

> The ark rested on the top of a certain mountain in Armenia... both he [Noah] and his family went out... the Armenians call this place "The place of descent"... the remains of the ark are shown by the inhabitants to this day.
>
> [Bailey, 1989, p. 71]

The claim by the inhabitants of Armenia to possess original pieces of the Ark should not be taken seriously. However, the location of Ararat in Armenia is attested on three occasions in the Bible: 2nd Kings 19:37; Isaiah 37:38; and Jeremiah 51:27 (although the first two references are verbatim copies of the same account on the downfall of Sennacherib, king of Assyria). This account describes how the sons of Sennacherib murdered him and then escaped to the 'land of Ararat'. Subsequently, Jeremiah describes Ararat as one of three kingdoms that will execute God's judgement against Babylon. Both of these accounts make it clear that Ararat is not a mountain as such but a region in Armenia.

Fig. 4.4 View of the extinct volcano Agri Dagi (Mt. Ararat) in eastern Turkey.

Despite these evidences, it is clear that if the Flood was restricted to the southern Mesopotamian plain, the Ark could not possibly have rested on the present-day 5000 m high Mt. Ararat in Armenia. Indeed, Ararat is so distant from the Mesopotamian plain that it would not even make sense to speak of the Ark grounding on mountains in the region of Ararat (Fig. 4.5). However, there are many cases in antiquity of more than one place having the same name, so we should not fix our eyes so firmly on the Ararat of Armenia that we close our eyes to the overall context of the Flood story, which is clearly southern Mesopotamia.

Since the evidence quoted above for the location of Ararat is from several thousand years after the Flood, it is quite possible that in the intervening time period a region of Ararat came to prominence that was different from the Ararat of the Flood. Indeed, ancient Babylonian literature provides evidence for a different location for the mountains of Ararat (called Aratta) in Iran. Since the Iranian mountains line the eastern side of the Mesopotamian plain, this could mean simply that the Ark grounded on these mountains. The ancient literary evidence will be discussed in more detail below (section 8.2).

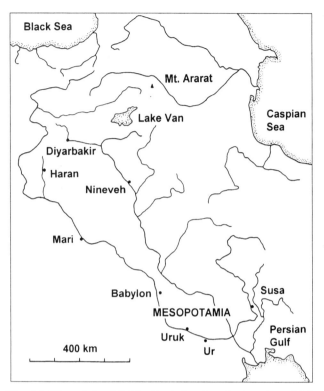

Fig. 4.5 Map of the Middle East showing the location of Mt. Ararat in eastern Turkey relative to the Mesopotamian plain.

After the grounding on the mountains of Ararat, the continued abatement of the Flood is described in Genesis 8:5 and 8:13-14 as follows:

The waters continued to recede... and on the 1st day of the 10th month the tops of the mountains became visible.
By the 1st day of the 1st month... the water had dried up from the earth.
By the 27th day of the 2nd month the earth was completely dry.

The account of the emergence of the *'tops of the mountains'* in Gen 8:5 has long caused consternation, since this did not occur until 10 weeks after the Ark grounded on the mountains of Ararat. A host of questions arise... Were the mountains whose tops emerged the mountains of Ararat? If so, did the Ark ground by a miracle on the pinnacle of the highest mountain? If not, then surely the top of at least one mountain was visible before the Ark grounded. And so on...

50

All of these questions are avoided if we understand that the Flood Story describes the view of Noah and his family from the Ark as they looked back towards the plain of Mesopotamia from whence they had come. They were not interested in the Mountains of Ararat behind them, a wilderness which was described earlier in Genesis as the *'Land of Nod, east of Eden'* (Genesis 4:16). Instead, I would argue that they were looking out across the Mesopotamian plain, trying to spot any recognisable land-marks, such as the remains of temple mountains that had been the site of mankind's corruption, now reduced to mountains of mud.

We can get an idea of what was in Noah's mind from an account by the 19th century Assyriologist, Austen Henry Layard. While visiting Tel Afer, located on the edge of the Assyrian plain in northern Iraq, Layard ascended the citadel mound and looked out over a vast plain, stretching westward towards the Euphrates and losing itself in the hazy distance (Layard, 1849, p. 258):

As the sun went down, I counted above one hundred mounds, throwing their dark and lengthening shadows across the plain. These were the remains of Assyrian civilisation and prosperity. Now not even the tent of the Bedouin could be seen. The whole was a barren, deserted waste.

4.5 The prediction and the promise

If this quote from Layard gives an impression of Noah's view of the aftermath of the Flood, what can we learn about God's view of the Flood? Light is shed on this question by an examination of God's declarations about the Flood, reported in Genesis 6:13 and 17:

So God said to Noah 'I am going to put an end to all people, for the earth is filled with violence because of them. I am surely going to destroy both them and the earth.
I am going to bring floodwaters on the earth to destroy all life under the heavens, every creature that has the breath of life in it.

Although these verses are spoken *by* God, we have to remember that they are spoken *to* Noah. Just as God described the Creation from Adam's point of view, so He describes the Flood from Noah's point of view. When God says in verse 13 that the Flood will destroy the earth, he does not mean that it will destroy the Globe, which is a modern concept and a misreading of the Genesis text. Indeed, the Hebrew word usually translated as 'earth' (*eretz* in Roman script) has a meaning much closer to 'land' than to 'globe'. Therefore, in these verses God is telling Noah that the Flood will destroy the earth as Noah knows it, which is the Land of Mesopotamia. This viewpoint is confirmed in verse 17 by the threat to destroy all life *under* the heavens. Here, the expression 'under the heavens' should be a reminder that we are dealing with the ancient view of the world as a flat plain bounded by a great sea, not a globe floating in space (Seely, 1997).

Later, Gen Ch 9:11 describes the covenant of the rainbow that God established with Noah after the Flood:

> *Never again will all life be cut off by the waters of a flood;*
> *never again will there be a flood to destroy the earth.*

This promise raises a puzzling question: If the Flood was confined to Lower Mesopotamia, why did God promise that a flood of such magnitude would never be repeated? We know, indeed, of subsequent floods which have been of similar geographic extent and have caused massive loss of human life. However, the mystery of the covenant can be understood if we consider the significance of the Flood for the revelation of God to mankind. The focus of God's judgement was the perversion of his name that had occurred in the invention and worship of idols. The Flood represented the potential jeopardy of the totality of God's revelation of himself to mankind, so that if Noah had not been saved, God would have had to start again 'from scratch'. The significance of the covenant of the rainbow is that God promised never again to jeopardise his revelation to all of mankind.

One group of Middle Eastern people who apparently did survive the Flood, according to the Bible, were the descendants of Cain. According to Genesis 4:20-22, the three sons of Cain's corrupt descendant, Lamech, were Jabal, Jubal and Tubal-Cain. The first is stated as the *'father of those who live in tents and raise livestock'*, the second as the *'father of all who play the harp and flute'*, while the third *'forged all kinds of tools out of bronze and iron'*. These three professions were all practised by the nomadic peoples who lived on the northern borderlands of the Mesopotamian plain and who periodically ventured onto the plain to pasture their flocks, to trade, or to loot the cities of the plain.

Ironically, Creationists do not take these claims in Genesis 4:20 literally, because to do so would be to admit that the Flood was not a global catastrophe. Instead, they argue that Jabal, Jubal and Tubal were only figuratively the fathers of those who practice these professions. However, this interpretation goes against the spirit of the text (as well as against the Creationists' own claims of literalism). If the descendants of Jabal, Jubal and Tubal were all drowned in the Flood, then they must have passed these professions on to Noah's family so that Noah's family could preserve them for posterity. But that is an unreasonable proposal because it would imply intimate social interaction between Noah, God's elect, and the descendants of Cain, God's outcasts who lived in the land of Nod, east of Eden.

Instead, what the Bible is clearly doing here is to look back in time from a much later period in order to explain how the peoples in the wilderness lands to the north and east of the Mesopotamian plain came to possess these arts of civilisation. The relatively late date of this comment can be deduced from the fact that bronze was not invented until 3000 BC, and iron not until 1000 BC, several millennia after the Flood. Nevertheless, the account is essentially accurate. For example, the Mesopotamian plain was always totally lacking in mineral resources, and the art of metalwork was introduced to Mesopotamia by trade from the wilderness lands of Iran and Anatolia (Turkey) which were rich in ore deposits. Indeed, the earliest use of metal, dating to around 7000 BC, is documented from Cayonu, near Diyarbakir in SE Turkey (Fig. 4.4). At this site early copper implements have been found that were made by cold-hammering naturally occurring 'native' copper (Lloyd, 1978, p. 30).

CHAPTER 5

THE RUINS OF MESOPOTAMIA

Scattered across the plain of Mesopotamia are dozens of mounds or 'tells', each of which represents the accumulated debris of centuries of human habitation. In a land of few natural resources, the ruins of past civilisations are preserved in the clay bricks, broken clay tablets and pottery sherds which together form these accumulated piles of debris. In order to find out how the story of Genesis and the biblical Flood fit into human history we must try to understand these ancient civilisations, whose remains go back over 7000 years.

5.1 Deciphering the ancient scripts

The first Europeans to encounter the Middle Eastern civilisations of Egypt and Mesopotamia were the ancient Greeks. They observed that Egyptian temples were covered in a pictorial script that they could not read, which they called 'holy writing' or *hieroglyphics*. Modern archaeological interest in the Middle East began in the 17th century when French and British diplomats observed fascinating monumental sculptures which they coveted to adorn the great museums of Europe. In the course of an expedition under Napoleon's command, a stone was discovered at Rosetta in Egypt which bore an inscription repeated in three languages; Greek, Egyptian demotic script and Egyptian hieroglyphics. This 'Rosetta Stone' was the key which allowed the decipherment of hieroglyphics by Champollion in 1823.

The Mesopotamian equivalents of the Rosetta Stone are tomb inscriptions from Persepolis in SW Iran and a monumental inscription carved on a mountain-side at Bisitun (Behistun) in western Iran (Fig. 5.1). Both inscriptions were written in three different scripts, but all using indentations whose wedge-shaped form gave the name 'cuneiform' (wedge-like) to this style of writing. One of the scripts was recognised as alphabetic by Niebuhr in 1775, since it contained about

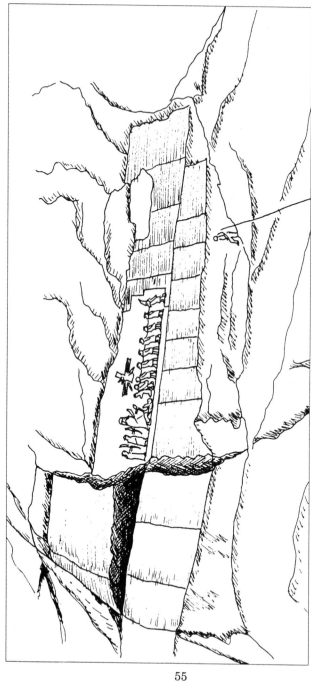

Fig. 5.1 A view of the monumental inscription of Behistun, located on a carved rock face 100m above the road. The Persian script is on the lower right and the Elamite script on the lower left. The Assyrian script is on the most inaccessible part, located to the top left above an overhang.

55

forty different signs. The decipherment of this 'Old Persian' script was begun by Grotefend in 1802, based on recognising the names of kings such as Darius and Xerxes who reigned from Persepolis. The decipherment of Old Persian was finally completed by Rawlinson in 1847, based on the particularly long trilingual inscription at Behistun (Mitchell, 1988, p. 85).

The second script at Persepolis and Behistun (in Elamite) was of lesser interest, since it is not widely distributed. However, the third script (originally called Assyrian) matched the writing on numerous clay tablets that were being discovered during excavations by Layard of the ancient city of Nineveh in northern Mesopotamia. This script was based on over four thousand different signs, suggesting that it represented a style of writing like Chinese, based on characters. However, the language which these characters expressed turned out to be of a Semitic type, from the same family of languages that includes Hebrew.

Because of the great number of signs in the third script, it was necessary to use the long Behistun inscription in order to decipher it. However, this part of the inscription was particularly inaccessible. A copy was only made possible when a heroic Kurdish boy clawed his way across the polished rock face using his fingernails and took 'squeezes' of the inscription under the direction of Rawlinson (Lloyd, 1947, p. 77). This procedure involves pressing papier mache into the indentations and then peeling it off when it has dried somewhat, yielding a reverse image of the inscription. Again using names such as Darius and Xerxes as a starting point, Rawlinson was able to determine the pronunciation of some of the characters, and by 1851 he had completed the translation of this third script at Behistun.

This script had barely been deciphered when Rawlinson discovered yet another kind of cuneiform writing on inscriptions from Southern Mesopotamian cities such as Uruk (biblical Erech). This script was clearly different from any of the three types at Persepolis and Behistun. However, once the new script had been recognised, it was also found on bilingual tablets from Nineveh, along with the newly deciphered 'Assyrian' writing. By studying how Semitic names were transliterated into this new script it was also possible to determine the pronunciation of the unknown language associated with the script. The results showed that the new script represented a completely new language that was not of a Semitic type at all, but of completely unknown linguistic affinity.

56

One of the earliest texts published in this new language (Rawlinson and Norris, 1861) was a royal inscription written on the bricks of a temple built around 2000 BC (Fig. 5.2). This inscription can be transcribed into Roman script as follows[5]:

*Ish-me-*Da-gan / u.a Nibru ^{ki} / sag.ush / Urim ^{ki}.ma /
u₄. da gub / Eridu ^{ki}.ga / en Unug ^{ki}.ga /

lugal kalag.ga / lugal I.si.in ^{ki}.na /
lugal Ki.en.gi Ki.uri / dam.ki.aga / *Inanna.ka

Fig. 5.2 Copper engraving of a royal inscription from a clay brick. The inscription is shown in its historical orientation. After Rawlinson and Norris (1861, engraving V).

The inscription commemorates the piety of Ishme Dagan, king of the city of Isin, for his support of temples in the cities of Nippur, Ur, Eridu and Uruk. However, most interestingly, the inscription also refers to the kingship of 'Sumer and Akkad', the two main political regions of Mesopotamia:

Ishme-Dagan / provider of Nippur / support / of Ur /
who daily stands for / Eridu / priest of Uruk /
mighty king / king of Isin /
king of Sumer and Akkad / beloved "spouse" / of Inanna
[translation: Bottero, 1987/92, p. 62]

Based on this evidence, Oppert (1869) recognised Akkad as the kingdom of northern Mesopotamia whose language had initially been called Assyrian, but is properly called Akkadian. This in turn meant that the second kingdom (from southern Mesopotamia) must be Sumer, and the newly discovered language was therefore Sumerian.

At first, many Assyriologists refused to recognise the Sumerians as a separate linguistic and cultural group, leading to a controversy that was called the 'Sumerian Problem' (Jones, 1969). This was ironic because we now know that it was the Sumerians who invented the art of writing and passed it onto the Semitic peoples of northern Mesopotamia, who adapted it for writing their own language of Akkadian. The weight of evidence in favour of the Sumerians as a distinct cultural group is now overwhelming, but a relic of the Sumerian Problem is the fact that we still refer to these people as Sumerians- the name given to them by the Akkadians.

5.2 Digging up the ancient past

The history and prehistory of Sumer and Akkad must be reconstructed using archaeological evidence from excavated sites. Strictly speaking, the historical period is defined by the appearance of contemporary written records. This is usually taken to begin at 3000 BC, when written records first provide evidence about commodities, professions, and names of cities, gods and people (e.g. Nissen, 1988, p. 81). However, archaeological evidence suggests that the development of writing actually took about 1000 years to progress from its first tentative steps to an instrument which could be used for the writing of literature. Hence, the first royal inscriptions, which provide detailed contemporary accounts of Mesopotamian history, begin around 2600 BC.

Due to the scarcity of suitable material for absolute (radiocarbon) dating in archaeological sites, the general chronological framework of Mesopotamia is based on relative dating methods. The most important of these methods is the study of changing pottery styles. This is a powerful tool because of the very wide distribution, excellent preservation, and distinctive features of pottery fragments (sherds). This framework of relative age periods is then converted to actual years by radiocarbon dating of carbonised wood from critical horizons. We will now review this chronological framework (Table 5.1) including some of the characteristic pottery styles of different periods.

Agricultural settlements in the Middle East have been dated back to ca. 8000 BC using calibrated radiocarbon ages (e.g. Moore *et al.*, 2000). These settlements are scattered widely in Syria, Turkey, Iraq and Iran,

Table 5.1 Summary of Major Mesopotamian Periods

~~~~~~

C-14 age BC	Name of Period in Mesopotamia		General name of Period

~~~~~~

1600 ~~~~~~~~~~~~~~~~~~~~~~~~

	Old Babylonian Period	Babylon Larsa Isin	Middle Bronze

2020 ~~~~~~~~~~~~~~~~~~~~~

	3rd Dynasty of Ur		~~~~~~~~
2200	Gutian period		
	Akkadian Dynasty		

2370 ~~~~~~~~~~~~~~~~~~~~~~~

		III	
2600	Early		
	Dynastic	II	Early Bronze
2750	Period		
		I	

3000 ~~~~~~~~~~~~~~~~~~~~~

| | Protoliterate (Jemdet Nasr) | | ~~~~~~~~ |

3200 ~~~~~~~~~~~~~~~~~~~~~~~

		Late	
3600	Uruk		Chalcolithic
		Early	

4000 ~~~~~~~~~~~~~~~~~~~~~~

		Late	
4500	Ubaid		~~~~~~~~
		Early	

5400 ~~~~~~~~~~~~~~~~~~~~~~~   Neolithic

		Late	
5700	Halaf		
		Early	

6100 ~~~~~~~~~~~~~~~~~~~~~~

~~~~~~

Note that according to some systems of nomenclature, the Ubaid period extends back and overlaps with the Halaf (Lloyd, 1978, p. 66; Roux, 2001, p. 21).

and seem to grow gradually in size and sophistication. Their ages are distinguished based on changing styles of pottery. The most elaborate painted designs are found in the Halaf period, dated at approximately 6100 to 5400 BC by calibrated radiocarbon dates (Campbell, 1992,

p. 187). This style of pottery is named after Tell Halaf in northern Syria, where a large pot was found with an intricately painted animal motif on the upper body (Schmidt, 1943). This period is also well represented at Tell Arpachiyah, near Nineveh in northern Iraq. Here, some pots with complex multi-colour decoration are seen, but these are present in less than 1% of the total pottery deposit, suggesting that they were luxury items. More typical ware of this period is shown in Fig. 5.3, but even these smaller pieces are often intricately painted (Mallowan, 1933).

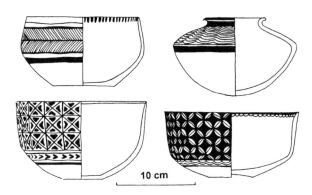

Fig. 5.3 Typical pottery styles from the Halaf period at Tell Arpachiyah. Iraq Museum, Baghdad.

On the Mesopotamian plain, the Prehistoric (pre-Dynastic) period is divided into the Ubaid, Uruk and Jemdet Nasr periods, also based on distinct pottery styles named after specific sites. The oldest of these is Tell al-'Ubaid (Hall *et al.*, 1927), excavated at the beginning of Sir Leonard Woolley's major work at the nearby city of Ur. Ubaid pottery shows simple painted designs (Fig. 5.4), many of which were probably applied using a kind of 'Lazy Susan' device to rotate the pot during painting. The use of the 'Lazy Susan' represented a kind of primitive mass production technique. The result was that pot designs became less elaborate than those seen in the earlier Halaf period, but a much higher proportion of the total pottery output could be decorated (Nissen, 1988, p. 46). This technical development evidently spread rapidly around the ancient world because previously distinct local painting styles give way to a uniform Ubaid 'horizon' that can be widely recognised. The best archaeological record of the Ubaid period is seen at Eridu, which is the oldest city in southern Mesopotamia, based on both archaeological and literary evidence.

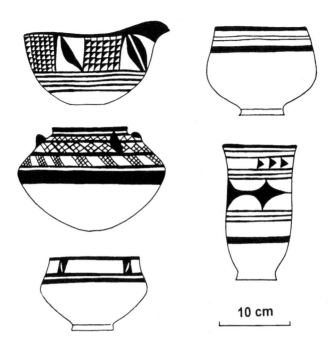

10 cm

Fig. 5.4 Pottery styles found in the Ubaid period from Tell Al Ubaid (on the left) and the city of Ur (on the right). British Museum and Iraq Museum (Baghdad).

Further technical development is seen in the Uruk period, lasting from approximately 4000 to 3200 BC. This level marks the appearance of wheel-thrown pottery, as the Lazy Susan was developed into a true potter's wheel. During this stage, more specialisation in pot shape is observed, but pot decoration largely disappears. Typically, the pots were dipped in slip (liquid clay) and burnished after firing, resulting in so-called 'grey' and 'red' ware. Because of the paucity of painted decoration at this stage, these wares are often drawn simply as cross-sections in order to highlight the variety of shapes (Fig. 5.5a). Painted designs return in the Jemdet Nasr period, named after a tell 50 km NE of Babylon in the north-central part of the Mesopotamian plain. During this period multi-coloured geometric decorations are often found (Fig. 5.5b), and a ware with distinctive purple slip is also seen. It was during this last period that the first writing was developed, and hence Jemdet Nasr is often called the Proto-literate period (Nissen 1988, p. 86), a convention that will be adopted here.

61

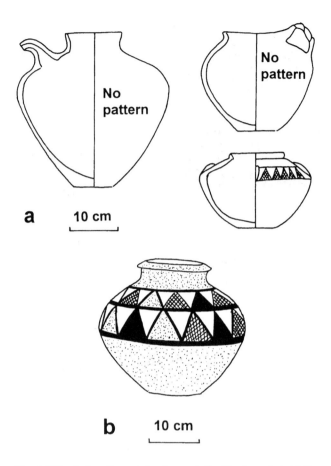

Fig. 5.5 Typical pottery styles from a) the Uruk period; b) the
Jemdet Nasr period. After Nissen (1983/1988, p. 91).

The buildings of ancient cities were made of a mixture of unbaked
and baked clay bricks. The latter material was used for facing major
buildings such as temples, and for the foundations of houses (Fig. 5.6).
However, the remainder of buildings were of unbaked clay bricks that
were continually in a gradual process of disintegration. The result was
that the ground surface in ancient cities was continually rising as a mixture of clay and refuse accumulated on the streets. Even during the
'lifetime' of a private dwelling, the street level would rise so fast that it
was necessary to construct a flight of steps downwards from the new
street level to the level of the occupied rooms (Fig. 5.6).

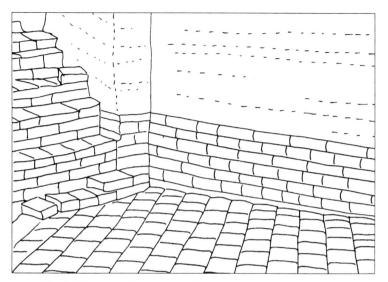

Fig. 5.6 Excavated house from Ur showing flight of steps from 'street level' down into a house. Only the lowest six courses of bricks were baked. From a photo by Woolley (1954, p. 180).

The build-up of city mounds over time provides a great bonus to the archaeologist by separating successive periods of occupation of a city into distinct 'levels' that can be excavated as separate units. The later prehistoric periods are very well displayed at Eridu and Uruk, where sections up to 20m thick, with up to eighteen distinct levels, span periods of over 1000 years each. The late prehistoric period at Eridu and Uruk was also a period of great temple building, and a long series of superimposed temple structures is seen at both sites. The excavations at Ur also go back through a similar time period, but because of the good state of preservation of the late Third Millennium ziggurat it was not possible to excavate the prehistoric temples which are thought to underlie the ziggurat (Woolley, 1954, p. 38-39).

5.3 The beginning of history

The early Historical period in Mesopotamia begins around 3000 BC and is essentially divided into two halves. The first half, comprising the 600 year long Early Dynastic Period, was a time characterised by rival city states, during which each of a dozen or so major centres of Mesopotamian civilisation strove for dominance over the plain. The result was a rapid succession of dynasties, in which first one city, then another, achieved dominance over the other cities of the plain. During this period, written evidence becomes progressively more and more important as a dating tool. At first, the style of writing is itself an indicator of the age of a tablet or inscription. Later, the historical contents of inscriptions provide a dating method, since each year of the king's reign was named after an important event of that year, such as a military victory or the completion of a monument. Successive reigns were then linked together and recorded in the form of King Lists.

By the end of the Early Dynastic Period, Mesopotamian civilisation had reached a mature stage, and the next four hundred years was characterised by the development of two empires which spread, for the first time, beyond the limits of the Mesopotamian plain. However, these empires were in turn susceptible to attack from nomadic peoples who lived in the mountainous areas to the north and east. Consequently, both of the ruling dynasties were brought to an end by the invasion of the Mesopotamian plain by barbarians from the mountains of the east or northwest. Eventually, order was re-established with the appearance of a new dominant king, and the overthrow of the earlier civilisation was then commemorated in a lament.

The first of the empires of the early historic period was the greatest. Its area of direct control reached from the Persian Gulf to the upper reaches of the Euphrates (Fig. 5.7), but military campaigns ranged as far as the Mediterranean. This Akkadian empire was established by Sargon, who founded its capital named Akkad (or Agade). This is thought to have been located near present day Baghdad in the northern part of the Mesopotamian plain, but its site has not been discovered. The Akkadian dynasty was Semitic, but to a large extent it maintained the traditions of earlier Sumerian kings. The dynasty was brought to an end by the Gutian invasion from the Iranian mountains, but eventually the Sumerians were able to throw off the Gutian yoke and re-establish central government from Ur in the south. This empire is referred to as the Third Dynasty of Ur (Ur III), because two previous dynasties had ruled from Ur during the Early Dynastic period. The Ur III empire was not quite as large as the Akkadian (Fig. 5.7), but it marked a return to Sumerian dominance of Mesopotamia, and a revival of Sumerian culture.

The Ur III empire collapsed from a combination of circumstances, including climatic deterioration and pressure from invading Amorite peoples. However, Amorite immigrants had already been assimilated by this time into Sumerian civilisation, and after the sack of Ur by Elamite invaders, an Amorite dynasty was established at Isin in the centre of the Mesopotamian plain. The rise of the Amorite peoples to power marks the final end of Sumerian dominance in Mesopotamia, and the beginning of the Old Babylonian Period. However, the rulers of Isin sought to present themselves as upholders of the traditions of Sumerian civilisation. Therefore, many of the institutions of this civilisation were continued during this period, as symbolised in the famous Sumerian King List.

The dynasty of Isin ruled for over 200 years, but gradually lost influence to another Amorite dynasty which had become established at the city of Larsa, located near Ur. Larsa finally conquered Isin, only to fall 30 years later to Hammurabi of Babylon. The conquest of Mesopotamia by Hammurabi around 1760 BC established the dominance of the first Dynasty of Babylon, with an area of influence similar to the Akkadian empire. This dynasty gave its name to the Old Babylonian Period and marks the end of Sumerian civilisation.

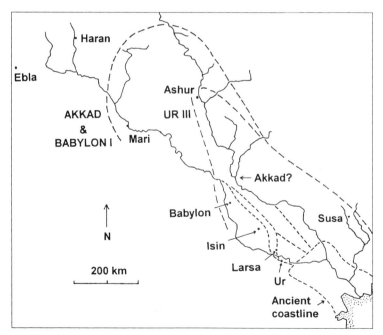

Fig. 5.7 Empires of the early historic and the Old Babylonian periods in Mesopotamia, showing their areas of influence. After Postgate (1992, p. 44).

CHAPTER 6

THE MESOPOTAMIAN FLOOD

Having sketched out the history and prehistory of Mesopotamia, we are now ready to examine the Great Flood from a Mesopotamian perspective, and in particular to search for evidence of the Flood in the ancient record. Unfortunately, this is one of the most difficult (and unsolved) problems in Mesopotamian archaeology. However, we will examine three main lines of evidence for the timing of the Flood. Firstly the biblical evidence (including genealogies and the social context of the Flood presented in Genesis); secondly the evidence from Mesopotamian written records (the Flood Stories and the Sumerian King List); and thirdly the archaeological evidence for flood deposits in excavated sections.

If we take the biblical account of the Masoretic text at face value, the Flood occurred in 2350 BC, after the Early Dynastic period and immediately before the empire of Akkad. This would be a very late date for the Flood, since it is a mature stage in Mesopotamian history, after the period of 'rival city states' and at the beginning of the period of empire building. Such a context is not consistent with the Bible's own portrayal of the social context of the Flood, at an early stage in human history. Therefore, we must conclude that the Shemite genealogy of Genesis Ch 11 (Table 2.2, column 2) is a schematic rather than a complete record of Abram's ancestry, and not intended to give an accurate date for the Flood. On the other hand, evidence in Genesis for an early date comes from the claim that all life in the known earth was killed by the Flood, and that all the nations were descended from Noah's sons after the Flood (Gen 7:23; 10:32). These claims are only reasonable if the Flood occurred in prehistory, not at a time when sophisticated civilisations had trade links spanning half the globe.

In the Samaritan Pentateuch text, most of the patriarchs in the line of descent from Shem to Abram are claimed to have their first son 100 years later in their lifetime than in the Masoretic text. This increases the time-span from the Flood to Abram's departure from Ur by 650 years, from 367 to 1017 years. The Greek Septuagint translation adds an additional generation to the line of descent, yielding a total of 1147 years. However, since these changes solve obvious technical problems, it is likely that they reflect later modifications of the text, and that the Masoretic text preserves the oldest account (Larsson, 1983). Hence, we cannot use these later manuscript versions of Genesis to estimate the date of the Flood, and we are forced to rely on the available Mesopotamian evidence.

The story of a devastating flood represents the closest parallel between the biblical account and the myths and epics of Sumerian and Akkadian literature. To allow the reader to judge the extent of the similarities, and also the differences, between the biblical and Mesopotamian accounts, we will now review some of the most important Mesopotamian documents.

6.1 The Sumerian Flood Story

The Sumerian version of the Flood Story is preserved as the bottom third of a tablet found in a temple library from Nippur, and was first published by Poebel (1914). The tablet itself dates from around 1600 BC but the composition probably goes back to the 3rd Dynasty of Ur, more than 400 years earlier. Jacobsen (1981) called this myth the 'Eridu Genesis' because it begins with the creation of man, describes the founding of the first city (Eridu) and ends with the story of the Flood. The tablet has three columns on the front and three on the back (Fig. 6.1). Because we only have a third of the tablet there are large gaps, and no other Sumerian copy of the material is known. However, the extant part is sufficient to show that this material shares a common source with the flood stories in the Akkadian epics of Atrahasis and Gilgamesh. The following account is summarised from the translation of Jacobsen (1987, p. 145):

After a long gap, the first column opens with one of the gods (not identified) addressing an assembly of the gods. This god is asking for the people to come back (from a nomadic existence?) to build cities and cult places. The column ends with a statement that the four chief gods of the Sumerian pantheon, An, En-lil, En-ki, and Nin-hursaga created the 'dark-haired people' (Sumerians) and various animals. After the second gap, the second column describes the lowering of kingship from heaven to earth, and the giving of the first five Sumerian cities to their patron

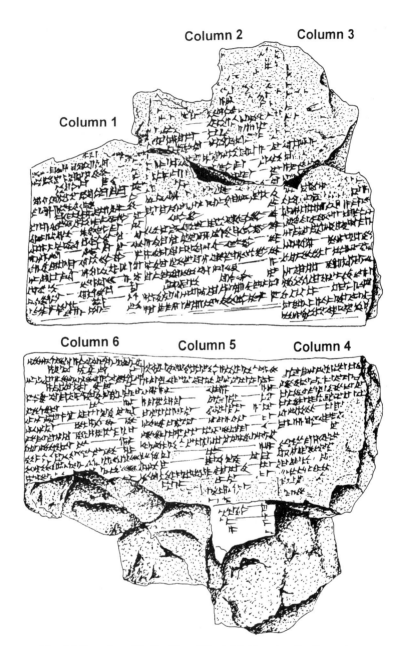

Fig. 6.1 Drawing of both sides of the tablet bearing the Sumerian Flood Story, based on drawings and photos by Poebel (1914, vol. 5). University Museum, Philadelphia.

gods: Firstly Eridu to Enki (god of sweet water and god of wisdom); then Bad-tibira to Dumuzi (god of the harvest) and Inanna (goddess of passion and guardian of the storehouse); Larak to the god of trees; Sippar to the sun god; and finally Shuruppak to the grain goddess.

With the beginning of the extant part of the third column we understand that some calamity is going to occur. Nintur (goddess of birth) and Inanna are full of grief but Enki is making a plan (of rescue?). Then we are introduced to the pious king Ziusudra, who appears to be seeking a revelation of the gods' plan. At the end of the third column, the tablet is flipped over to reveal the top of the fourth column, which is therefore consecutive with the bottom of the third (Fig. 6.1). This describes how Ziusudra, standing by a wall, hears the voice of a god, known from the Akkadian versions of the Flood story to be Enki. Enki tells how mankind will be destroyed by a great flood on the orders of the two chief gods, An (god of heaven) and Enlil (god of the wind.) After another gap, the fifth column describes how Ziusudra survives the storm in a big boat (whose actual size is not however recorded). After the storm has swept over the country for seven days and nights, the sun comes out and Ziusudra makes an opening in the boat and emerges. He bows down before the sun god and sacrifices many bulls and sheep. In the last column, Ziusudra bows down before An and Enlil, and is rewarded for saving mankind with the gift of eternal life. He goes to live in a supernatural land in the east called Dilmun.

6.2 The Flood Story in the Akkadian epics

The Flood Story plays an important part in two of the great Akkadian epics, Atrahasis and Gilgamesh. The Atrahasis Epic describes the origin of mankind and the story of how the man Atrahasis (meaning 'Extra-wise') survived the Flood. It claims to have been written in Akkadian by Nur-Aya at Sippar during the reign of Ammi-saduqa (ca. 1645-1625 BC), fourth king after Hammurabi in the Old Babylonian period. Late Assyrian versions come from the palace library of Ashurbanipal at Nineveh. However, these are close to the Old Babylonian version. Since the purpose of the present examination is to focus on the flood story, we will continue to use the Sumerian names for the gods rather than their Akkadian equivalents, which will be discussed later. The story is summarised here from the translation of Dalley (1991, p. 9).

The epic begins with a revolt by a class of working gods (Igigi) · against the 'great gods' (Anunnaki). The most important of these were

Enlil, and Enki, besides An, the father of the gods. The working gods complain that their work of digging irrigation canals is too arduous, and in response, Enki (god of wisdom) suggests that mankind be created to take the place of the Igigi in serving the great gods. Following this suggestion, the gods kill one of the Igigi and mix his blood with clay to make seven men and seven women. The spirit of the dead god is then imbued into them to make them alive.

Man begins his work, but after less than 600 years his noise becomes so great that Enlil (counsellor of the gods) cannot sleep. He gives an order that disease should break out in order to reduce the population, but Enki tells Atrahasis how to make a sacrifice in order to deliver mankind from the disease. This pattern is repeated twice more, the second time with a scourge of famine, the third time with plague and famine, but evidently these scourges are likewise not effective in reducing mankind's numbers. There is a gap of 36 lines here, but presumably it told how Enki again informed Atrahasis how to defeat the plagues. Finally, Enlil determines to wipe out mankind with a flood and Enki has to swear not to reveal this to Atrahasis. However, he manages to inform Atrahasis indirectly, apparently by revealing the plan to a reed hut, which in turn would whisper the secret to Atrahasis (this is much clearer in the same story from the Gilgamesh Epic).

Next, the story describes the building of the Ark, made by dismantling the reed hut, also describing the excuse made by Atrahasis that he must leave the city in order to worship his god, presumably so that he could carry on the work without harassment. The beginning of the deluge is described (torrent, storm and flood), lasting seven days and nights. However, following a gap of 58 lines we find Atrahasis sacrificing to the gods after the flood. In the end, Enlil and Enki are reconciled and they devise other means of population control, including female infertility and human mortality.

The Gilgamesh Epic relates the heroic exploits of Gilgamesh, King of Uruk. The Old Babylonian Version (OBV), written in Akkadian during the early Second Millennium, was probably made by joining together several short stories first written in Sumerian during the 3rd Dynasty of Ur. These Sumerian works were mostly a variety of stories about the exploits of the hero Gilgamesh, but by skilfully selecting material the creators of the Gilgamesh Epic put together a story of majestic sweep about man's vain search for eternal life. The most complete version of the Epic, the Standard Babylonian Version (SBV), was found in the library of Ashur-banipal at Nineveh.

Unlike most of the stories in the Gilgamesh Epic, the Flood Story does not involve Gilgamesh directly. However, it is woven into the epic by having the Flood Hero relate his story to Gilgamesh. The Flood Hero is here named Ut-napishtim, meaning 'He found Life', and the story is used on the pretext of Ut-napishtim explaining how he found eternal life. The Flood Story is told essentially as in the Atrahasis Epic, but fewer details are missing because the text is in near perfect condition. Fig. 6.2 shows the famous 11th tablet of the epic from Nineveh, bearing the Flood Story.

Fig. 6.2 The Flood Tablet of the Epic of Gilgamesh from the 7th century Assyrian palace at Nineveh. British Museum.

The Old Babylonian version of the Gilgamesh Epic is only known in fragments, which do not include the Flood Story itself. However, the direction of the story at the end of the last OBV fragment suggests that it probably did include the Flood Story. In this fragment (equivalent to Tablet 10 of the SBV), Gilgamesh is asking the boatman of Ut-napishtim to take him to the Flood Hero, presumably in order to learn the secret of eternal life. Evidence to be examined below demonstrates that Gilgamesh did actually exist as a king of Uruk, albeit with less glory than the epic suggests. This information can therefore be used to estimate a minimum age for the Flood, as discussed below.

6.3 The Flood in the Sumerian King List

The Sumerian King List is one of the few sources in Mesopotamian literature which somewhat resembles a historical document. However, its main purpose was to demonstrate the antiquity and continuity of Sumerian civilisation, rather than to provide a chronological record. The King List probably dates from around the time of the 3rd Dynasty of Ur, and describes a succession of dynasties from different cities of the Mesopotamian plain which are supposed to have ruled over the whole plain in consecutive periods. According to the Sumerian King List, kingship came down from heaven twice; once at the beginning of human civilisation and once after the Flood. Following each of these divine initiatives, a succession of kings is named. A summary of these dynasties to the end of the Early Dynastic period is given in Table 6.1, and the location of these cities on the Mesopotamian plain is shown in Fig. 6.3.

The most complete version of the King List is the Weld-Blundell prism (section 22.1), which begins with 8 kings who ruled before the Flood and ends with Sin-magir of the Isin dynasty. The authoritative translation of the King List was published by Jacobsen (1939), from which the following excerpts are quoted from the beginning of the ante-diluvian and post-diluvian sections (revised according to Finkelstein, 1963, p. 42):

After kingship had descended from heaven the kingship was in
*   Eridu*
(In) Eridu A-lulim reigned 28,800 years as king; Alalgar reigned
*   36,000 years.*
2 kings reigned its 64,800 years
I will bring to an end Eridu; its kingship was carried to Bad-tibira.

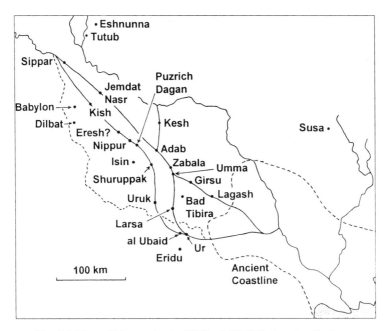

Fig. 6.3 Map of Mesopotamia (3200 - 1600 BC) showing the locations of ancient cities relative to the two ancient branches of the River Euphrates and the ancient coastline. Eresh(?) = modern Tell Abu Salabikh. Dotted line = modern course of River Euphrates.

The antediluvian section continues in this manner, with three kings from Bad-tibira, followed by one king from Larak and one king from Sippar (the location of Larak is unknown). It then concludes as follows:

> *I will bring to an end Sippar; its kingship was carried to Shuruppak.*
> *(In) Shuruppak Ubar-Tutu reigned 18,600 years as king: 1 king reigned its 18,600 years.*
> *5 cities were they; 8 kings reigned their 241,200 years.*
> *The Flood swept there-over.*
> *After the Flood swept there-over, when kingship was lowered from heaven the kingship was in Kish. In Kish Ga(lac)ur reigned 1,200 years as king...*

The account then lists 23 kings who reigned in Kish[6], before Kish was 'smitten with weapons' and its kingship carried to Uruk. Gilgamesh himself is described as the fifth king of this dynasty (Uruk 1).

73

Table 6.1. Summary of the Sumerian King List

Name of Dynasty		Number of kings	Total length of reigns, yr
Eridu		2	64,800
Badtibira		3	108,000
Larak		1	28,800
Sippar		1	21,000
Shuruppak		1	18,600
~~The Flood~~~~~~~~~~~~~~~~~			
Kish	1	23	24,510
Uruk	1	12	2,310
Ur	1	4	177
Awan		3	356
Kish	2	8	3,195
Hamazi		1	360
Uruk	2	3	187
Ur	2	4	116
Adab		1	90
Mari		6	136
Kish	3	1 (queen)	100
Akshak		6	99
Kish	4	7	491
Uruk	3	1	25

After Finegan (1979, p. 24, 28).

Because the King List was composed as a piece of political propaganda, hundreds of years after many of the kingdoms it lists, it should not be treated as a modern historical document. For example, the immense regnal spans before the Flood are clearly not credible, and in fact the antediluvian section is regarded as a later addition to the postdiluvian king list (section 22.1). In addition, the dynasties after the Flood are thought to have been largely overlapping, with the exception of the first dynasty of Kish which may genuinely have held pre-eminence over all of Sumer.

It has been suggested (Hallo and Simpson, 1971/98, p. 35) that the compilers of the King List knew that several of the dynasties were overlapping, but chose to ignore the fact. This was probably because they copied the regnal lists of different city dynasties verbatim, then arranged all of the records in a grand order, not wanting to omit any of their material. Therefore, we should realise that the King List presents a formulaic view of the dynastic period of Mesopotamia, in that different cities did hold supremacy at different times, but lordship did not pass from one city to another in the simple consecutive manner that the King List implies. Despite these complexities, attempts have been made to use the King List to date Early Dynastic kings by cross-checking the concurrent reigns of kings from different cities and then assigning an arbitrary length to each reign.

Assuming an average reign of 30 years, Jacobsen interpreted the King List to suggest a period of about 270 years going back from Sargon, first king of Akkad, to Gilgamesh, king of Uruk. Given a widely agreed date for the beginning of the Akkadian period (2370 BC, Table 5.1), this puts Gilgamesh at about 2640 BC, in the Early Dynastic II period. This estimate was supported by the discovery of a fragment of stone offering bowl of Early Dynastic II age in the Oval Temple (level 1) at Tutub in northern Mesopotamia (Finegan, 1979, p. 29). This fragment bears the name of (En)Me-baragesi, a king of Kish who was a contemporary of Gilgamesh according to a later Royal Hymn (Hallo and Simpson, 1971/98, p. 42).

The period before Gilgamesh is less easy to date because it is based only on the genealogy of the kings of Kish. Furthermore, the 23 kings of this dynasty are generally believed to represent two or more separate lineages, perhaps one comprising kings and the other comprising high priests. Taking this possibility into account, Jacobsen estimated a further 230 years between Gilgamesh and the Flood, placing the Flood at around 2850 BC, during the Early Dynastic I period. This is much earlier than the genealogy of Genesis suggests, but still at a fairly mature stage in Sumerian civilisation. This date will be compared with archaeological evidence below.

6.4 Flood deposits in the archaeological record

Archaeological records of floods are preserved in three of the ancient cities of the Mesopotamian plain. We will examine the evidence for each of these as being the biblical Flood, but we must note at the outset that these flood horizons appear to be at different levels in the different cities, and therefore do not represent a single flood which inundated the whole plain. The most recent of these deposits is found in Kish, where there are flood horizons between ED II and III (ca. 2600 BC). However, these appear to be quite local (Moorey, 1978, p. 98-99). They are also very late relative to the rise of Sumerian civilisation, so I reject them as viable candidates.

A better candidate for the Flood deposit is seen in the ancient city of Shuruppak, where an 'alluvial soil' possibly deposited by flood-waters was observed (excavation reports cited by Mallowan, 1964 p. 80) between the Protoliterate and Early Dynastic levels (ca. 3000 BC). In a review of this archaeological evidence, Mallowan (1964) argued that the flood of Shuruppak was indeed the flood recorded in Sumerian mythology and in Genesis. However, we need to consider the possibility that elements of the Flood Story of Sumerian mythology and of Genesis are actually derived from two different events, even if the stories share a common heritage.

As a candidate for the flood of Sumerian mythology, the flood of Shuruppak is reasonable, because in the Gilgamesh Epic, Shuruppak is stated to be the home of the Flood Hero Ut-napishtim. The Gilgamesh Epic also names Ubar-Tutu as the father of Ut-napishtim, and this Ubar-Tutu is himself named in the Sumerian King List as the king of Shuruppak before the Flood. A date for this flood between the Protoliterate and early Dynastic periods is also supported by the late Babylonian chronicler Berossus (Dalley, 1991, p. 6), since Berossus claims that ancient writings were buried at Sippar before the Flood and later retrieved. However, it is recognised (e.g. Mallowan, 1964) that the proposed flood horizon at Shuruppak did not markedly inter-rupt the continuity of Sumerian civilisation. Indeed, there is no evidence whatsoever for such a flood at this level at Uruk or Ur, which were already at this time great cities with monumental temple architecture. Such a local flood is therefore not in accord with the sense of the biblical narrative.

If we look for an older candidate for the biblical Flood Horizon, we are led to Ur, where Woolley made a major excavation 20 m square and approximately 20m deep to test indications of a flood deposit at Ur, based on previous exploratory soundings. This excavation involved the removal of ca. 20,000 tons of material, beginning from the level of a Royal Cemetery of Early Dynastic age and reaching down to present day sea-level (Fig. 6.4).

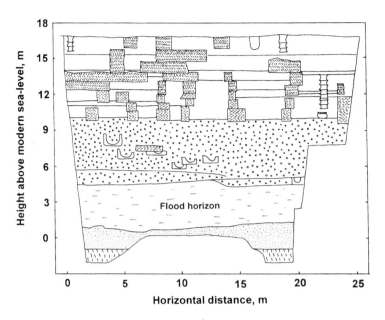

Fig. 6.4 Cross section of Woolley's great Flood Pit at Ur, with heights relative to modern sea-level: 17 to 10 m = remains of walls; 10 to 5 m = pottery debris; 5 to 1 m = Flood deposit; +1 to -1 m = pre-Flood debris. After Woolley (1954, p. 29).

Below the Early Dynastic cemetery, Woolley cut down through eight levels of house walls, the top five levels with plano-convex bricks laid in a herring-bone fashion, and the bottom three with flat bricks laid in the normal way. This transition in style of brick is recognised as a marker of the beginning of the Early Dynastic period, and was found at the 12 m level (Fig. 6.4). Below the houses, Woolley encountered a vast deposit of broken pottery, totalling over 5m thick and containing pottery kilns at various levels. This was interpreted as an ancient vase factory. This factory must have operated over a prolonged period of time because the style of the pottery changed with depth through the section. At the top it was of the Protoliterate type, in the middle of the Uruk type, and finally at the bottom a thin layer of Ubaid type. Below this stratum, Woolley encountered a 3 - 4 m thick layer of water-lain silt which he had previously seen in the test pits... the Flood Layer itself. Below the Flood Layer, Woolley again encountered Ubaid type pottery with three successive floor levels, and finally, near present day sea-level, green clay pierced by brown root stains. This was interpreted as the virgin soil of a small island which must have risen slightly above the level of the surrounding marsh.

Based on the style of pottery fragments, the age of the Flood layer at Ur is thought to correspond approximately to Level 6 at Eridu, to be described shortly. However, there is no evidence for any flood at this level at Eridu, only 20 km SW of Ur. Neither is there evidence for a flood at the corresponding level in Uruk, only 60 km upstream from Ur along the River Euphrates. Furthermore, Woolley suggested that even at Ur the whole city was not covered by the Flood Stratum, but only the side of the city that was towards the Euphrates, which flowed close to the city at that time. Since Uruk, Eridu and Ur were the three greatest cities in the world at that time, and since the Bible describes the Flood as destroying the whole known world, we are forced to conclude that the biblical Flood predates Woolley's flood stratum, and indeed predates both Eridu and Uruk. This leads us to examine the oldest archaeological records of these two great cities.

CHAPTER 7

THE EARLY HIGH CIVILISATION

The word 'civilisation' literally means 'life in cities' and is an apt word to describe the culture of Eridu and Uruk as the two great cities of the fifth and fourth millennia (5000 - 3000) BC. Eridu, literally 'the good city' (Jacobsen, 1967) is attested by both archaeology and by the Sumerian King List as the First City of Mesopotamian civilisation. On the other hand, Uruk displays the flowering of this civilisation, and the building of a city whose size was not exceeded worldwide for over 2000 years. Following an examination of the archaeological record from these cities, we can attempt to relate their development to the biblical account of the Flood.

7.1 The rise and eclipse of Eridu

There are no historical records describing the founding of Eridu but we can make some deductions about its origins from pictorial evidence. Cylinder seals of Protoliterate age (e.g. Fig. 7.1a) show herds of animals near byres built of reeds. These byres resemble structures which are still built today from reeds by Marsh Arabs who live in the Euphrates delta (Fig. 7.1b).

An interesting feature of the Protoliterate cylinder seal is the series of upright bundles, each with three pairs of loops attached. Modern reed-built structures have similar upright pillars, but lack the loops, implying that these loops were probably some kind of totem. The same looped totem is seen on another seal associated with what appears to be brick-built temple architecture (Fig. 7.2). Elsewhere, a single-looped variant is seen, either associated with a reed-built byre or as a temple doorpost (e.g. Saggs, 2000, p. 44, 57). Furthermore, this single-looped version later becomes the cuneiform sign for the goddess Inanna. Hence, this totem provides a clear link between the early reed-built structures and the later brick-built storehouses and temples. The many-pillared architecture of the later temples may also have been inspired by the reed-bundle pillars.

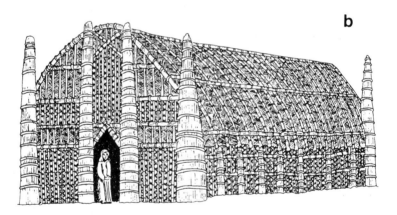

Fig. 7.1 Comparison of an ancient depiction of a reed-built byre with a modern reed-built strcture: a) Protoliterate cylinder seal impression, Ashmoleum Museum, Oxford; b) Modern reed-built house of the Marsh Arabs of SE Iraq.

Fig. 7.2 Uruk-age cylinder seal impression, showing the multiple looped totem next to a brick-built temple. British Museum.

Archaeological evidence points to a continuous succession of mud-brick temple architecture at Eridu from ca. 5500 BC to 3200 BC. Starting at level 18 of the excavation, which is founded on a small sand dune, these temples were built one on top of another. By building on the site of an earlier shrine, each new temple would inherit the consecrated site of its predecessor. However, it was probably regarded as sacrilegious to demolish the earlier shrine completely. Therefore, the normal procedure was to remove the roof of the old temple and partly dismantle its walls before filling up the interior space with mud bricks or sand to form a level platform on which a new temple was erected. This, no doubt, was the origin of the ziggurat, and it has also allowed the reconstruction of the successive stages of development of the site. These stages are shown in a partially exploded view in Fig. 7.3. An interesting point is that all of the temples were oriented with their corners to the cardinal points of the compass (N-S-E-W).

The first complete temple plan preserved at Eridu is from the 16th level, corresponding to the end of the Late Halaf period defined by pottery types (Table 7.1). The building consisted of sun-dried bricks, and measured only 4 m square. It contained two platforms, one of which was probably the main altar, as evidenced by the remains of burnt offerings. By Late Ubaid time, the level 7 temple had grown to a size of 20 m square, with numerous small alcoves round the edge. The level 6 temple was similar, although slightly larger. This was accompanied during the Early Uruk period by the development of a cluster of religious buildings which grew up around the temple.

81

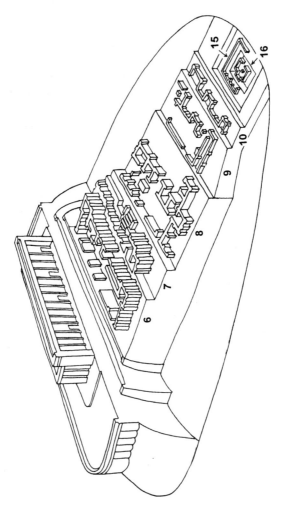

Fig. 7.3 Exploded view of successive temple ruins at Eridu. The wall bases were preserved when they were incorporated into successively higher temple platforms. Modified after Heinrich and Seidl (1982).

Table 7.1 Excavation levels at Eridu and Uruk

Years BC	Name of Period	Level Eridu	Level Uruk
2750 ~~~~~~~~~~~~~~~~~~~~~			
	Early Dynastic I		1
3000 ~~~~~~~~~~~~~~~~~~~~~			
			2
	Protoliterate		3a
	(Jemdet Nasr)		3b
			3c
3200 ~~~~~~~~~~~~~~~~~~~~~			
		1	4a
	Late Uruk		4b
		2	5
3600 ~~~~~~~~~~~			
			6
			7
		3	8
			9
	Early Uruk		10
		4	11
			12
			13
		5	14
4000 ~~~~~~~~~~~~~~~~~~~~~			
			15
	Ur Flood layer	6	16
	Ubaid 4		17
		7	18
		8	
	Ubaid 3	9	
		10	
		11	
		12	
	Ubaid 2	13	
		14	
5000?			
		15	
		16	
	Ubaid 1	17	
		18	
		19	

Ubaid 1 & 2 = 'Eridu ware'; Ubaid 3 & 4 = Early and Late Ubaid from Ur. (Jawad, 1974, p. 31; Lloyd, 1978, p. 36, 45).

The succession of temples described above represented the centre of worship, probably for the whole Sumerian plain, for 2000 years, from around 5500 to 3500 BC. However, near the end of the Early Uruk period the temple apparently fell into decline because the subsidiary buildings around it were abandoned and filled by blown sand (Lloyd, 1978, p. 39). The timing of this decline ties in with evidence of changing environmental conditions around the middle of the Fourth Millennium, involving the drying of the regional climate and the encroachment of the sea towards Eridu (Nissen, 1988, p. 55-56).

Eridu had originally been near a freshwater lake but it was not on the main channel of the Euphrates River. Hence, if the water supply from the lake was compromised by drought or by contamination with sea-water, this would have caused salination of the soil, reducing agricultural production. To offset these effects, a canal was dug to link Eridu to the main river. However, the city of Uruk, located on the main channel of the Euphrates River 70 km upstream of Eridu, would have had more plentiful access to water, giving it an advantage during dryer climatic conditions. Indeed, practically all of the prominent Sumerian cities of the early Third Millennium (the Early Dynastic period) were situated on one of the two main channels of the Euphrates River. Hence the transition between climatic periods probably corresponds to the time when Uruk eclipsed Eridu in importance as the leading city of Sumer, and reflects the different geographical situation of the two cities.

The continuity of the traditions of Eridu and Uruk, in the eyes of the Sumerians themselves, is illustrated by the myth of Enki and Inanna, found in the Nippur temple library and thought to date from near the end of the Third Millennium. At this later time, Enki (god of fresh waters and god of wisdom) was regarded as the patron god of Eridu, and Inanna as the patron goddess of Uruk. This does not necessarily mean that these were the principal deities of these sites during the Fourth Millennium, although evidence from the Uruk Vase (see below) points to the prominence of Inanna at this time. What is most important is the relationship between the two cities that is expressed in the myth.

The myth describes how Inanna goes from Uruk to Eridu in search of the divine decrees that confer civilisation, in the hope of obtaining them from Enki, described in the myth as her father. Enki invites Inanna to a banquet where he becomes intoxicated and, in a display of liberality, starts to present the decrees of civilisation to her. For example:

O name of my power, O name of my power...
To the pure Inanna, my daughter, I shall present...
Lordship, ...-ship, godship, the crown exalted and enduring,
   the throne of kingship...

[Kramer 1944, p. 66]

Hence, in groups, Enki presents over 100 decrees to Inanna, who loads the decrees in her 'boat of heaven' and sets off for Uruk with the precious cargo. When Enki has sobered up he realises that the decrees are missing, and, upon questioning his assistant Isimud, he learns that he himself presented them to Inanna during the banquet. Greatly upset, Enki sends Isimud and a group of sea monsters after Inanna to try to intercept her before she can reach Uruk. There are seven stopping stations where Isimud intercepts Inanna, but at each one she is rescued by her assistant Ninshubar. Hence, she finally arrives at Uruk and unloads the decrees, one at a time, to the jubilation of the inhabitants.

7.2 The flowering of Uruk

The period from 3600 BC to 2900 BC (Late Uruk - Early Dynastic I) represents the flowering of Sumerian civilisation in Uruk. During this time of great prosperity it appears that Uruk had two principal cultic centres, devoted to An (the god of heaven) and Inanna (goddess of passion). The first of these sites probably saw a progressive development similar to Eridu, with successive temples built on top of the foundations of the old shrine. Archaeological evidence (e.g. Salman, 1972) shows that temples on this site go back to the Ubaid period. Eventually, at the beginning of the Protoliterate period, it was built into the proto-type of the ziggurat, termed the Anu Ziggurat by the German excavators, after the Akkadian name of the god of heaven, Anu.

The second cultic site in Uruk is the Eanna complex, referred to in both the Sumerian King List and the Gilgamesh Epic. Literally, Eanna means 'House of Heaven' or 'House of An' but according to the Gilgamesh Epic it was the home of Ishtar (the Akkadian name for the goddess Inanna). It is difficult to reconstruct the process by which the 'House of An' became the 'House of Inanna', but this seems to involve the 'promotion' of Inanna from an original role as the goddess of the date harvest to being the 'Queen of Heaven'. Putting this the other way round, it implies that the god of heaven (An) was eclipsed in importance by the cult of the goddess.

Evidence that the 'promotion' of Inanna was well advanced by the Protoliterate period is provided by the 'Uruk Vase' (Fig. 7.4), a 1m high alabaster pedestal vase which was found in the level 3 buildings of Eanna. The vase depicts the presentation of offerings, probably the date harvest, to a goddess (or a priestess representing her) who is standing in front of a shrine containing various pieces of temple furniture. The evidence that the goddess is Inanna comes from two reed bundles with curled tops in front of the shrine, objects which became the pictographic sign for Inanna. Other inferences that can be drawn from the Uruk vase will be discussed later in the wider context of the development of Sumerian religion.

**Fig. 7.4 General view of the Uruk Vase. Iraq Museum, Baghdad.
For a detailed view of the upper frieze, see Fig. 11.2 (p. 137).**

The Eanna complex developed in stages, but during the Late Uruk period (levels 5, 4b and 4a), it was truly a monumental example of cultic architecture, justly described as a 'Cathedral City' (Burney, 1977, p. 59). Two large temple buildings were constructed during the period of level 5, termed the Stone Mosaic and Limestone temples. The Stone Mosaic temple exemplifies a style of decoration in which the walls were plastered, and while still wet, intricate patterns were made by pressing thousands of cone-shaped stones of different colours into the surface. The name of the Limestone Temple refers to its foundation, which was composed of limestone blocks rather than clay bricks. These temples were supplemented in level 4b by a double row of eight massive columns, themselves decorated with cones now made of baked clay, but painted to match the stone mosaic temple (Fig. 7.5).

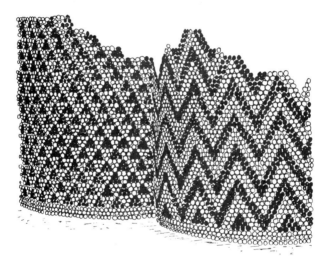

Fig. 7.5 Restoration of part of a row of joined columns from level 4b at Uruk, showing the spectacular appearance of cone mosaic decoration.

Despite the magnificence of these buildings of the Late Uruk period, they were quite soon partially demolished and filled with clay bricks to make a new platform at least 100 x 200 m in size. This platform bore a collection of even larger temple buildings, identified as Eanna level 4a (Fig. 7.6). Among these buildings were a second and larger Limestone Temple, a huge temple measuring 40 x 50 m, and a very large square building that has been described as a palace but could have been a great storehouse.

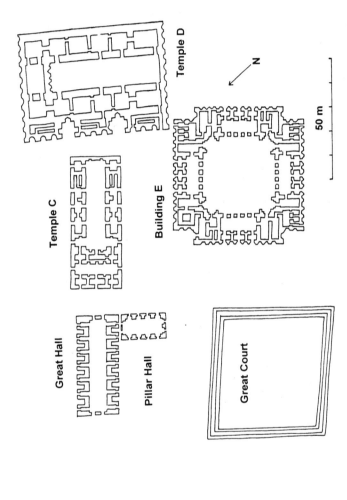

Fig. 7.6 Plan of part of the Eanna Complex of Uruk at Level 4a, showing the second Limestone Temple (C), the immense Temple D, the Hall of Pillars, and 'Palace E'. After Nissen et al. (1993, p. 6).

Level 4a of the Eanna Complex was apparently destroyed by fire, and was not rebuilt for some period of time. In the meantime, the pre-existing temple site to the west of Eanna was incorporated into a new very high platform, forming the 'Anu ziggurat'. On this platform was built the 'White Temple', composed of clay bricks covered with white gypsum plaster. This must have created a dazzling spectacle, situated on top of its 13 m high platform (Fig. 7.7). The final (level 1) temple at Eridu was also constructed around this time, probably under the influence of Uruk. As at the Anu ziggurat, earlier buildings were filled in to make a high raised platform which was faced at the top with limestone blocks.

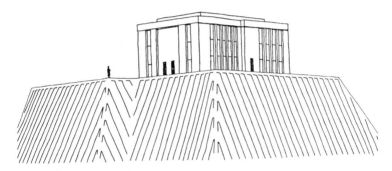

Fig. 7.7 Artist's impression of the White Temple of Uruk on its 13m (45 foot) high platform. Modified after Noldecke (1936).

The dominance of the Anu temple at Uruk was apparently not to last, and it was finally superceded when a new high terrace was constructed on the west end of the Eanna complex. This now rivalled the Anu ziggurat in height, but was also much larger in area. On this terrace, three phases of development are identified in the Protoliterate period, recognised as levels 3c -3a, but these temple outlines are not well established because they were buried under the huge ziggurat of the Ur III dynasty, built nearly 1000 years later. However, several treasures were found within the Protoliterate (level 3) buildings, including the Uruk Vase mentioned above, a beautifully sculpted white marble head, and several metal objects.

As noted before, the beginning of the Early Dynastic period is marked by the appearance of a new style of clay brick with a humped back, in contrast to the earlier prismatic shape. This seems a regressive step, since the new brick was less suitable for neat brickwork, but the use of greater amounts of clay mortar may have allowed the more rapid construction of 'Jerry-built' structures by unskilled labour (Nissen, 1988, p. 93). Based on the distribution of Early Dynastic I pottery, Uruk continued to flourish during this period, but changes were on the way, and by Early Dynastic II times the population of Uruk was in decline. Nissen (1988 p. 131) has suggested that the decline of Uruk was caused by water shortages, partly due to an overall decrease in the volume of the Euphrates with an increasingly drier climate, but also exacerbated by a shift in the course of the river about 200 km upstream of Uruk, near the city of Sippar. This change in the river's behaviour may have diverted some water from the western to the eastern channel of the river (Fig. 6.3). As the largest city on the western channel, and the one furthest downstream, Uruk was most vulnerable to this change. With the decline in Uruk's population, the political situation in Mesopotamia was about to change. From being the pre-eminent city of the world, Uruk would now become only one amongst half a dozen rival city states.

7.3 The rise of Kish

The archaeological records of Eridu and Uruk described above imply a continuous 2500-year period of uninterrupted architectural and social development, followed by a decline to second-rank status as one city amongst several on the Sumerian plain. Many archaeologists have suggested that the biblical Flood occurred at the end of this period, as marked by the Flood Deposit at Shuruppak. However, the 'fall' of Uruk is not marked by a cataclysm such as we would expect from the biblical Flood, but by a gradual decline in influence, while other cities such as Kish rise to equal Uruk in importance. Hence, I argued above that the biblical Flood must have occurred *before* the rise of Eridu and Uruk.

If Eridu was founded after the biblical Flood, what are we to make of the claim in the Sumerian King List that Eridu was the first city to be established with kingship *before* the flood, and Kish as the first city of kingship *after* the flood? To understand this contradiction we must remember that the King List was written around the time of the 3rd dynasty of Ur, in about 2100 BC, and hence nearly 1000 years after the beginning of the Early Dynastic period. Furthermore, the King List does not even know about the 500-year supremacy of Uruk before the establishment of the first dynasty of Kish. Finally, the King List advertises its own unreliability concerning the prehistoric period, based on the incredible lengths of kingly reigns both before and after the flood (Table 6.1).

The claim in the King List for the early supremacy of Eridu seems well founded, and there is also evidence that Kish was an important centre in Early Dynastic times. This is based on the fact that when other cities later achieved lordship over Sumer, rather than proclaiming their kingship in the name of their own cities, they proclaimed it in the name of Kish. For example, inscriptions concerning the first two kings of Akkad (ca. 2300 BC) describe them as 'King of Kish'.

Of the 23 kings listed in the King List as comprising the first dynasty of Kish, two are known from outside sources. Most importantly, the penultimate king, Me-baragesi is actually described on the first known contemporary royal inscription as *'Me-baragesi, King of Kish'* (Fig. 7.8a). The inscription reads from right to left, with the pictogram for 'king' being a stylised view of a man with a crown on his head. This inscription is on a fragment of a stone bowl which was bought on the antiquities market, and therefore has no provenance. However, the three signs which make up the king's name were also found on a smaller fragment from the city of Tutub, 60 km north of Babylon (Fig. 7.8b). The match-up suggests that the inscription is genuine, and it therefore anchors the first dynasty of Kish in the Early Dynastic period. Indeed, it can be called the very first contemporary political record.

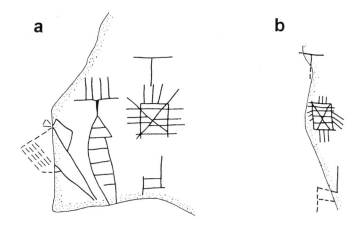

Fig. 7.8 Drawings of the earliest known royal inscriptions. a) 'Me-baragesi, King of Kish'. Iraq museum, Baghdad. b) fragment bearing the king's name only. Oriental Institute, Chicago.

According to the King List, the 13th king in the dynasty of Kish was Etana, who is described as:

Etana, the shepherd, he who ascended to heaven,
who consolidated all the lands, reigned 1560 years as king

This king is also known from an outside source, the myth 'Etana and the Eagle' (Kramer, 1963, p. 43-44). This myth describes how the pious king Etana, who was nevertheless childless, ascended to heaven with the help of an eagle in order to obtain the 'plant of birth'. The King List seems to recognise the story of ascending to heaven which is recounted in the myth, but it also suggests that Etana himself founded the dynasty of Kish by conquering 'all of the lands'. Hence, Jacobsen (1939, p. 152) suggested that Etana was actually the first king of Kish, and the first twelve rulers named in the King List were actually priests who served concurrently with the kings numbered 13 - 23.

We can conclude from the above evidence that the King List rests on a basis of historical fact, but that it represents a poor judge of chronology. Given that flooding was a relatively common occurrence in Mesopotamia during the 4th and 3rd millennia, and that there were no written records at this time, it seems very likely that the biblical Flood, which perhaps occurred more than 3000 years before the King List was composed (2100 BC), became conflated with more local floods that occurred around 3000 BC (still nearly 1000 years before the composition of the King List). Essentially, Mesopotamian literature has brought the Flood 'forward' into human history, whereas it actually occurred in prehistory. In other words, Mesopotamian literature has re-invented history in a telescoped way. To compensate for the shortness of the genealogical record in the King List, all the kings are then given fantastically long reigns to place the Flood back into the remote past.

Placing the biblical Flood before the foundation of Eridu and Uruk reconciles the archaeological evidence with the biblical account. The Sumerians appear mysteriously in Mesopotamia before the development of their Early High Civilisation, without any apparent provenance, and speaking a language which is not related to any other in the world. This is consistent with the arrival of Noah and his family from the Ark, having been isolated from their original homeland by the Flood.

CHAPTER 8

THE FLOOD IN CONTEXT

It was argued above that the founding of Eridu, probably around 5500 BC, places a minimum age constraint on the time of the Flood. However, there are also wider environmental constraints on the possible timing of the Flood. These constraints have to do with the global changes in climate which followed the end of the last ice age, and the effects that these climatic changes had on global sea-level. Superimposed on these global environmental changes, and in part arising from them, there were also more short-lived local changes in climate which could place important constraints on the probability of catastrophic flooding of the Mesopotamian plain at different time periods.

8.1 The environmental context

For much of the last million years of geological history the Earth has been through a series of climatic cycles that have involved successive ice ages interspersed with warm periods. Recently, considerable attention has been focussed on this period because of its importance in trying to predict future climate change in response to the 'Greenhouse Effect'.

One consequence of this climatic cycle, with alternating glacial and interglacial periods, is the variation in global sea-level. These variations, more than 100m in magnitude, occur as water is temporarily locked up in glaciers, then released back to the sea as the glaciers melt. We can chart the extent of sea-level fall during glacial periods because caves that are now deep under the sea were, only a few thousand years ago, above sea level. During the time that these caves were above sea-level, stalactites and stalagmites grew, and these have been dated by radiocarbon and the new uranium-thorium dating method (section 3.2; Dickin, 1995, p. 323).

Another way of charting sea-level changes is to date coral reefs that grow on the fringes of tropical islands. This evidence shows that sea level did not change smoothly, but went up and down in small jumps.

During a period when sea-level was only changing slowly, a coral reef would flourish in the shallow water just off shore. However, sea-level would then change more rapidly, either stranding the reef above sea-level or drowning it below the depth of light penetration. Since coral reefs rely on a 'symbiotic' partnership with green algae to get their energy, this drowning of the reef kills it.

Using the radiocarbon and uranium-thorium dating methods, coral reefs from several tropical islands have yielded consistent records of sea-level rise since the peak of the last glacial period. One of the most reliable of these records is from Tahiti (Fig. 8.1), which shows that global sea-level rose about 110m since the maximum extent of the last glaciation, about 16,000 years ago. Since the maximum depth of the Persian Gulf is less than 100m, it would have been a dry valley during the last glacial maximum. As the glaciers melted, the sea rose at an average rate of about 1 cm per year, causing it to advance up the Persian Gulf at about 100m per year until sea-level reached its present-day height at about 4000 BC (Fig. 8.1).

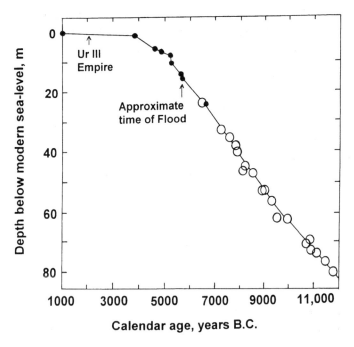

Fig. 8.1 Plot of global sea-level rise since 12,000 BC, based on coral reefs from Tahiti. Open circles = U-Th dates; closed circles = radiocarbon dates. After Bard et al. (1996).

94

Olson (1967) suggested that because the slope of the Gulf floor is not smooth, rising sea-level might have over-topped natural ridges and then rapidly flooded low-lying areas which were previously dry ground. He speculated that this could have caused localised flooding events, giving rise to the Mesopotamian and biblical stories of the Flood. However, there are geological objections to this theory. Even during the glacial period, the Persian Gulf was drained by a river which was equivalent to the present-day Tigris and Euphrates. Any low-lying areas would have filled with lake-water, and were therefore not susceptible to 'flash-flooding' when the sea broke through a natural ridge. The only way in which Olson's theory could work would be if water in the low-lying areas evaporated as fast as it was supplied by the rivers, as seen in the present Dead Sea. In this case we would expect to see salt layers in sediment cores which have been taken from the floor of the Western Basin. However, these are not seen (Sarnthein, 1972, p. 255).

Another locality where the 'Sea-water Flood' model has been proposed is the Bosporus Strait between the Mediterranean and Black seas. Since the Bosporus has a shelf only 20 m deep, the Black Sea lost communication with the Mediterranean during the last glacial maximum, and cores from its floor reveal thick salt layers, showing that it largely dried up during the last glacial period. If the level of the Black Sea remained low during deglaciation, the rising of sea-level until it overtopped the Bosporus Strait would lead to the formation of a giant waterfall. Ryan and Pitman (1998) suggested that this Black Sea flooding event occurred at about 5500 BC, marked by the appearance of marine shells in the Black Sea. Hence, they suggested that this flooding event could have led to the biblical and Mesopotamian flood stories. Again, however, there are major problems with this model.

Firstly, the geological basis of the Black Sea Flood model has been challenged by Aksu *et al.* (1999, 2002). These authors argued that sea-level actually overtopped the Bosporus Strait over 1000 years earlier than the time proposed by Ryan and Pitman, but by this time the Black Sea had been refilled by glacial melt-water. The outflow of this fresh water would have prevented sea-water from penetrating the Black Sea for over a thousand years, until sea-level rose higher than the level of the Black Sea and finally allowed saline bottom water to enter through the Bosporus Strait.

Even if the geological reasoning of Ryan and Pitman proves correct, the Black Sea waterfall would be a very poor fit to the biblical/Mesopotamian Flood Story. Firstly, this type of flood would have been sufficiently gradual to allow the population to escape; and secondly (and fatally) this flood did not dry up, unlike the biblical flood. Ryan and Pitman (1998, p. 252) tried to get round this problem by arguing that the story of the 'Black Sea Flood' was carried by migrating peoples who later settled in Mesopotamia and mixed it into a story of the annual flooding of the Euphrates River. However, there is no basis for this argument in the ancient texts.

If the Flood was not caused by sea-level rise, one might ask why this phenomenon is important for the context of the Flood. The reason is that sea-level variations affect the gradients of rivers and thus the tendency of these rivers to flood. In a review of this question, Nutzel (1978) showed that the present gradient of the Euphrates and Tigris rivers corresponds to a river in 'old age' which is very susceptible to widespread flooding (Fig. 8.2). Hence, the important question with regard to the date of the Flood is when such conditions pertained in the past.

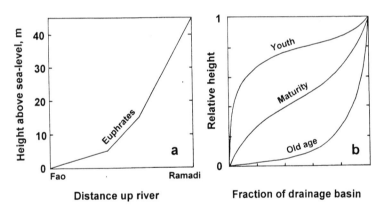

Fig. 8.2 Comparison of the average present day gradient of the Euphrates with gradients of rivers in different stages of their development. After Nutzel (1978).

In order to answer this question, Nutzel drew a topographic section approximately along the mid line of the Mesopotamian plain and the Persian Gulf (Fig. 8.3). The bathymetric data he used have been superceded (Uchupi et al., 1996), but Nutzel's general conclusions remain. The present day topographic section along the floor of the Gulf shows a 'step' with markedly steeper gradient just off shore, compared with the more gentle gradient further out to sea. Some of the step is the

96

result of sediment accumulation on the Mesopotamian delta over the past 8000 years. However, based on the thickness of this accumulation seen in drill cores, it appears that even before 8000 BC there was a marked step in the topography of the Gulf at point X in Fig. 8.3, marking the ancient edge of the Mesopotamian plain. This means that after 8000 BC the sea would have lapped onto the edge of the plain for the first time, thus preventing the rapid escape of flood-waters from the plain. This had two effects. Firstly, it caused the rapid accumulation of sediment which built the Mesopotamian delta (shaded area in Fig. 8.3). Secondly, it meant that river floods occurring after this time would tend to get backed up when they met the sea, so that major flooding of the Mesopotamian plain was much more likely after 8000 BC.

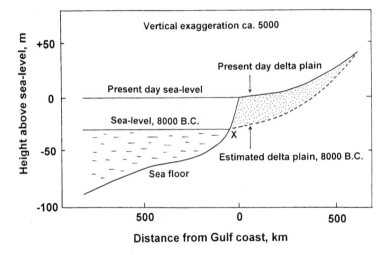

Fig. 8.3 Longitudinal section along the mid line of the Persian Gulf and Mesopotamian plain to show proposed changes of topography from 8000 BC to the present day. Note vertical exaggeration! After Nutzel (1978).

A second factor that may have constrained the timing of the Flood is the changing climate of the Middle East. This would have affected the amount of rain and snow that fell in the headwaters of the Tigris and Euphrates, and hence the tendency of these rivers to flood. Pertinent evidence of past variations of precipitation in this region comes from Lake Van, a self-contained drainage basin in southeast Turkey that lies between the headwaters of the Tigris and Euphrates rivers (Fig. 4.5).

Lake Van is an example of a 'Terminal Lake', which is fed by rivers but has no outflow. The levels of such lakes are determined by a balance between river influx and water loss by evaporation, and they are therefore very useful as monitors of past climate. During wet periods the lake level rises, whereas in dry periods the lake level falls and salinity increases to the point where salt deposits may form (as seen around the Dead Sea). Water level variations of about 0.5 m occur on a seasonal basis in Lake Van, with a marked rise in May from a combination of snow melt and spring rains, followed by a drop over the summer due to enhanced evaporation. Lake level variations of over 1m also occur between wet and dry years. However, sediment records from the floor of the lake record changes in lake level of over 400 m over the past 15,000 years, and these records can be precisely dated because the bottom sediments in Lake Van are varved (for an explanation of this process, see section 3.3).

Recent sample coring of the lake bed by Landmann *et al.* (1996a) allowed accurate counting of a continuous record of varves from the present day to 12,280 BC. This calibration was validated by dating the beginning of the Holocene, a sudden warming of the climate which is detected at 8,970 +/- 130 BC in the Lake Van sediments, compared with 9,020 BC in the European dendrochronology timescale. The varve ages were then used to date the beginnings of sediment deposition from cores in different parts of the lake, at different depths below the present day lake surface. Hence Landmann *et al.* (1996b) reconstructed lake level fluctuations for the past 15,000 years, based on a series of 'anchor' points (Fig. 8.4).

The results in Fig. 8.4 show three periods when the level of Lake Van rose very sharply, corresponding to periods of prolonged wet conditions. These are from around 9000-8500 BC, 7500-6500 BC and 6200-5500 BC. The latter two periods fall below the date of 8000 BC discussed above, when encroachment of the sea onto the Mesopotamian plain would have caused river floods to back up, and cause catastrophic flooding of the plain. However, bathymetric data from Lake Van show that the most recent increase in Lake volume (ca. 6000 BC) was much more substantial in its volume than the earlier increase, even though the lake level rose by 100 m in each interval (Fig. 8.4). This is because the shelving lake bed causes its volume to increase at a faster rate than its area. Thus, data from Landmann (1996b) suggest that the wet period around 6000 BC saw an increase in lake volume nearly three times as great as the earlier period, over a similar time interval.

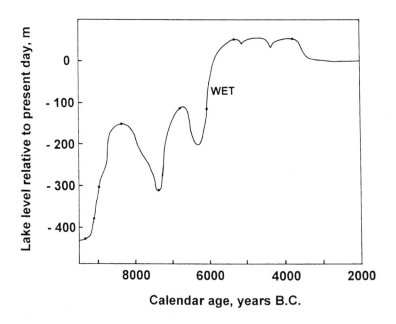

Fig. 8.4 Reconstruction of lake level fluctuation in Lake Van since the last glacial period. Anchor points for the curve are shown by solid dots. After Landmann et al. (1996).

There is substantial evidence from the Eastern Mediterranean region that the two wet intervals from 7500 to 5500 BC at Lake Van were unusually wet over the whole of the Fertile Crescent. For example, a cave stalactite from Jerusalem records two periods of extensive local flooding, represented by large perturbations in the stable carbon isotope composition of water entering the cave system (Bar-Matthews et al., 1997). Dating of these periods of flooding by the U-Th method (Bar-Matthews et al., 2000) showed that the two wet intervals lasted over almost exactly the same periods as the increases in the level of Lake Van (Fig. 8.5). These data therefore imply that the period of 6000 to 5000 BC was not only unusually wet, but that precipitation in this interval may have been more seasonal, leading to more frequent flooding over the whole Fertile Crescent. Hence, when this paleoclimatic evidence is combined with the archaeological evidence from Mesopotamian cities, it seems most likely that the Great Flood occurred between 5500 and 6000 BC, shortly before the founding of Eridu.

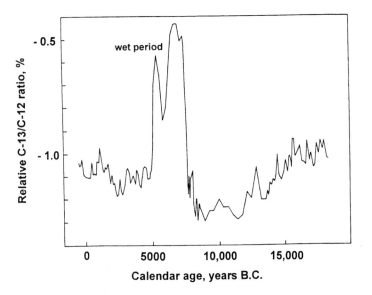

Fig. 8.5 Carbon isotope record from a cave stalactite near Jerusalem, indicating two periods of frequent local flooding, around 8000 - 6500 and 6000 - 5000 BC. After Bar-Matthews et al. (1997, 2000).

8.2 The landing place of the Ark

According to the Bible, the landing of the Ark on the mountains of Ararat after the Flood begins a new phase of the human story. The landing place of the Ark on the mountains of Ararat cannot be identified with the Ararat in eastern Turkey, which is hundreds of miles north of the Mesopotamian plain. Instead, I suggest that the mountains of Ararat can be identified with the mountainous land of Aratta in Iran. This is based on the fact that both Ararat and Aratta can be derived from the word 'Ararta', meaning the 'land of Ara' (Deimel, in Kavoukjian, 1987, p. 68). We know about Aratta because it was the subject of a series of Sumerian epic stories which describe the struggles between two city states: the kingdom of Aratta in the Iranian mountains, and the cities of Uruk and Eridu in Sumer. These stories show that there was an intimate relationship between the lands of Sumer and Aratta, so that Aratta would have been an obvious landmark to identify the landing place of the Ark.

The two most important stories about Aratta are the epic of 'En-merkar and the Lord of Aratta' and the epic of 'Lugal-banda and En-merkar'. Both of these epics are concerned with a power struggle between the king of

100

Aratta and En-merkar, thought to have been a king of Uruk during the Early Dynastic period. During this time, Aratta was a supplier of precious stones for the temples of Uruk and Eridu. The power struggle arises from the fact that En-merkar demands these building materials as his right, whereas the lord of Aratta resists the demand to bow to the power of Uruk. The myth of Lugal-banda and En-merkar (also called Lugal-banda and the Thunderbird) concerns the adventures of Lugal-banda, a commander in En-merkar's army, on his way to fight against Aratta. It is part of a larger corpus of stories on this subject which have not all been preserved.

A remarkable feature of the Aratta epics is that both Uruk and Aratta share the same patron goddess, Inanna. This implies a special relationship between the two cities, most likely due to one of them being a colony of the other. Since En-merkar claims to be the 'father' of the Lord of Aratta (Jacobsen, 1987, p. 291), the implication is that Uruk is the parent city and Aratta the daughter colony, hence explaining the demand by En-merkar for tribute from Aratta.

The myth of En-merkar and the Lord of Aratta describes a contest of wits between the two kings, rather than an armed struggle. The contest of wits is in three stages, each of which requires an envoy to travel back and forwards between the two cities, reciting his message in the court of the king. In the course of this journey, landmarks are described that help us to determine the location of Aratta. The key lines are as follows:

> Whither did he (the envoy) *take Inanna's great words*
> *in the reed canister for her?*
> He had to go up into the Zubi ranges
> *had to come down with it out of the Zubi ranges*
> (The people of) Susa toward Anshan's mountains
> *saluted him like tiny mice,*
> And (people of) all the great ranges, grown populous on their own
> *at (word of) it grovelled in the dust for him.*
> Five mountain ranges, six mountain ranges,
> *seven mountain ranges, he crossed over,*
> Lifted up his eyes, he was approaching Aratta;
> *and joyfully he set foot in Aratta's courtyard*

[Jacobsen, 1987, p. 291: lines 164-174]

Anshan was identified by Sumner (1973) as Tepe Malyan, near Persepolis, in the Zagros mountains east of Mesopotamia (Fig. 8.6).

101

Hence, as the envoy climbed the steep mountain road towards Anshan and looked back at Susa on the plain below, her people would indeed have looked like tiny mice (Jacobsen, 1987, p. 284). Thereafter, the envoy crossed 'seven ranges of mountains' before reaching Aratta. This aptly describes the Zagros mountains between Persepolis and the province of Kerman in south-central Iran, where the topography consists of alternating mountain ridges and valleys. In the Kerman region there is also evidence for the working of lapis lazuli, which was imported from Afghanistan and probably then exported to Mesopotamia. Hence, Majidzadeh (1976) suggested that Aratta was located in the Kerman region on an early Third Millennium trade route from Mesopotamia, through Susa, to Afghanistan. The story of Inanna and Ebih (Kinnier Wilson, 1979, p. 5) provides additional evidence for this location.

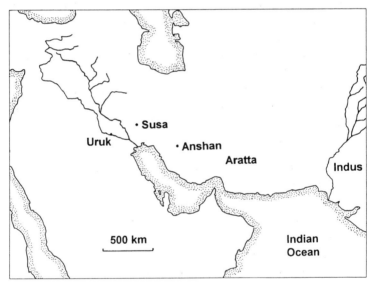

Fig. 8.6 Map of the Middle East to show proposed location of Aratta and other cities mentioned in the epic of En-merkar.

Not all scholars have accepted the proposed location of the city of Aratta in Iran, since the name Aratta is also attested in Armenia to the north of Mesopotamia (e.g. Kavoukjian, 1987). However, the Aratta in Armenia does not fit with the epic of En-merkar. The natural route from Uruk to Armenia is along the Euphrates River (Fig. 8.6), a well-attested trade route of ancient times. This route goes nowhere near Susa, and although it runs parallel to the Zagros mountains, these ranges are so far away from the Euphrates that they are not even visible for most of the route. Hence, it is concluded that the location of Aratta in the epic of En-merkar is in central Iran, and that the biblical 'mountains of Ararat' correspond to the Zagros range on the eastern side of the Mesopotamian plain. From this location 'in the east', Noah's descendants could have spread out over the Mesopotamian plain (Shinar) after the Flood, as described in Genesis 11:2.

8.3 The lost Eden

Mesopotamian myths display a deep sense of longing for the lost age 'before the Flood' and the lost immortality of the Garden of Eden. The quest for this lost secret of immortality is nowhere seen more poignantly than in the great Akkadian work, the Epic of Gilgamesh, itself constructed by the amalgamation of older Sumerian myths and epics.

After the death of Enkidu, his sparring partner and soul-mate, Gilgamesh sets out on a quest to find the lost secret of immortality and is directed to search for the Flood Hero, Ut-napishtim. According to tablet 11 of the epic, Ut-napishtim had built the Ark in obedience to the god Enki and was rewarded for this obedience with eternal life *'in a far-away place at the mouth of the rivers'*. The fact that the place of immortality is located where rivers meet suggests that this is an echo, in Akkadian mythology, of the Garden of Eden described in Genesis.

The Sumerian Flood Story (Eridu Genesis) has a similar account, with the Flood Hero (here named Ziusudra) again receiving eternal life from the gods. However, in this version of the myth he is made the king of a paradise called Dilmun:

> *Toward the east, over the mountains, in Mount Dilmun*
> [Jacobsen, 1987, p. 150]

The earliest contemporary written references to Dilmun, in economic tablets from around 2500 BC, suggest that Dilmun was exporting dates to Mesopotamia at this time (Cornwall, 1952, p. 137). From the time of Sargon (2350 BC), Dilmun was clearly a trade centre involved in the importation of many commodities into Mesopotamia from the Persian Gulf, and we can confidently identify it with the modern island of Bahrein (Fig. 2.1), which provides one of the few sheltered anchorages in the Gulf. Evidence in support of this identification comes from the abundance of Mesopotamian artifacts found in Bahrein from the late

Third Millennium onwards, and is confirmed in two letters from 1370 BC (Cornwall, 1952).

Extensive excavations have been carried out in Bahrein ever since Rawlinson identified it as the land of Dilmun in 1861. These excavations revealed an immense number of burial tombs, numbering around 170,000 (Lamberg-Karlovsky, 1982). A typical tomb has a rectangular stone chamber with a large stone lid, surrounded by a ring-shaped wall which may have smaller chambers around its perimeter (Fig. 8.7). The whole structure was then covered by an earth mound or 'tumulus' up to 5 m high. Many of these tomb-tumuli contain multiple burials, although others were left empty, perhaps still awaiting their future occupants. Lamberg-Karlovsky argued that the immense number of people buried at Dilmun, perhaps involving half a million individuals from the time of Ur III onwards, could not possibly be accounted for by the indigenous population of Bahrein, but instead pointed to a Mesopotamian funerary cult of major proportions. Such a cult makes perfect sense when we remember that Dilmun (Bahrein) was regarded as the land of immortality. No doubt wealthy Mesopotamians thought that they would have a better chance of spending the after-life in paradise if their bodies were buried in the very spot.

Fig. 8.7 Cross section through a Bahrein tumulus. After Lowe (1986).

The legendary, pristine and virginal state of Dilmun is described further in the Sumerian Paradise Myth (the myth of Enki and Ninhursag, section 13.3). This myth begins by describing the pure and holy state of Dilmun:

Holy is the city... The land Dilmun is holy.
Sumer is holy... The land Dilmun is holy.
The land Dilmun is holy, the land Dilmun is pure,
The land Dilmun is pure, the land Dilmun is bright.

[Kramer and Maier, 1989, p. 23]

There are also no crowing birds to disturb the peace of Dilmun, the lion and the wolf do not kill there, and there is no sickness or old age. However, one thing is lacking in Dilmun: it has no fresh (sweet) water. Therefore, the goddess Ninsikilia (also called Ninhursaga) entreats the god Enki (god of sweet waters) to bring forth these waters. This Enki does with a decree:

> *At the stepping onto heaven by Utu* (the sun god)
> *May, from the standing bollards on the shore of Izin,*
> *From Nanna's radiant temple on high,* (at Ur)
> *From the mouth of the waters running underground,*
> *Sweet waters run out of the ground for you*
> [Jacobsen, 1987, p. 187]

It has been suggested (e.g. Dalley, 1991, p. 44) that the Sumerians believed that a river of fresh water flowed across the bottom of the Persian Gulf from the mouth of the Euphrates (Izin) to the island of Bahrein, where in fact fresh-water springs are known, both on land and under the sea. Jacobsen suggested further that the temple of Nanna (the moon god) at Ur is mentioned as the source of the sweet waters because Ur was the capital city of Sumer at the time of composition of the myth (during the 3rd dynasty of Ur).

Although the location of Dilmun at Bahrein is very well established from the time of the Ur III dynasty (2100 BC), this could not have been the original location of the biblical Garden of Eden (at the meeting of the Tigris and Euphrates), or of the land of immortality described in the Gilgamesh Epic (at the 'mouth' of the rivers). Therefore, Howard-Carter (1981) suggested that Dilmun was originally located near Qurna, at the present confluence of the rivers.

Geological evidence suggests that sea-level rose by over 10m between the time of the Flood (ca. 5500 BC) and the time of the Ur III dynasty (Fig. 8.1). This sea-level rise probably caused the shore-line to migrate inland by as much as 200 km in the 3000 years following the Flood, drowning the original site of the Garden of Eden near the conflu-ence of the rivers. This could have prompted the Sumerian tradition that Dilmun lay on an island across the sea, and can explain the idea of the river Euphrates flowing across the floor of the sea to provide sweet waters in Bahrein. It may also explain the story in the Gilgamesh Epic where the hero is told of a spiky 'plant of rejuvenation' that lies at the bottom of the sea. This plant may be an echo of the biblical 'Tree of Life', presumed by the Sumerians to have been drowned along with the Garden of Eden.

CHAPTER 9

THE BABBLE AT BABEL

Unlike the permanent sense of longing for the land of immortality in Sumerian mythology, the Bible has a purposeful forward sense of history. After the Flood, God tells Noah to be fruitful, to increase in number and fill the earth. The 'Table of Nations' in Genesis Chapter 10 gives the biblical view of how this occurred. However, just as Adam's descendants were cut off by God's judgement in the Flood, so Noah's descendants were humbled and divided by God's judgement at Babel. As the Flood separates human history (in the broad sense) into the period 'before the Flood' and 'after the Flood', so Babel separates human history after the Flood into a blissful era 'before the earth was divided' and the modern era 'after the earth was divided'. With this perspective, we will now examine the story of the Tower of Babel in order to explore its meaning and its origins.

9.1 Babel in history

The story of Babel begins with a picture of universal harmony: *'Now the whole world had one language and a common speech'*. It then describes mankind's aspiration to build a city, *'with a tower that reaches to the heavens'*. However, to prevent mankind from attaining some kind of invincibility, God confuses their language and scatters them over the whole Earth. The story has a basic chiastic form (e.g. Radday, 1972) which is similar to the Flood Story. It is probably intended to echo the Flood Story on a smaller scale; just as Babel itself was a disaster for mankind, but on a smaller scale than the Flood. The chiasmus can be summarised as follows:

Human unity (Ch 11:1-2)
  Man speaks and acts (v. 3-4)
    God comes down to see (v. 5)
  God speaks and acts (v. 6-7)
Human dispersion (v. 8-9)

This structure seems to fit the theological objective of the story quite well in focussing attention on God's judgement of the hubris (arrogant pride) of mankind. The turning point is when God comes down to see what mankind is doing. This turning point emphasises the comparison between humanity, which seeks to build a tower that will reach to heaven, and God, who has to come *down* to see it because it is so pathetically insignificant from his perspective. Based on this observation it is usually assumed that the Tower of Babel story is a diatribe against human pride. This may be true in the general sense, but Laurin (1978) argued that it is inconceivable that the building of a ziggurat tower in Mesopotamia was an enterprise of secular engineering, since the whole of their society was focussed on the service of the gods. For example, the great ziggurat of Ur, which is the most completely restored Mesopotamian tower (Fig. 9.1), was dedicated to the moon god Nanna. Therefore, in seeking to *'make a name for ourselves'* the builders must in fact have been acting in the name of a Mesopotamian deity. In other words, the rebellion at Babel was not atheistic pride but idolatry.

Fig. 9.1 Architectural impression of the Great Ziggurat of Ur. After Woolley (1939).

Despite its clear Mesopotamian setting, the actual narrative of the Babel story has less clear Mesopotamian origins. Indeed, the narrative has several characteristics that point to a non-Mesopotamian composition. An obvious one is the aside to the reader (verse 3b) that the Babylonians *'used brick instead of stone, and tar instead of mortar'*. This comment clearly has a post-Mesopotamian origin, explaining to the Israelite reader the style of Mesopotamian architecture. However, this is probably a later editorial addition (a 'gloss') and does not have any significance for the age of the main narrative. On the other hand, an important post-Mesopotamian characteristic of the text as a whole is the pervasive extent of Hebrew word-play (e.g. Wenham, 1987, p. 234). For example (expressing the Hebrew in Roman phonics) man's *nilbenah*, meaning "let us make (bricks)" sounds like God's *nabelah*, meaning "let us mix up", and of course *Babhel* = 'Babylon' sounds like *Balal* = 'confused'. This word-play suggests at least that the present form of the narrative represents a Hebrew composition. However, we must remember that Hebrew is one of the Semitic group of languages, so that these puns in the Hebrew might have been taken over from an earlier story in Akkadian. Furthermore, there are other features of the story which clearly have pre-Hebrew origins.

One of these features is the use of the plural form for God in Gen 11:7 "Come, let *us* go down and confuse their language". In view of the Hebrew passion for monotheism, it would be unthinkable for a Hebrew author after the Exodus to use the plural form for God, who revealed himself to Moses as 'I AM'. Therefore the plural form suggests that the basis of the story goes back to primitive Mesopotamian roots.

The actual construction of the great ziggurat of Babylon (Fig. 9.2) is described in the Akkadian Epic of Creation, usually referred to by the first two words of its text, *Enuma Elish* ('When Above'). It describes the origin of the gods, including Marduk, a god who was originally the city god of Babylon but was 'promoted' to the chief god of the Mesopotamian pantheon when Hammurabi made Babylon the capital of Mesopotamia around 1760 BC. According to a tablet of ritual instructions for the New Year Festival in Babylon, the Creation Epic was to be recited on the fourth day of that Festival (Dalley, 1991, p. 231). In Book 6 of the Epic, the building of Babylon and its ziggurat is described, as in the following excerpt. It will be noticed that, according to this account, the gods themselves built the ziggurat for their chief god, Marduk. However, this projection of human actions onto the divine plane is the normal mode of expression in Mesopotamian literature.

> *Create Babylon, whose construction you requested;*
> *Let its mud bricks be molded, and build high the shrine!*
> *The Anunnaki (gods) began shovelling,*
> *For a whole year they made bricks for it.*
> *When the second year arrived,*
> *They had raised the top of Esaglia in front of the Apsu;*
> *They had built a high ziggurat for the Apsu.*
>
> [Dalley, 1991, p. 262]

It seems likely that this description of the building of the great ziggurat of Babylon did inspire the Tower of Babel story in Genesis (e.g. Speiser 1964, p. 75). However, we need to compare the Mesopotamian and biblical chronologies to see whether the building of the ziggurat of Babylon could actually have occurred between the Flood and Abram's departure from Mesopotamia.

Fig. 9.2 Model reconstruction of the ziggurat of Babylon from the time of Nebuchadnezzar II. Staatliche Museen, Berlin.

Dates for Mesopotamian dynasties in the Old Babylonian period are determined from astronomical records of the rising and setting of the planet Venus during the reign of Ammi-saduqa, the fourth king to reign after Hammurabi. This dynasty has been securely linked by king lists and date lists to the preceding Isin and the Ur III dynasties (e.g. Reade, 2001, p. 11). However, because there are several possible fits to the astronomical data, this has led to the so-called 'High, Middle and Low' alternative chronologies, spread over a range of more than 100 years (Astrom, 1987). Because of the difficulty of choosing between the relative merits of the competing chronologies, most scholars have used the Middle chronology, as adopted by the Cambridge Ancient History encyclopedia (e.g. Postgate, 1992, p. 39). This chronology has recently been linked to the very well dated 'Anatolian tree ring chronology' from southern Turkey (Kuniholm *et al.*, 1996; Manning *et al.*, 2001). The links between the two chronologies are not 100% secure (Reade, 2001, p. 10), but the 'Middle' chronology represents a good working hypothesis and will therefore be used here. This places the beginning of the reign of Hammurabi at 1792 BC.

Most evidence puts Abram earlier than the time of Hammurabi (see section 17.3), while the genealogy of Shem suggests that the Tower of Babel was built at least several generations before Abram. Therefore, the setting of the story is probably hundreds of years before the ziggurat of Babylon was built. This implies that the story of Babel is a deliberate anachronism (an event which is set in a different time from when it really occurred). Most likely the story combines two (or more) events which actually occurred at different times into a single object lesson.

While the building of Marduk's temple at Babylon probably inspired the association of the Tower with Babylon, we must also look for an origin for the story in a much earlier event between the time of Noah and Abram. If the reference to the 'division of the earth' in the time of Peleg (Gen 10:25) refers to the division of languages after Babel, this implies that the building of the Tower occurred about half way between the time of Noah and Abram, around 3500 BC. However, since this genealogy is primarily schematic rather than chronological (section 2.3), any date between 2500 and 4500 BC would be reasonable. On the other hand, the reference to the baking of the bricks (Gen 11:3) implies a date after 3500 BC, when this technique was first applied to building materials (Seely, 2001).

In support of an early Third Millennium date, Kramer (1968) suggested that elements of the Babel story go back to the Sumerian myth of Lugal-banda and Enmerkar. This myth describes an early blissful state of mankind, to be contrasted with the 'modern' state of the world at the time of its composition. A 'catalogue tablet' from the Nippur library of the Old Babylonian period lists this myth along with several other compositions believed to date from the Third Dynasty of Ur (ca. 2100 BC). Hence this is probably the date of composition of the myth, but it describes a much more ancient time. Kramer (1944) translated the relevant part as follows: (note that the compass points in brackets are not in the original but were included for explanation):

110

In those days the land of Shubur (East), the place of plenty,
  of righteous decrees,
Harmony-tongued Sumer (South), the great land of the
  "decrees of princeship"
Uri (North), the land of all that is needful
The land Martu (West), resting in security,
The whole universe, the people in unison,
To Enlil in one tongue gave praise.

[Kramer, 1944, p. 107]

Over twenty years later, Kramer (1968) published the next piece of the story which had been found in the meantime by Gurney. Kramer translated this piece as follows:

Then a-da the lord, a-da the prince, a-da the king,
Enki a-da the lord, a-da the prince, a-da the king,
Enki, the lord of abundance, (whose) commands are trustworthy,
The lord of wisdom, who understands the land,
The leader of the gods,
Endowed with wisdom, the lord of Eridu,
Changed the speech of their mouths, brought (?) contention into it,
Into the speech of man that had been one.

On the basis of this translation, Kramer argued that the Sumerians believed that there had been a period of universal harmony which was brought to an end by Enki, god of wisdom, possibly because he was jealous of the pre-eminent position of the god Enlil. The roles of these gods will be discussed in detail below; however, it is sufficient for now to note that this interpretation of the Sumerian myth presents the confounding of human speech as the result of rivalry between the gods. If we adopt the interpretation of Laurin (1978) then we can see how the Sumerian myth could have arisen from an account of how the True God judged the peoples of the earth for their idolatry. However, I will argue (section 14.5) that this was primarily a battle between the True God and the goddess Inanna, rather than between Enlil and Enki.

Regarding the historical setting of the Tower story, archaeological and linguistic evidence is not in accord with a period of *global* unity, any more than geological evidence is consistent with a *global* flood. However, from the viewpoint of the Sumerians there was a time when one city dominated the civilisation of the known earth, and that city was

111

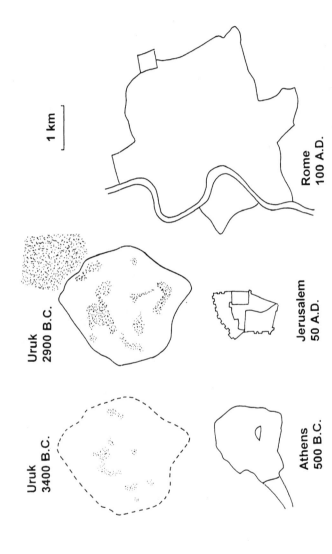

Fig. 9.3 Plans of Uruk showing evidence of occupied areas shaded during the Late Uruk and the Early Dynastic I period, compared with the size of Athens, Jerusalem and Rome. After Nissen (1983/1988, p. 71-2).

1 km

Uruk
3400 B.C.

Uruk
2900 B.C.

Athens
500 B.C.

Jerusalem
50 A.D.

Rome
100 A.D.

Uruk. Hence, there are several important reasons why the origin of the Tower of Babel story (rather than its name) might date to the end of the golden age of Uruk.

Firstly, the decline of Uruk was preceded by the building of great temples placed on huge raised platforms, the forerunners of the classic ziggurat of later Babylonian history. In this context, it should be noted that the Bible describes a *'tower that reaches to the heavens'* (Gen 11:4) rather than the particular design of ziggurat that was developed over subsequent centuries. Furthermore, the high towers of Uruk known as the Anu Ziggurat and the Eanna Complex were devoted to the heavenly god, An, and the Queen of Heaven, Inanna. Hence, it was perfectly natural that a special emphasis should be placed on building a tower that *'reaches to the heavens'*.

The second point concerns the pre-eminent political position of Uruk in the ancient world. Archaeological evidence suggests that at the beginning of the Third Millennium, Uruk was by far the largest city in the world. The approximate extent of the settled area of the city can be determined from the surface distribution of pottery of different styles (and hence ages). This evidence shows that during the Early Dynastic I period, the occupied extent was greater than the limits defined by the city walls, and the extent of the city during Late Uruk times was probably almost as large (Fig. 9.3). A comparison with other great world cities shows the truly immense size of Uruk, which was greater than Athens or Jerusalem at their height and almost as large as Imperial Rome.

Other evidence suggests that during the Protoliterate period, Uruk also had a major influence on world civilisation. The sudden appearance of Egyptian hieroglyphics around 3100 BC suggests that the Egyptians were influenced by the earlier development of writing in Sumer (e.g. Hawkins, 1979, p. 146), and this cultural influence is also demonstrated by the Mesopotamian (Jemdet Nasr style) cylinder seals found in Egyptian graves at this time (Kantor, 1952; Finegan, 1979, p. 168). Elamite writing was probably also inspired by the Sumerian script, which is understandable in view of its close proximity. However, Elamite may in turn have influenced the later development of writing by the Indus Valley civilisation, located in modern Pakistan (Parpola, 1994, p. 53). There is also evidence that patterned designs seen in Indus Valley art were ultimately derived from Mesopotamia (Parpola, 1985, p. 143).

A third point which supports Uruk as the original subject of the Tower story is the reference in the Table of Nations (Gen 10:25), to the name Peleg, *'because in his time the earth was divided'*. This reference is generally linked to the scattering of peoples after Babel, and it aptly describes the end of the period of supremacy of Eridu and Uruk, and the beginning of the period of 'Rival City States' (Reimer, 1996).

The final point concerns the confusion of language at Babel, which aptly describes the encounter between Sumerian and Semitic (Akkadian) speakers. The peoples who built Eridu and Uruk were clearly Sumerian, but several of the kings in the succeeding dynasty at Kish were evidently of Semitic race. This can be inferred because several of these kings have names which are recognisable as words in the Akkadian language. This correspondence demonstrates that these are native Semitic names and not transliterations from Sumerian into Akkadian. Hence, the decline of Uruk and the rise of Kish also signalled a cultural shift, in which the Sumerians lost their dominance of civilisation for the first time.

9.2 The Table of Nations

Just as the Tower of Babel represents the major turning point in human history after the Flood, the Table of Nations (Genesis Ch 10) describes the major direction of human civilisation after the Flood. It does this by tracing the ancestry of the major people-groups of the Middle East back to Noah's sons, Shem, Ham and Japheth. However, we must recognise that the Table of Nations is a highly stylised account. This is demonstrated by the large number of seven-fold groups. For example, Japheth apparently had seven sons (which is quite natural), but only seven of his grandsons are named (Gen 10:2-4), which can hardly represent the total number of such offspring. This suggests that seven grandsons have been chosen for stylistic reasons. Similarly, five sons of Cush are named, but only two grandsons, again achieving a total of seven (Gen 10:6-7). This total excludes Nimrod, who is identified as a city builder rather than the ancestor of a nation (Gen 10:8-12). Again, in Gen 10:13, seven nations are named as descendants from Egypt (Mizraim). Finally, the total number of nations represented in the account is seventy (again excluding Nimrod). This total matches the total number of Jacob's descendants who entered Egypt (Gen 46:27). Thus Jacob (Israel) is a 'microcosm of the wider family of humanity' (Wenham, 1987, p. 214).

The Table of Nations is not intended as a genealogy connecting Shem to Abram (the line of God's Elect). That function is accomplished by the genealogy in Gen Ch 11. In contrast, the main function of the

Table of Nations is to describe the relationship between God's Elect and the non-elect peoples of the ancient world. It has a symmetrical overall form in which the distribution of peoples is simplified into three major swathes: the Semites in the fertile crescent, the Hamitic peoples from Canaan to North Africa, and the descendants of Japheth in the more remote northern and western areas of the ancient known world. In this context, Eber, ancestor of the Hebrews, takes his place as a great-grandson of Shem (Table. 9.1).

Table 9.1 The descendants of Shem

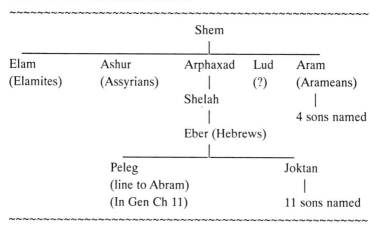

Names in brackets are people groups identified with this ancestor.

Each of the main sections of the Table of Nations ends with a similar formulaic summary. For example, the genealogy of Shem (Gen 10.31) ends as follows:

These are the descendants/sons of Shem by their clans and languages, in their territories and nations.

Based on this claim, we can compare the people groups defined in the Table of Nations (e.g. Tables 9.1 and 9.3) with a modern linguistic analysis of Middle Eastern peoples (Table 9.2). This comparison reveals some areas of disagreement between the groupings based on biblical and linguistic analysis. Assuming that linguistic analysis yields the most accurate evidence for ethnic relationships, this suggests that the biblical Table expresses primarily political (and hence theological) relationships. This is perfectly reasonable when we remember that biblical genealogies are intended to show relationships in a schematic rather than literal way, and are not taken literally, even by Creationists (section 2.3)

Table 9.2 Recognised linguistic groups of the Middle East

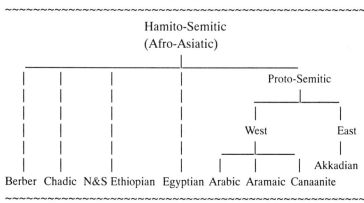

Both the biblical and linguistic classifications recognise major differences between the Semitic peoples and the North African (Hamitic) peoples (Egyptians, Ethiopians, Libyans etc). However, linguistic analysis places the Canaanites within the Semitic family, whereas the Bible places them in the Hamitic family (Table 9.3). It is commonly suggested that this placing of the Canaanites into the Hamitic branch reflects the fact that both Egyptians and Canaanites were the greatest enemies of God's people at the time of the Exodus from Egypt and the entry into the Promised Land. This would suggest that the table of Nations was composed after the time of Moses. Such a date is usually inferred from the wording of Gen 10:18b-19, which contains information that could not have been known before the Israelite invasion of Canaan:

Later the Canaanite clans scattered and the borders of Canaan reached from Sidon towards Gerar as far as Gaza, and then towards Sodom, Gomorrah, Admah and Zeboiim, as far as Lasha.

However, these verses, located at the very end of the genealogy of Ham, have all the marks of an editorial comment added to the main text long after its composition. Therefore, an alternative possibility is that the main body of the Table was composed during the sojourn of the Israelites in Egypt, when the Canaanites were under Egyptian rule. The close association between Egypt and Canaan during this period is attested by the

'Amarna Letters', which record correspondence between Canaanite princes and their Egyptian overlords in the 14th century BC.

The description of the exploits of Nimrod (Gen 10:8-12) is probably another late addition to the Table of Nations, and several scholars (e.g. Dalley, 1998, p. 66-67) have suggested that Nimrod is actually Tukulti-Ninurta I, who was the first Assyrian king to conquer Babylon in ca. 1220 BC. He was named after Ninurta, god of the hunt, who was the patron god of the city of Nimrud. The description of Nimrod as a descendant of Cush (and hence Hamitic) is at variance with the Semitic affinity of the Mesopotamian peoples described in Gen 10:22 and is probably an indication that this comment was added at a late date when the Assyrians were the enemies of the Israelites.

9.3 Sumerians and Semites

One group of people who are not named anywhere in the Table of Nations are the Sumerians. However, if the Tower of Babel story reflects events that originally occurred at Uruk then the implication is that Shem and his immediate descendants were (by modern linguistic analysis) Sumerian rather than Semitic. Exactly this proposal was made by Poebel (1941), as cited by Kramer (1963, p. 297). Kramer suggested that Shem and Sumer are actually one and the same, since the word we pronounce as 'Sumer' would have been pronounced *Shumi* by the Akkadians. When this was translated into Hebrew, the final *i* could have been dropped and the vowel changed from *u* to *e*, as we see for the word 'name', which changes from *shumu* in Akkadian to *shem* in Hebrew.

Whether or not the above explanation is correct, there is a clear parallel in the Table of Nations which shows how the Sumerians could have become 'Shemitic'. This is based on the treatment of Elam, who is included as one of the sons of Shem (Table 9.1), even though the Elamites represent a distinct people group on the basis of linguistic analysis of the pronunciation of the Elamite script. As argued above, this placement of the Elamites suggests that relationships in the Table of Nations are political rather than ethnic. The inclusion of the Elamites as Semitic is reasonable from a political perspective since these people are situated immediately to the east of the Mesopotamian plain.

The treatment of Elam shows how the Sumerians would be regarded as Semitic in the Table of Nations, based on political relationships. Historical evidence discussed by Jacobsen (1939b) shows that the assimilation of Sumerian culture by the Semitic peoples of Mesopotamia was a peaceful process resulting from continual Semitic immigration into the Mesopotamian plain. Therefore, in the cultural sense, the transition from Sumerian to Semitic civilisation was almost seamless. By the time Abram left Mesopotamia (sometime around 2000 BC), the Sumerians had effectively been absorbed by the Semitic peoples of Mesopotamia and the Sumerian language remained only as a scholarly and religious language, with a role similar to Latin in the European Middle Ages.

The passing of this Sumerian linguistic, cultural and theological heritage to the Semitic peoples and then to the Hebrews is succinctly represented in the Table of Nations by the line of descent Shem-Arphaxad-Shelah-Eber. The name of Shem's son, Arphaxad, is non-Semitic, whereas Shelah is an archetype of the Semitic peoples, and Eber is the archetype of the Hebrews. We can see that this archetype is symbolic rather than literal because although Abram was called a Hebrew, not even all of his own descendants (Ishmael, Edom) were regarded as Hebrews. Instead, the symbolic genealogy in the Table of Nations is designed to show that the Hebrews have long cultural roots, extending back to the dawn of history (Malamat, 1968, p. 167).

Table 9.3 The descendants of Ham

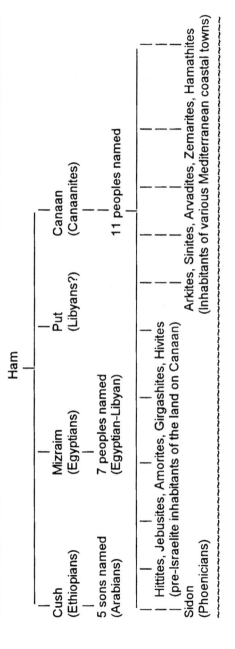

Ham

Cush (Ethiopians)	Mizraim (Egyptians)	Put (Libyans?)	Canaan (Canaanites)
5 sons named (Arabians)	7 peoples named (Egyptian-Libyan)		11 peoples named

Sidon (Phoenicians)

Hittites, Jebusites, Amorites, Girgashites, Hivites (pre-Israelite inhabitants of the land on Canaan)

Arkites, Sinites, Arvadites, Zemarites, Hamathites (Inhabitants of various Mediterranean coastal towns)

CHAPTER 10

THE ORIGIN OF LITERATURE

10.1 The origin of writing

Written history is taken to begin at the start of the Early Dynastic period (ca. 3000 BC), but human records go considerably further back in time. In the general sense, we could argue that cave paintings are a form of historical record. However, the earliest systematic record keeping was the development of stamp seals shortly after the Neolithic agricultural revolution. Good examples of these seals and their impressions have been found at Arpachiyah (near Nineveh) during the Halaf period (around 6000 BC). Because these seals have been found with impressions of fabric or string, they may have been used to label sacks of goods with their owners' identity (Campbell, 1992).

Another aspect of record keeping that goes back to the Halaf period is the use of tokens to represent different commodities (Amiet, 1966). These tokens are usually made of stone or clay, and their plain shape and form meant that for a long time they were overlooked during excavations. Study of these artifacts was taken up by Schmandt-Besserat, who developed a theory as to how the use of tokens could have given rise, over a period of time, to more sophisticated forms of record keeping (Schmandt-Besserat, 1992).

Evidence for the development of token records into the first writing comes from Uruk, in levels 6 to 3 of the Eanna Complex (spanning the Late Uruk to Protoliterate periods). The Eanna complex contained elaborately decorated temples and temple storehouses, probably representing the world's largest religious-economic institution. The storage of food offerings in the temple complex is shown on cylinder seals of the Uruk period (e.g. Lloyd, 1978, p. 60; Senner, 1989, p. 31), and on the Protoliterate-age Uruk vase (Fig. 7.4). As the population of Uruk grew and the economy of the temple expanded it must have become more and more important to keep records of the receipt of commodities into the temple storehouses and their distribution as temple offerings and as food for the temple servants.

The first stage in the development of record keeping, during the early Fourth Millennium, was the elaboration of tokens from a small number of simple shapes into a greater variety of 'complex tokens' with surface markings. This allowed tokens to be used to identify a wider range of specific commodities, such as jars of oil and wine, and different kinds of livestock. For example, the token for a sheep is believed to have been a ball of clay with a cross on it, while a ewe was represented in a similar way, but with an extra indentation in one quadrant (Fig. 10.1).

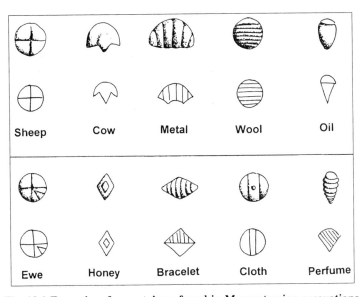

Fig. 10.1 Examples of some tokens found in Mesopotamian excavations, along with their proto-cuneiform equivalents from archaic book-keeping records. Examples from Schmandt-Besserat (1992).

Around this time, methods of recording transactions were developed, perhaps first by making tokens with holes and threading them on a string. The ends of the string could be sealed into a clay ball, which was then marked with a seal to prevent tampering. Alternatively, and perhaps later, the tokens were pressed directly into a clay ball that was marked with a seal to denote ownership or the witnessing of a transaction. It is thought that this procedure finally led to the practice of 'drawing' the tokens directly on the surface of the clay ball with a sharp stylus, before sealing it in the usual way. Examples of tokens and their drawn equivalents are shown in Fig. 10.1.

Using the system of tokens described above, multiple units of a given commodity (e.g. sheep) were represented by multiple tokens, one for each unit. However, the crucial stage in the development from token-based accounting to writing was the realisation that the concept of number could be separated from the identity of the commodity. Thus, instead of drawing five complex sheep tokens on a lump of clay, the transaction could be recorded by drawing only one sheep token, alongside five simple indentations to represent the quantity. This separation of the quantity from the type of commodity must have greatly increased efficiency and it opened the door to the separate development of counting and writing.

With this development, a tablet could record a more complex transaction, such as the allotment of food offerings for the temple. This is seen, for example, on a proto-cuneiform tablet from Uruk level 4 (Fig. 10.2a). This tablet shows that two sheep were to be used for an offering at the temple (a house on a platform, whose sign in this case is partially obscured by damage). The signs on the left hand side of the tablet show that this was the temple of the goddess Inanna, represented by the combination of a star (divinity) and the looped totem associated with her temple storehouse. The latter symbol is seen on the Uruk vase, and also on an early cylinder seal (Fig. 10.2b). We know that this 'pictogram' means Inanna because it evolves into the cuneiform sign for Inanna in later Sumerian literature.

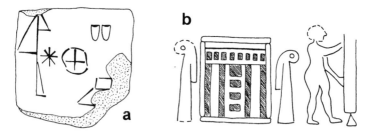

Fig. 10.2 a) Proto-cuneiform tablet from Uruk level 4 showing the offering of two sheep at the temple of Inanna. Deutsches Archaologisches Institut, University of Heidelberg. b) cylinder seal impression showing the juxtaposition of the looped totem with an image of the temple. Yale Babylonian Collection (Goff and Buchanan, 1956).

To enlarge the vocabulary of pictographic signs, graphic elements were combined to portray additional objects. For example, stippling could modify the sign for 'jar' to indicate 'beer'; modify 'oil' to mean 'perfume', and modify 'sheep' to mean 'ewe' (Fig. 10.3a). Similarly, the addition of two ticks modified the pictogram for 'head' to mean 'mouth'. Modifications of signs were also used to create signs for abstract concepts, called ideograms, which represent a further step in the development of writing. For example, the pictogram for 'head' was modified by adding the pictogram for 'food' (a rimmed bowl), to mean eat, while 'mouth' + 'water' were combined to signify 'drink'. Other abstract concepts were described by broadening the meaning of certain pictograms to include related abstract words. For example, the pictogram for 'mouth' could also be the ideograms 'word', 'voice' and 'speak'. However, this broadening would actually have a negative impact on the later development of writing because it made the language rather imprecise.

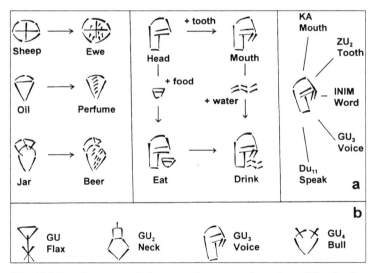

Fig. 10.3 Developments of pictogram interpretation: a) modification by pictograms by stippling; by addition of extra elements; and by broadening of meaning; b) variety of pictograms representing homophones of the Sumerian word 'GU'.

Pictograms are the oldest form of writing, and involve a pictorial representation of a complete word. Hence, these signs are also called logograms. Clay tablets of different ages can be compared to show the development of pictograms from the earliest forms, which are essentially drawings of objects, to later forms which became more and more stylised to accelerate the process of writing. The most important development is a change from semi-continuous lines on the clay surface to a series of separate indentations, each of which has the wedge-shaped form which gives us the word 'cuneiform'.

Probably as a result of this development, the clay tablet was later turned through 90º to facilitate writing, so that columns of signs become rows, with each sign on its side. Hence, by this double step in the evolution of writing the cuneiform character became almost entirely dissociated in appearance from the original object. For example, this rotation makes a man's head and a ration bowl stand on their side and it makes the horns of a cow or bull come out of the side its head, (Fig. 10.4). However, this evolution in writing style took much longer than previously thought.

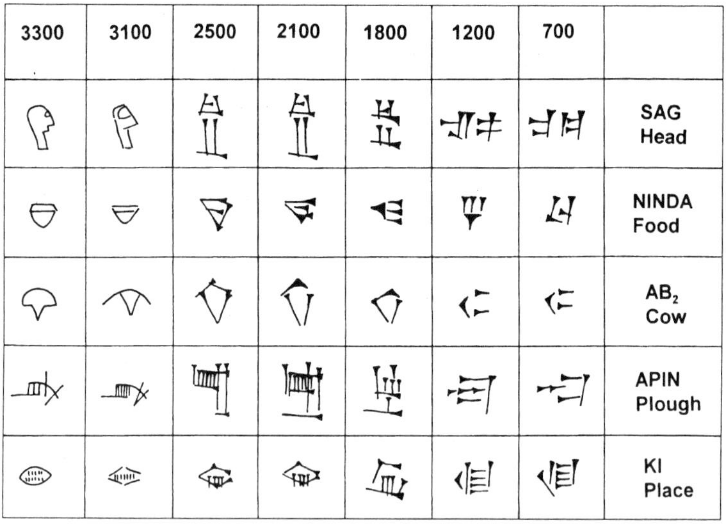

3300	3100	2500	2100	1800	1200	700	
							SAG Head
							NINDA Food
							AB$_2$ Cow
							APIN Plough
							KI Place

Fig. 10.4 Diagram showing the progression from incised pictograms (ca. 3300 BC) to early Sumerian cuneiform (2500 BC) and late Assyrian cuneiform (700 BC). Modified after Nissen et al. (1993, p. 124).

Beginning with Rawlinson and Norris (1861), early Assyriologists assumed that Sumerian tablets were written in horizontal rows because that was the orientation of the Assyrian cuneiform with which they were familiar (section 5.1). However, evidence from numerous artifacts shows that Sumerian cuneiform was written in vertical columns, reading from right to left, like traditional Chinese characters. These artifacts include bricks (Fig. 5.2), statues (e.g. Fig. 16.1) and stelae (e.g. Fig. 16.3) which show that cuneiform inscriptions were still being written in the original orientation as late as the Old Babylonian period. An example of cuneiform script written vertically on clay is provided by the Cylinders of Gudea (2200 BC), one of the greatest early Sumerian literary works. The text is written on large clay cylinders, about 1m in length and 50 cm across, which have holes in the ends. These were doubtless designed to mount the cylinders on horizontal wooden poles for public reading (Fig. 10.5). Therefore, Sumerian cuneiform may have been read in the old vertical orientation until well into the Old Babylonian period[7].

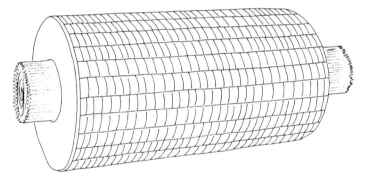

Fig. 10.5 Drawing of one of the cylinders of Gudea as it might originally have been mounted for public recitation. These artifacts are now too fragile to mount in this orientation. Musee du Louvre.

10.2 From pictograms to phonograms

It is a long way from a series of pictograms and ideograms to a written account. However, Bottero (1987, p. 77 ff) pointed out that a series of pictograms for objects can be useful as an aid to the memory (a mnemonic device). For example, if we know a story, we can recollect it with the help of a series of pictograms. However, a fully developed system of writing allows an educated reader to reconstruct a train of ideas without prior knowledge of the subject matter. Because this requires a much more sophisticated written vocabulary, another developmental step was needed to progress from a mnemonic device to a means of literary communication. This was the invention of phonograms.

A major barrier to the development of a pictographic language is the difficulty of representing abstract words or names that cannot easily be communicated in pictorial form. Sometime around the end of the Late Uruk period, when writing had become established as a reliable means of book-keeping, scribes probably encountered the need to record the names of people who were contributing temple offerings. Perhaps some of these people were foreigners from the north or east of Sumer whose names could not be expressed in Sumerian pictograms. It must have occurred to some ingenious scribe that a name which could not be written directly could nevertheless be 'spelled out' phonetically. This was done by borrowing a group of otherwise unrelated words (logograms) which had the same sound as the syllables of the name they were trying to pronounce. Such words with the same sounds are called homophones. We can illustrate the process with the name of Hammurabi of Babylon, even though this comes from a later period. Hammurabi is a Semitic name but was written in Sumerian by writing each syllable of the name phonetically: 'Ha-am-mu-ra-bi'.

Some further thought would lead to a realisation: many regular words in a language, apart from names, could be used as homophones. For example, the word 'can' in English can be used as a verb (I *can* see you) or as a noun (a tin *can*). So if we are using a pictogram for writing then we can use the same sign to represent an unrelated homophone. This sign is then called a phonogram. For example, a drawing of a tin can could be used to express the word 'can' in the phrase 'I can see you'. Such an abstract concept would be impossible to represent using a pictogram.

Our evidence suggests that because of its linguistic structure, the Sumerian spoken language had many words with only one syllable, and consequently had many homophones. Modern Chinese also has many homophones, which are distinguished in speech by different tones. Presumably the Sumerians used a similar system. For example, the word pronounced *gu* could mean the nouns 'flax', 'neck', 'voice', or 'bull' (Fig. 10.3b). These different meanings are distinguished in the Romanised transliteration of Sumerian cuneiform by the addition of numerical subscripts (e.g. gu_4= bull). An example of a verb with several homophones is the word pronounced *du*, which could mean 'to go', 'to build', 'to butt', or 'to free' (Bottero, 1987, p. 69). Verbs of this type were modified for different tenses or persons (i.e. I go, you go, I will go etc) by adding prefixes or suffixes to the original word. Hence, Sumerian is described as an 'agglutinative' language. In contrast,

Semitic languages typically have words of more than one syllable whose phonetic pronunciation is modified ('inflected') to express person or tense.

An example of the development of a phonogram to convey an abstract concept is provided by the Sumerian word for 'arrow' (*ti*) which apparently sounded the same as the word for 'life'. Hence, in an inscription from the Jemdet Nasr (Protoliterate) period, we read *En lil ti* (Fig. 10.6). Based on comparison with other similar inscriptions, the deduced meaning is: 'The Lord (*En*) breath (*lil*) is life (*ti*)'. The intended meaning of the phonogram (out of all the possible homophones) must be deduced by the context, but this can usually, though not invariably, be achieved by the modern scholar.

Fig. 10.6 Signs for *En lil ti* from a Protoliterate inscription (Bermant and Weitzman, 1979).

The words 'life' and 'arrow' are homophones in Sumerian, but not in Semitic languages such as Akkadian. Therefore, we deduce from such examples that it was the Sumerians who made the step from pictographic to phonetic writing. Thus by adapting a pictogram to make a phonogram for every syllabic sound in Sumerian speech, the Sumerians now opened up to themselves the opportunity of expressing the total meaning of their spoken language in writing. It was this step, thought to have occurred at the end of the Jemdet Nasr period around 3000 BC, which opened the way to written history (Bottero, 1987, p. 81).

Human conservatism being what it is, the Sumerians did not immediately switch from pictographic to phonographic writing, but exploited the two alongside each other. A given character could be used as either pictogram or phonogram, and to help distinguish between them, extra characters called 'classifiers' were introduced. Indeed, it took several hundred years for writing to exploit the full potential of the phonetic system. With the increasing dominance of Semitic speakers, the process became more and more complete, but to the very end of Sumerian culture, numerous archaic logograms remained in the script.

There were probably some good reasons for extreme conservatism in the development of writing. One is the need to retain continuity between any new system and the existing system of writing ('backwards compatibility'). Without backwards compatibility, new writing systems do not catch on because they cannot be used by a majority of the literate population. The second reason for conservatism is that early writers may not have perceived a need for anything more than a mnemonic device. In the same way, computer programmers often do not see the need for full documentation of their programs. Thus it may have taken some time to appreciate the usefulness of a complete written communication system.

10.3 The development of Sumerian literature

Literature is generally taken to be one of the highest achievements of human society, but the question of what constitutes literature can be hard to answer. A useful approach is the classification proposed by Hallo (1958), which divides cuneiform records into three categories: *archival*, such as bureaucratic records and letters; *monumental*, such as royal inscriptions; and *canonical*, comprising literature. The first two categories are usually known only from single copies, but the latter material is normally known from multiple copies because it represents material that has entered what Oppenheim (1964, p. 13) called the 'Stream of Tradition'. Some material in the Stream of Tradition was intended at the time of its composition to be of literary value; for example, epics, myths, hymns, laments, poems and wisdom literature. Other material in the Stream of Tradition was originally archival or monumental but was adopted for the curriculum of the scribal schools as material for copying exercises.

Apart from book-keeping records, the earliest written materials consist of different kinds of word lists. These first appear during the Jemdet Nasr period and many are then copied verbatim for more than 700 years (Nissen, 1988, p. 80). Examples are the Standard List of Professions (Fig. 10.7), lists of cities and gods, lists of different kinds of animal used for food (e.g. fish, birds, pigs), and lists of different kinds of metal (Pollock, 1999, p. 164). These word lists were presumably used for teaching scribal students. They help us to see the development in the cuneiform signs through time and also provide us with information about the organisation of Sumerian society at the time when the lists first appeared.

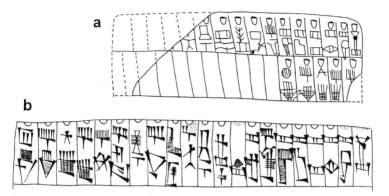

Fig. 10.7 Beginning of the Standard Professions List. a) from the Protoliterate level at Uruk (ca 3100), Freie Universitat, Berlin; b) from an excellently preserved tablet of Early Dynastic III age from Tell Abu Salabikh (ca 2600 BC), Oriental Institute, Chicago. The tablets are shown in their original pictographic orientation and are read horizontally from right to left, panel by panel. After Nissen (1983/1988, p. 81) and Biggs (1974, pl. 1).

Two of the earliest examples of what we would call true literature are the Instructions of Shuruppak and the Hymn to Kesh. The former is a collection of proverbs attributed to the father of the Flood Hero, after whom the city of Shuruppak is named. The latter is a hymn to the temple of Kesh, a city near the Tigris in eastern Mesopotamia. The reasons for writing hymns are similar to the reasons for writing down temple offerings. A hymn represents a sacrificial offering to the temple god and if the hymn was composed by a gifted individual, perhaps for an auspicious occasion such as the dedication of the temple, it would be desirable to reproduce it exactly on future occasions. Hence a particular importance would be attached to exact reproduction of the ritual, which could best be achieved by adherence to a written script.

Fragments of the Hymn to Kesh are known from the Early Dynastic period around 2600 BC from Tell Abu Salabikh (possibly ancient Eresh, Fig. 6.3). The content of this work is well known from the Old Babylonian period, which allows comparisons to be made between versions which were written hundreds of years apart. The Early Dynastic version of the Hymn (Biggs, 1974) comprises only scattered fragments, but these are enough to suggest that the text was accurately reproduced over a period of 800 years. Nevertheless, the accurate reading of these early texts is extremely difficult. To quote Alster (1976, p. 114): *'The signs are written in arbitrary order within each case, rare signs with unknown readings are used, grammatical elements are often not written at all, abbreviated writings occur, and at times signs well known from later periods have readings not later ascribed to them'*. Hence we can conclude that at this stage in the middle of the Third Millennium, Sumerian writing was only beginning to achieve the necessary sophistication to allow the writing of complex works of literature.

Most Sumerian myths and epics have a repetitive structure which is considered to be a sign of oral rather than written transmission (e.g. Rasheed, 1972; Vanstiphout, 1992, p. 247). The repetitive nature of the story acts as a memory aid and is pleasing to the ear when orally recited. Other evidence for the oral nature of poetry in Early Dynastic times is provided by the pictogram for the word 'poetry', which is a jug. Rasheed (1972) suggested that this is a representation of a copper jug used to contain wine, suggesting that poetry was recited at feasts or relaxed social settings, where people would gather to hear the recitation of their cultural traditions. When these oral traditions were written down, their repetitive structure was preserved. For example, in the very earliest collections of literature, discovered in Shuruppak and Tell Abu Salabikh and dating from around 2600 BC, several tablets begin with an introduction which was standard for later mythological texts:

On a faraway day, indeed on a faraway day,
On a faraway night, indeed on a faraway night,
In a faraway time, indeed in a faraway time...

[Biggs, 1966, p. 81]

One of the tablets bearing this text can be identified, from its style, as a school tablet copied as an exercise. The discovery of this form of introduction in a school tablet implies that the form itself was well established, and probably had a long history prior to 2600 BC. It seems staggering that texts written more than 4600 years ago should begin with an introduction that suggests a people who were themselves looking back into the mists of time. However, if the Flood did occur around 5500 BC then this was nearly 3000 years earlier than the text, ample time to conjure the phrase *'On a faraway day...*

CHAPTER 11

THE SUMERIAN PANTHEON

The invention of writing initiated the historical period, when our understanding of ancient societies no longer has to rely only on our inferences from archaeological evidence but can be informed by the contemporary records of the ancient peoples themselves. Such evidence is particularly important in our attempts to deduce the nature of the ancient world view, and the identity of the ancient gods.

The Sumerians believed that man was created for the sole purpose of serving the gods, and accordingly their whole civilisation was completely centred on the offering of food to the gods in their temples. However, even the earliest historical records show that the Sumerians were polytheistic, worshipping a pantheon of tens or hundreds of gods. The biblical view of God shares with the Sumerians the idea that the worship of God is the first duty of mankind. For example, the Great Commandment (Deut 6:5):

> *"Love the LORD your God with all your heart and with all your soul and with all your strength."*

However, the preceding verse (also quoted in Mark 12:29) declares emphatically that the God of Israel was One God:

> *"Hear, O Israel: The LORD our God, the LORD is one."*

Thus it is generally assumed that monotheism was developed at the time of Moses as a 'refinement' of early polytheistic religion. However, Genesis maintains that the True God revealed himself at the dawn of human history to the patriarchs Adam, Noah and Abram. Genesis also emphasises the continuity of this revelation through the generations. For example, Gen 4:26 establishes the continuity of the identity of God in terms of his *name* (normally translated as LORD in English), whereas other texts emphasise the continuity of the religion of the patriarchs,

131

where the worship of God was passed down from father to son. Thus, Genesis 9:26 implies that Shem worshipped the same god as his father Noah, since Noah pronounces the blessing: *"Blessed be the LORD, the God of Shem"*.

If the continuity of worship of the True God is accepted, it could nevertheless be argued that the knowledge of this God was preserved for the 4000 or so years between Adam and Abram in some kind of religious 'hermit colony' that was totally isolated from the rest of human civilisation. However, it is much more reasonable to suppose that the knowledge of God was preserved as a thread of truth somewhere amongst the many false gods of Mesopotamia. In order to search for this thread, we must examine some of the more important Mesopotamian gods, their roles, and the relationships between them.

11.1 The Sumerian Pantheon through time

The Mesopotamian pantheon was not immutable and unchanging. Instead, individual gods often increased or decreased in importance over time. Therefore, one of the most important, but also one of the most difficult tasks in understanding the Mesopotamian view of the gods is to understand how the pantheon *changed* in the period between the foundation of Eridu and Abram's departure from Ur. If we can do this it may tell us how belief in the True God was preserved amongst a plethora of idols. However, a major problem that faces us in reconstructing the evolution of Mesopotamian theology is that the most detailed information comes from the time after the departure of Abram for the Promised Land. This information comes from the great Akkadian epics of Gilgamesh, Atrahasis and Enuma Elish, mainly composed during the Second Millennium BC.

Sumerian myths yield more ancient information about the Mesopotamian gods. For example, the tablets in the Temple Library of Nippur date to the Old Babylonian period but the content clearly comes from older sources. However, the original Sumerian written versions do not often seem to date back beyond the 3rd Dynasty of Ur (ca. 2100 - 2000 BC). Under the rule of king Shulgi, this period saw a 'renaissance' of the then-ancient Sumerian culture, in which a concerted attempt was made to record its mythology. However, we must realise that the positions which different gods occupied in the pantheon at this time (Ur III) may have been different from those of a millennium earlier.

A somewhat older source of information about the Mesopotamian pantheon is represented by the Sumerian Temple Hymns. This is a collection of 42 hymns, each directed to a god who was the patron deity of a specific city. Thirty five cities are named, but some of these had more than one patron god. The text claims as its author/compiler En-heduanna, high priestess of Nanna (the moon god) at Ur and daughter of Sargon of Akkad. This would correspond to a date of ca. 2350 BC, although some of the material is known in older sources from the Early Dynastic period. Also in the Early Dynastic period, some royal inscriptions from ED III give us a vital snap-shot of religious belief in the middle of the Third Millennium, around 2500 BC. Finally, the oldest information we have about Sumerian theology comes from lexical lists and from pictorial representations on temple furniture. One of the most important pictorial sources is the Uruk Vase discussed above (section 7.2).

Before examining some of the earlier (Third Millennium) evidence in detail, it is necessary to get an overview of the Mesopotamian pantheon from the Old Babylonian period. However, since nearly all of the Akkadian gods were inherited from the Sumerians, we will use the Sumerian names, with Akkadian versions in brackets. Firstly we list the 'great gods' which are clearly identified by Sumerian myths as the heads of the pantheon. These comprise a 'Cosmic Triad' of male gods (An, Enlil and Enki), along with the Mother goddess Ninhursaga:

> An (Anu), the god of heaven (his sign is simply that for 'heaven' or 'sky')
> Enlil (Ellil or Bel), the Lord-wind/air/breath/spirit, also the warrior god
> Enki (Ea), 'Lord of the Earth', the god of fresh waters and also of wisdom
> Ninhursag or Nintur (Nintu), goddess of the foothills and also the Mother goddess

There were also dozens of other gods who oversaw different aspects of the natural world and human life. Only a few of the most important are listed here:

> Inanna (Ishtar) goddess of passion and of the harvest, 'promoted' to Queen of Heaven
> Utu (Shamash) the sun god, also god of justice
> Nanna (Sin) the moon god
> Ninurta (Hadad) god of the thunderstorm

133

By the time the Akkadian epics were written (in the Second Millennium), the heavenly gods were collectively referred to as the Igigi, and distinguished from gods of the underworld, called the Anunna gods or Anunnaki. However, the name Anunnaki implies that these were originally the sons of An (god of heaven), and this is confirmed by the first line of the Sumerian myth 'Disputation between Cattle and Grain' (Kramer, 1956, p. 82). The reason why the Anunnaki were 'demoted' from the heavens to the underworld is unclear, but a hymn to the god Enlil at Nippur implies that he may have been responsible. This is one example of how the Mesopotamian pantheon evolved over time.

One source of information about the evolution of the pantheon is provided by lexical lists of gods (e.g. Fig. 11.1). This type of 'god list' parallels the standard list of professions discussed in section 10.3, and it appears that these lists were copied as school exercises. The list of professions is arranged in hierarchical order, with the greatest offices listed first, beginning with the king. A notable feature of the standard list of professions is that it was copied for over 1000 years, from the Protoliterate period to the Old Babylonian period, yet in all this time the order of the entries was preserved unchanged (Fig. 10.7). This might imply that the god list would also be in hierarchical order, which would allow us to understand the relative importance of each god in the pantheon.

Fig. 11.1 The beginning of the god list from Shuruppak (tablet VAT 12626). The tablet reads from right to left and the star sign in each element is the indicator of divinity. After Deimel (1923, p. 5).

Unfortunately, an examination of god-lists from different cities shows a rather different picture. The results of this examination are shown in Table 11.1 for the first six gods in each list (Deimel, 1923, p. 5; van Dijk, 1964, p. 6; Biggs, 1974, p. 83). These show that even between tablets of the same age from a single city (Shuruppak) there is some variation in the order, although the great gods An, Enlil and Enki usually comprise three of the top four gods.

134

Table 11.1 Some god lists from the Third and Second Millennium

Shuruppak VAT 12573+12763 2600 BC	Shuruppak VAT 12760 2600 BC	Shuruppak VAT 12626 2600 BC	Abu Salabikh AbS-T 200 2600 BC	Nippur 1600 BC
En-ki	An	En-lil	-	An
En-lil	En-lil	En-ki	-	An-tum
En-girish	Inanna	?	Nin-ki?	Urash
En-bulug	En-ki	?	En-ki?	En-lil
En-du	Nanna	?	Shesh-ki	Nu-nam-nir
En-udu	Utu	?	Inanna	Nin-lil

The conflicting evidence from these ancient lists of gods was summed up by Van Dijk (1964, p. 2) something like this: *'Sumerian religion presents itself to our eyes like a monster with a hundred different heads'* (my translation from the French). This complexity is largely due to the changing importance of different cults over time, and a tendency to try to rationalise these changes within the Mesopotamian pantheon by constructing 'family' relationships between the gods.

11.2 The rite of 'Sacred Marriage'

Family relationships between the gods were established by means of the rite of 'Sacred Marriage', widely regarded (e.g. van Buren, 1944) as the pivotal element of Babylonian religion. In this rite, male and female gods had sexual relationships within or outside 'marriages' and gave birth to divine 'offspring'. The supposed family relationships changed according to time and place, so that if we tried to construct a meaningful 'family tree of the gods' we would get hopelessly tied in knots. For example, Inanna (goddess of Uruk) was regarded both as the daughter of Enki (god of Eridu) and also the consort of An, who was either the grandfather or the father of Enki. Alternatively, Inanna was also regarded as the daughter of An himself (Dalley, 1991, p. 41). Another example of a goddess with complex relationships is Ninhursaga, who is sometimes the wife of Enlil and sometimes sister of Enlil (when Ninlil is Enlil's wife).

The 'divine offspring' of the unions of the gods often supplanted their 'parents' in importance as time passed. We can see this process at work most clearly when we compare Babylonian myths such as the *Enuma Elish* with the much older Sumerian inscriptions, hymns and stories. By the end of the Second Millennium BC, when the *Enuma Elish* was composed, the god Marduk, originally the city god of Babylon, had become the chief god of the pantheon. This reflected the rise of Babylon to political supremacy after 1800 BC, and is justified in the Enuma Elish (Tablet 1) by his position as the son of Enki (Ea).

The Uruk Vase, found in the Protoliterate levels of the Eanna Complex (at Uruk) presents a picture of Sumerian religion that is approximately 600 years older than the lists of gods from Shuruppak and 1000 years older than the presumed date of composition of the Sumerian Myths. Although the vase has no text of its own to confirm our interpretation of its 'message', the scenes depicted are in such harmony with the later myths that there can be relatively little doubt about the events that are being depicted. The evidence is so critical to our understanding of the Mesopotamian view of the gods that a detailed description will be given.

The vase has four registers, of which the upper is shown enlarged and flattened in Fig. 11.2. The bottom register (Fig. 7.4) contains a frieze of alternating palm trees and wheat stalks growing next to water (represented by a wavy line). Above a narrow horizontal band, the next register shows alternating goats and sheep. Taken together, these two registers summarise the agricultural economy of Uruk, consisting of stock, grain, and date harvesting.

The top two registers show the fruits of the harvest being brought to the temple store-house of Eanna. The lower of the two shows naked men, presumed to be priests, bringing harvest products in open baskets, open clay vessels, and clay bottles (presumably containing oil or wine). The large upper register shows the presentation of the gifts at the sanctuary. The doorway to the shrine is marked by the 'doorposts of Inanna' (the looped totem), and contains a bull (probably a statue), behind which are two tables bearing human statuettes. These are probably cult statues from the shrine. Behind these statues is another doorpost, indicating a separate storeroom. This contains the stored fruits of the harvest in jars, along with pictures of animals probably representing stored meat.

In front of the shrine stands a female figure in a long bordered gown. She appears to be wearing a horned head-dress, indicating her divinity, although this part of the pot was damaged and repaired in antiquity, so the head-dress is unclear. Nevertheless, even without this evidence, the female figure must either be a goddess, or a priestess representing her.

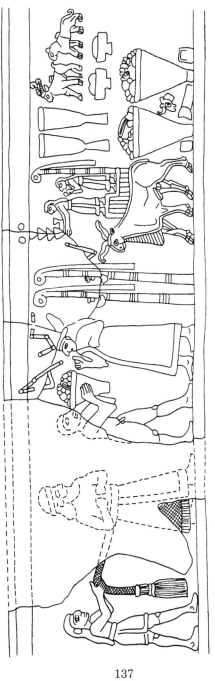

Fig. 11.2 Detailed view of the upper register of the Uruk vase, flattened out to show the scene in detail. Iraq Museum, Baghdad.

Facing the priestess or goddess are three figures. The first, resembling the naked priests on the register below, bears a large vessel of fruit, probably dates. The second figure is largely missing, due to a substantial area of damage, but we can see that the (smaller) third figure, who is female, is holding the train of a heavy gown. Therefore, we must presume that the second figure is a male god, or his representative, the high priest. Jacobsen (1976) identifies him as Dumuzi, god of the harvest (also known as Amau-shum-galanna). The overall interpretation of the scene (e.g. Jacobsen, 1976) is that it portrays the ritual of 'sacred marriage', which represents the entry of the harvest, personified as the god Dumuzi, into the storehouse, personified as the goddess Inanna.

Sumerian and Babylonian literature make it clear that in the ritual of Sacred Marriage the gods were 'impersonated' by priestesses and either priests or kings, and that the rite was sexually consummated. The general background to the ceremony is explained by the Sumerian myth of the Marriage of Dumuzi and Inanna. However, the way in which the Sacred Marriage was acted out by the King (impersonating Dumuzi) is explained all too clearly in the Hymn to Inanna, written in the time of king Iddin-Dagan of the Isin Dynasty (ca. 1970 BC).

The hymn praises Inanna as Queen of Heaven, explaining how Enki conferred this office on her in Eridu. This is clearly a reference to the myth of Inanna and Enki, describing the transfer of the arts of civilisation from Eridu to Uruk. After eight sections of the hymn in which Inanna's praises are sung, the ninth section describes the Sacred Marriage, in which king Iddin-Dagan (representing Dumuzi) enters the temple of Inanna and spends the night in sexual union with Inanna's representative (a priestess). The tenth section concludes the hymn as follows:

From heaven's midst Milady looks kindly down-
  Before holy Inanna, before her eyes, they walk
August is the queen, the evening star, unto the borders of heaven!
  Mighty she is, noble, elevated to high rank, great she is and august, in heroism surpassing.

[Jacobsen, 1987, p. 124]

However, in the Bible, we see a very different view of the rite of Sacred Marriage. In Gen Ch 6:2-3 there is an account which has often baffled commentators, but which, from the perspective of Sumerian culture is clearly a description of Sacred Marriage. In this case the 'sons of god'

138

are priests impersonating the Anunnaki (the lesser gods who were the sons of the heavenly god An):

> The sons of God saw that the daughters of men were beautiful, and they married any of them they chose. Then the LORD said, "My Spirit will not contend with (or remain in) man for ever, for he is mortal; his days will be a hundred and twenty years."

Because of the cryptic nature of this account, the following note (Gen 6:4) was probably inserted in the biblical text at a later time to explain the meaning of the rite in more detail:

> The Nephilim were on the earth in those days- and also afterwards- when the sons of God went to the daughters of men and had children by them. They were the heroes of old, men of renown.

The most famous example of such a hero was Gilgamesh, the king of Uruk whose super-human exploits are immortalised in the Epic of Gilgamesh, and after whom Greek heroes such as Hercules were modelled. According to the Gilgamesh Epic, he was the result of a union between king Lugal-banda and the goddess Ninsun, and was consequently two-thirds divine and one third mortal (tablet 1, Dalley, 1991, p. 51). However, according to the Sumerian King List he was the son of a High Priest of Kulab (one of the temples of Uruk), who is also referred to as a 'lillu demon' (Jacobsen, 1939, p. 142). This more sinister explanation of the rite of Sacred Marriage is consistent with the biblical view, which maintains that Sacred Marriage is not the elevated and holy rite portrayed in the Hymn to Inanna, but is actually ritual prostitution, which provoked the condemnation of the True God (Gen 6:5, 7):

> The LORD saw how great man's wickedness on the earth had become, and that every inclination of the thoughts of his heart was only evil all the time... So the LORD said, "I will wipe mankind, whom I have created, off from the face of the earth..."

In order to demonstrate that this is the correct interpretation of Sacred Marriage, we will examine several lines of evidence that point to Inanna as a divine usurper.

One line of evidence comes from the relationship between Dumuzi and Inanna in the gathering of the date harvest. In this relationship, Dumuzi is identified with Amau-shum-galanna, literally 'the one great source of the date clusters'. In other words, he is the deification of the power in the enormous bud of the date palm, which develops to provide the fruit (Jacobsen, 1976, p. 26). As such, Dumuzi is the provider of wealth, and Inanna (as the deified storehouse) is the receiver. However, in the development of the cult, Inanna usurps Dumuzi as the apparent provider of wealth. In addition, she ceases to be associated only with the date harvest, and becomes also the provider of blessings to the farmer, herder, fisherman and fowler (as illustrated in other myths, Jacobsen, 1976, p. 430). We can identify the elevation of Inanna to the position of universal provider with the development of agricultural bureaucracy in Uruk as it grew as a city. In this process, the power to store and distribute food came to eclipse in importance the power to produce food. Thus the power of Inanna's cult centre in Uruk (called Eanna) was probably based on the building of great storehouses. This is consistent with the portrayal of Inanna's shrine on the Uruk Vase.

Having usurped Dumuzi as the provider, Inanna was then elevated to the position of 'Queen of heaven'. This is described in the Hymn to Inanna by the phrase 'she is elevated to high rank' (line 131), implying promotion from a lower rank. Thus she obtains the decrees of office from Enki, and is then said to be taking her seat next to An, the god of heaven, on the great throne dias. This process of elevation may be seen in the architecture of Uruk, where Inanna seems gradually to assume the place of greatest importance. Eanna (the gate of heaven) must originally have been a temple to An, the god of heaven, but with Inanna's elevation to 'Queen of heaven', she displaces An in importance. Thus, by the time the Gilgamesh Epic achieves its completed form (possibly fairly late in the Second Millennium), Eanna is referred to as the 'home of Ishtar' (the Akkadian form of Inanna).

The character of Inanna, as presented in the Sumerian myths, is one of a 'beautiful, rather willful, young aristocrat' but 'never depicted as a wife and helpmate or as a mother' (Jacobsen, 1976, p. 141). To put it another way, she is a flirtatious and irresponsible young lover, prone to temper tantrums, who leaves a trail of emotional destruction in her wake; the personification of the spirit of instant gratification. As such she is an idol whose character appeals to the lusts of the flesh and to the desire for power. This in turn led to her status as the goddess of war (Fig. 11.3)

140

Fig. 11.3 Ishtar (Inanna) as the goddess of war, bringing prisoners to Anu-banini, king of the Lulubi. From
a Mid Third Millennium rock sculpture in the Zagros
mountains. After Jastrow (1915, pl. 29).

The promotion of Inanna in many ways exemplifies the way in
which gods were 'conceived' by ritual prostitution and then 'nurtured'
by the priesthood, building up a whole family tree of gods. In Genesis
Ch 6, ritual marriage or prostitution is described immediately before the
condemnation of the sinfulness of mankind that provoked the sending
of the Flood. Hence, it seems clear that it was the sin of idolatry, developed and expressed through ritual prostitution, that provoked the
sending of the Flood. The reason why this sin was so heinous was that
it was developed by the priesthood, which was intended to serve the
True God, but instead obscured the revelation of the True God so that
this was lost in a whole pantheon of false gods. Thus it was the priesthood itself that was the focus of God's wrath, and this is the significance
of the focus, in the biblical Flood Story, of the flooding of all the man-
made 'high mountains' where false worship took place.

Since all of these centres of false worship were apparently destroyed
during the Flood (and assuming that the Flood did indeed occur before
the foundation of Eridu), then it cannot have been the cult of Inanna in
particular that provoked God's wrath, since this was established after the
Flood. However, this cult is illustrative of the *process* by which false

141

gods and goddesses were conceived and then elevated to a place in the pantheon, ultimately obscuring the revelation of the True God.

Most likely, the cult of Sacred Marriage before the Flood was centred on the Mother Goddess, Nintur, a somewhat shadowy figure in later Mesopotamian mythology who was identified with Nin-hursaga, the goddess of the foothills. Significantly, Nintur is referred to as the 'Mistress of the Gods' in the Flood Story of the Gilgamesh Epic, and the 'Great Mistress' in the Flood Story of the Atrahasis Epic (Dalley, 1991, p. 114 [tablet 11, col. 3] and p. 32 [tablet 3, col. 3] respectively). In addition, it is she who blames the great gods, and especially Enlil, for causing the Flood in both of these epics. This part of the story may have been introduced by Nintur's later adherents, who were upset at the 'demotion' of their patron. If the worship of the Mother Goddess was eradicated from the whole of Mesopotamia by the Flood then this cult might have later 'diffused' back onto the plain from the pagan peoples of the surrounding mountains. It was argued above, based on Gen 4:20-22 that these people were not annihilated by the Flood (section 4.5).

CHAPTER 12

THE GODS IN
HYMNS AND INSCRIPTIONS

The proliferation of gods associated with the rite of 'Sacred Marriage' begs the question as to whether the True God is visible anywhere within the Sumerian pantheon. To attempt to answer this question we will search for evidence in the written record as to whether the ancient Mesopotamians recognised a Supreme God in their pantheon, and if so, to identify this god. We will look first at Royal Inscriptions, the first true historical records. We will then examine the earliest liturgical expression in the Sumerian hymns.

12.1 Early Dynastic royal inscriptions

Evidence for the hierarchy in the divine pantheon during the latter part of the Early Dynastic period (ca. 2500 BC) comes from a series of royal inscriptions from Girsu, a town within the city-state of Lagash. Lagash held brief sway over Sumer during Early Dynastic III, but is not even mentioned in the Sumerian King List, probably for political reasons. However, Lagash has yielded a rich harvest of Early Dynastic royal inscriptions which allow us to reconstruct a dynasty of nine kings founded by Ur-Nanshe (Table 12.1) and to identify the principal gods that they worshipped. These inscriptions were written as a result of a long-running border dispute between Lagash and its northerly neighbour, Umma, which is located in the east-central region of the plain (Fig. 6.3). We will examine the history of this dispute, and then discuss the evidence it provides about the Sumerian pantheon.

The dispute between Lagash and Umma seems to have begun around the beginning of ED III (2600 BC) when a Semitic king by the name of Me-salim had achieved the title 'King of Kish', indicating overall lordship over Sumer. This is recorded on a mace head from Lagash (Fig. 12.1). While holding this office, Me-salim arbitrated a border dispute between Lagash and Umma, which were both under his rule, and set up a stele (an inscribed pillar) to mark the new border (Kramer 63/70 p. 53).

Table 12.1   The Lagash dynasty of ED III

~~~~~~

Dynasty	King*	Start of reign

~~~~~~

Lagash:	UR-NANSHE	
	Akurgal	
	EANNA-TUM	~2500
	En-anatum I	
	EN-METENA	
	En-anatum II	
	En-entarzi	
	Lugal-anda	
	URU-KAGINA	~2400
Umma	LUGAL-ZAGESI	

~~~~~~

*Kings mentioned in the text are capitalised.

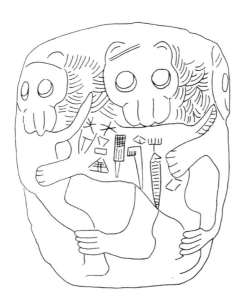

Fig. 12.1
The mace head of King Me-salim, decorated with lions. The inscription reads from right to left: 'Me-salim, King of Kish, builder of the temple of Ningirsu, set this up to Ningirsu. Lugal-sag-engur was the Ensi of Lagash.' (Postgate, 1992, p. 31). Sandstone, height 19 cm. Musee du Louvre.

The ruler of Umma soon broke the agreement arbitrated by Mesalim, but eventually Lagash became sufficiently powerful to defeat Umma and re-establish the original border. This success came under the leadership of Eanna-tum, who also defeated several other cities, including Elam to the east, Uruk and Ur to the south, and even Kish to the NW. Eanna-tum crowned his rule by claiming the title 'King of Kish' and recorded his achievements on the famous Stele of the Vultures. The 'historical' side of the stele (Fig. 12.2) shows various scenes from the battle, including Eanna-tum marching at the head of a phalanx of soldiers, leading his army in a chariot, and supervising a funeral pyre made of the dead bodies of the enemy. This side of the stele also shows vultures removing the dismembered bodies of the enemy, which gave rise to the name 'Stele of the Vultures'.

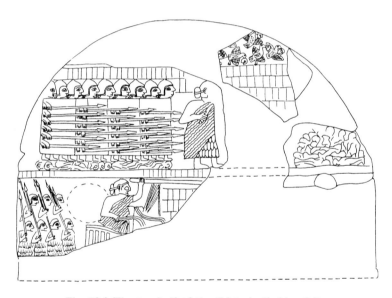

Fig. 12.2 The top half of the 'historical' side of the Stele of the Vultures. Sandstone, height 1.8 m, width 1.3 m. Musee du Louvre.

The other side of the Stele of the Vultures, which is actually the front side, shows the mythological interpretation of the war between Lagash and Umma. Here the god Ningirsu is shown with his mace, and with a net containing the dead bodies of Ummans (Fig. 12.3). Also shown in the figure are the elements of the inscription, which contained

145

the account of the war written in archaic pictograms. Much of the inscription has been translated by Kramer (1963, p. 310, 55). However, because it is quite long, only phrases pertinent to Eanna-tum's view of the gods are summarised here:

Fig. 12.3 Part of the 'mythological' side of the Stele of the Vultures showing the god Ningirsu with his mace and net. Part of the text is written in the top right area of the stele. Musee du Louvre.

Eanna-tum claims that he was set on the knee of his mother, the goddess Ninhursag, by the goddess Inanna (Eanna-tum is named after her sanctuary, Eanna, in Uruk). He then makes an oath several times in the name of several different gods and goddesses. This oath claims that Eanna-tum had laid a net over Umma to capture it in the name of each of these gods, and that henceforth he will respect the boundary between Umma and Lagash, but invokes the wrath of the god if Umma violates the boundary, so that the net will be hurled down from heaven on the violator. This oath is made in the name of the following gods: *'Enlil, the*

146

king of heaven and earth; my mother Ninhursag; Enki, the king of the Apsu; Sin, the spirited young bull of Enlil; and Utu, the king of .....' (word not understood). In return, Eanna-tum makes Umma swear in the name of Utu (the sun god), then finally he utters a curse against violators of the oath in the name of the snake Ninki, who will sink its fangs into the foot of Umma if Umma crosses the boundary line.

Notwithstanding these curses, Umma did invade again, but was defeated by Eanna-tum's nephew, En-metena. (The pre-fix *En-* originally meant High Priest but by the time of En-metena was probably a largely honorific title for the king). The victory was recorded on the Cone of En-metena (Fig. 12.4), which presents a summary of the whole dispute in terms of the jurisdiction of the respective city gods Ningirsu and Shara, and the supremacy of the god Enlil. The following quote is from Jacobsen (1994), but see also the version in Collingwood (1967):

> *The god Enlil, king of all lands, father of all gods, determined by his just ruling the territorial borderline for the god Ningirsu and the god Shara.*
>
> *Me-salim, king of Kish, checked at the bidding of his personal god Ishtaran the tautness of the measuring line and set up stelae at the spot indicated.*
>
> *Ush, ruler of Umma acted arrogantly, he tore out those stelae and carried them into the plain of Lagash.* (when he invaded)
>
> *Enlil's warrior, Ningirsu, did at his just command battle with the Ummeans and threw at Enlil's command the throw-net down upon them and ranged their burial mounds in the plain in that spot.*

Fig. 12.4
The Cone of En-metena, bearing the description of the Lagash--Umma dispute. The cone has a socket in the base which is designed to carry a wooden stake. Baked clay. Height 27 cm. Musee du Louvre.

147

The Lagash dynasty maintained the upper hand against Umma for another four generations after En-metena, but apparently at great cost to its citizens, who were severely taxed to maintain the war effort. We know of this because the last king of the dynasty, Uru-kagina, brought in political and economic reforms, which are recorded in the Reform Text of Uru-kagina (Postgate, 1992, p. 268). An excerpt from this reads:

> *When Ningirsu, warrior of Enlil, granted the kingship of Lagash to Uru-kagina, taking him by the hand from among the 36,000 people, he replaced the customs of former times...*

Unfortunately these reforms were soon followed by the invasion of Lagash by Lugal-zagesi of Umma. (The pre-fix *Lugal-* means 'big man' and was an alternative honorific title for the king). Lugal-zagesi seems to have taken advantage of the pacifist leanings of Uru-kagina to finally defeat Lagash in about 2400 BC. He went on to conquer Uruk, Ur, and even Kish, taking the titles of 'King of Uruk' and 'King of the Land', as described in the following vase inscription:

> *When to Lugal-zagesi*
>> *(King of Uruk, King of the Land, priest of An... looked on favourably by An, king of countries, the Chief Governor of Enlil, granted wisdom by Enki, chosen by Utu, High Vizier of Nanna, General of Utu, provider for Inanna, son born of Nisaba and suckled on the milk of Ninhursag...)*
>> *Enlil, King of countries, had given the Kingship of the Land, made the land obedient to him, thrown all countries at his feet, and subjected them to him from sunrise to sunset, -*
>> *at that time he made his way from the Lower Sea, via the Tigris and Euphrates, to the Upper Sea, and Enlil had allowed none to oppose him from sunrise to sunset.*
>> *If Enlil, King of all countries, would say a prayer for me to An, the father who loves him, and add life to my life, then will the country lie (contented) in its meadows under me, then surely will mankind spread abroad like grass, the udder of heaven will operate properly, the Land will experience comfort under me.*

> [Postgate, 1992, p. 35]

Despite these boastful claims, Lugal-zagesi's kingdom was short-lived, because his empire was in turn conquered by Sargon of Akkad in about 2370 BC. This conquest was seen as divine punishment for the desecration perpetrated by Lugal-zagesi against several temples. The destruction of these temples was described in the Lament for the Sacking of the Temples of Lagash, from which the following excerpt is taken (Postgate, 1992, p. 119):

> *The leader of Umma... set fire to the shrine Eanna of Inanna, looted*
> *its precious metals and lapis lazuli, and destroyed its sanctuary...*
> *The leader of Umma, having sacked Lagash, has committed a sin*
> *against Ningirsu.*
> *The hand which is raised against him will be cut off! It is not a sin*
> *of Uru-kagina, king of Girsu!*
> *May Nisaba, the goddess of Lugal-zagesi, ruler of Umma, make*
> *him bear the sin.*

Taken together, the most significant feature of these Royal Inscriptions from 2500 to 2400 BC is that each of the deadly enemies, Lagash and Umma, recognised the supreme authority of Enlil. This might be expected from Lagash, since Enlil was regarded as the father of Ninurta (a synonym of Ningirsu, the patron god of Girsu). However, it is more notable that Lugal-zagesi, who sacked the temples of the patron god of several cities, nevertheless recognised the supreme authority of Enlil.

Curiously, the Lagash inscriptions do not even mention An (the god of heaven), whereas in the vase inscription of Lugal-zagesi the god An is referred to first. This is interesting because An and Inanna were both the patron gods of Uruk, yet Lugal-zagesi evidently sacked the temple of Inanna but venerated the temple of An in Uruk. Taken together, the evidence from all of the inscriptions suggests that Enlil, as 'King of all Lands' was the effective head of the Sumerian pantheon. However, the reference to An as the 'father of Enlil' at the end of the inscription of Lugal-zagesi suggests that the god An may have held ultimate precedence.

12.2 Hymns to temples

Sumerian hymns represent one of the most important types of early literature and are of three main types: hymns to gods, hymns to temples, and royal hymns that extol the virtues of deified kings. The first two types reveal the identity of the chief gods of the Sumerian pantheon during the mid Third Millennium.

One of the earliest temple hymns is the Hymn to Kesh. The text of this hymn is well known from numerous versions in the Old Babylonian period, including three nearly complete copies (Gragg, 1969). In addition, it is also known in fragments from the Early Dynastic period in the middle of the Third Millennium, probably at the beginning of ED III around 2600 BC. This makes the Hymn to Kesh particularly important for its portrayal of the pantheon from this early period in the history of Sumerian literature. The following twelve lines introduce the hymn:

> *Princely office upon princely office he decided to bring them out of the house,*
> *Enlil decided to bring the princely offices out of the house,*
> *Decided to bring the princely offices and kingship out of the house.*
> *Enlil was looking at all lands*
> *In tiers rose the lands for Enlil*
> *The Four Quarters (of the world) were greening for Enlil like a garden.*
> *Kesh was there raising the head unto him*
> *Out of all lands Kesh was the one raising the head*
> *and (so) Enlil was moved to sing the praises of Kesh.*
> *Establisher of the standard version thereof was Nidaba* (goddess of writing)
> *She spun, as it were, a web out of those words*
> *And writing them down on a tablet she laid them (ready) to hand.*
>
> [Jacobsen, 1987, p. 378, lines 1-12]

Other gods associated with the temple are described as follows:

> *Who laid eyes ever on one as superior as Nintur, its mistress?*
> [line 20]
> *House founded by An, praised by Enlil...*
> [line 38]

These and other verses of the hymn make it plain that the temple of Kesh was devoted to the mother goddess Nintur, but Enlil was acknowledged as the divine ruler over 'All Lands', including the 'Four Quarters' of the earth. However, in line 38, An (god of heaven) is said to have founded the temple. Hence, it again seems clear that Enlil and An are chief gods of the pantheon, but the relationship between Enlil and An is unclear.

150

One aspect of the Hymn to Kesh that is very important is its description of temple ritual. For example, line 103 describes the ritual of prostitution which was at the heart of the operation of the temple, and line 104 makes it clear that the male chief priests (En-priests) impersonated the heavenly gods (Anunnaki = children of An) in this ritual. Finally, line 105 links the function of the temple's meat carvers with the institution of the temple storehouse, which was named after the 'House of Heaven', the temple of the goddess Inanna of Uruk.

> *The holy house of Kesh, the extravagant provider of which is the*
> *bedroom*
> *The house-- its En-priests are Anunnaki gods*
> *Its Nuesh-priests are Eanna's carvers*

[lines 103-105]

These lines help us to understand the origin of the cults of goddesses: If the high priest was a man, he was able to impersonate one of the sons of An in consummating the 'sacred marriage' with a female goddess. This would put him in a commanding position in the temple hierarchy. Hence it was in the interests of a corrupt priesthood to elevate the position of the goddess of the temple and dissipate the importance of the 'father god' by making him a remote figure. On the other hand we may see the continued veneration of Enlil at Nippur as indicative of a less corrupted tradition.

The Sumerian Temple Hymns consist of a set of 42 hymns with a standard pattern: an address to the temple of a particular city, followed by an address to the deity of the temple, and ending with a standard refrain. The collection is primarily represented from the Old Babylonian period, and is attributed to En-heduanna, daughter of Sargon, based on the wording of the final hymn, where she is named as the compiler of the tablet. However, since one of the hymns is addressed to Shulgi, the deified king of Ur who lived nearly 300 years after Sargon, it is clear that some of the hymns post-date En-heduanna. At the same time, some of the other hymns are known to go back at least to the end of the Early Dynastic period, since copies are found in the Abu Salabikh collection from ca. 2600 BC (Biggs, 1974).

If we compare the Old Babylonian collection of temple hymns, as attributed to En-heduanna, with the archaic (Abu Salabikh) collection then we see an interesting change. In the archaic collection the first hymn is addressed to Enlil at Nippur:

City, grown together with heaven, embracing heaven
God of Nippur, bond of Heaven and earth
Enlil, great mountain, Enlil, Lord
Nunamnir, whose command is irrevocable,
whose [.....] cannot be [.....]
Enlil, who placed the Anunna gods below earth
The great gods spoke his praise

[Alster, 1976, p. 121]

In contrast, the first hymn of the later collection is addressed to Enki at Eridu and begins as follows:

Eunir, which has grown high (uniting) heaven and earth
Foundation of Heaven and Earth, Holy of Holies, Eridu
[Sjoberg and Bergmann, 1969]

Comparison of the first two lines of each hymn suggest that perhaps the hymn to Enlil was replaced by one addressed to Enki, based on the tradition in the Sumerian Flood Story that Eridu was the site of the first city of Sumer, where kingship first came down from heaven. On this basis it would indeed be reasonable to expect that the hymn to the temple of Eridu should come first in the collection. But it is also interesting that Enki is not directly mentioned in the Early Dynastic collection, suggesting that perhaps he was less important during this phase of Sumerian history.

12.3 The Hymn to Enlil

The Hymn to Enlil is of uncertain date but is one of the most majestic expressions of Sumerian praise. The quotes below represent two excerpts from different translators, one from the first 14 lines and one from near the end of the hymn which refers to the relationship between Enlil and An. This reference seems to imply that they are one and the same god, but is rather ambiguous. The relationship between them will be examined further in a survey of Sumerian literature.

Enlil! His authority is far-reaching
his word is sublime and holy
His decisions are unalterable
he decides fates forever!
His eyes scrutinise the entire world!

152

When the honourable Enlil sits down in majesty
on his sacred and sublime throne,
when he exercises with perfection
his power as Lord and King
Spontaneously the other gods prostrate before him
and obey his orders without protest
He is the great and powerful ruler
who dominates Heaven and Earth
Who knows all and understands all

[Lines 1-14, source unknown]

Enlil- by your skilful planning in intricate designs
their inner workings a blur of threads not to be unravelled,
thread entwined in thread, not to be traced by the eye-
you excel in your task of divine providence.
You are your own counsellor, adviser, and manager,
who [else] could comprehend what you do?
Your tasks are tasks that are not apparent, your guise [of] a god,
Invisible to the eye; you are lord An and king Enlil,
judge and decision maker for heaven and earth,
you know no rescinder of your great decrees, they being as
respected as An
to [hear] your words the gods of high descent undergo ritual
purification.

[Lines 131-142; Jacobsen, 1987]

CHAPTER 13

THE GODS IN
SUMERIAN LITERATURE

Sumerian myths and epics represent the earliest true literature, and as such can present a much more detailed picture of ancient religion than monuments and inscriptions. However, the reader immediately realises that the Sumerian myths and epics are a corrupt source of information about theology and history. Nevertheless, useful information may still be obtained from these sources in certain areas.

13.1 Types of Sumerian literature

The principal focus of epics is on heroic deeds of men. These stories may be exaggerated accounts of actual historical events, or they may be fiction. However, by extracting evidence that is unwittingly given by the author, we may discover information that accurately portrays aspects of ancient Sumerian culture. For example, the account of a battle may present the losing side as if they were actually the winners. However, in describing the preparations for a battle, the author may unwittingly reveal accurate information about the divination practices of the king and about the gods in his pantheon.

The principal focus of the myths is to explain the origins of the gods. These myths can be used to explore relationships with the biblical account of the creation and early history of the earth. In this approach we do not use the myths to discover factual information about the pantheon, since such information may have been deliberately distorted. Instead, we can use those myths that are consistent with the biblical account to discern any threads of biblical truth running through Mesopotamian religion.

Some of the most important types of tablet yet found are ancient literary catalogues of other tablets. The first one of these to be translated was from the Nippur library of the Old Babylonian period. Its contents are listed here (Table 13.1) as an example of an ancient library of Sumerian 'classics'; however, other catalogues list other works, so that the total number known now exceeds 200 (Kramer, 1963). The entries are listed by their first line, which was the customary way of referring to a composition; and, almost incredibly, we now have translations of at least part of every work listed in this catalogue.

Table 13.1 Literary works listed in the Nippur Catalogue

~~~~~~

Title of composition	English translation
Hymn of King Shulgi (there are many)	Sjoberg & Bergmann (1969)
Hymn of King Lipit-Ishtar	Jacobsen (1976) p. 98
Myth: The Creation of the Pickaxe	Jacobsen (1976) p. 103
Hymn to Inanna (by En-heduanna, H & S 71, p. 59)	Jacobsen (1987) p. 112
Hymn to Enlil	Jacobsen (1987) p. 101
Hymn to the temple of Ninhursag (= Kesh?)	?Gragg (1969)
Epic: Gilgamesh, Enkidu, and the Nether World	Kramer (1979) p. 21
Epic: Inanna and (mount) Ebih	Eichler (Kinnier Wilson, 1979, p. 6)
Epic: Gilgamesh and Huwawa	Kramer (1963) p. 192
Epic: Gilgamesh and Agga	Jacobsen (1987) p. 345
Myth: Dispute between Cattle and Grain	Kramer (1963) p. 220
Lamentation for the Fall of Akkad	Jacobsen (1987) p. 359
Lamentation for the destruction of Ur	Jacobsen (1987) p. 447
Lamentation for the destruction of Nippur	Frankfort *et al.* (1946), p. 202, Kramer (1948)
Lamentation for the destruction of Sumer	Michalowski (1989)
Epic: Lugal-banda and Enmerkar	Jacobsen (1987) p. 320
Myth: Inanna's descent to the nether world	Jacobsen (1987) p. 205
Hymn to Inanna	Jacobsen (1987) p. 124
Collection of hymns to Sumerian temples	Sjoberg & Bergmann (1969)
Wisdom: training to be a scribe	Kramer (1963) p. 237
Wisdom: instructions of a peasant to his son	Kramer (1963) p. 340

~~~~~~

The good recovery of the works in the Nippur Catalogue should not be taken to imply that we have now recovered the 'Complete Works' of Sumerian civilisation. More likely, the inclusion of particular works in the catalogue reflects the fact that these were particularly popular, either for entertainment or for teaching purposes. On the other hand, to see how much of the Sumerian literary heritage has *not* been recovered, we should remember that only one broken fragment has been recovered of the critically important Sumerian Flood Story, despite decades of searching for additional copies of this work. Thus, if it were not for the providential discovery of this fragment, we would not even know for sure that there was a Sumerian version of the Flood Story in addition to the two Akkadian versions. Hence, we must infer that many other important Sumerian works have been altogether lost (section 20.3).

Most Sumerian myths and epics were probably first written down near the end of the Third Millennium, during the Third Dynasty of Ur and the dynasty of Isin. In particular, King Shulgi of Ur oversaw the recording of older stories and the composition of new myths and epics during his reign as an expression of the 'Sumerian Revival'. Evidence for this time of composition is provided, for example, in the Myth of Enki and Sumer (Kramer, 1944, p. 60). Enki goes to Ur rather than Eridu immediately after decreeing the fate of Sumer, suggesting that Ur was the capital of Sumer at the time the myth was first written down. Other myths, such as The Separation of Heaven and Earth have small fragments preserved from the Ur III dynasty (Alster, 1976, p. 122); however, most of the copies that we have of these myths are from the Old Babylonian period, many of them from the Nippur Library (ca. 1600 BC). Some of the other important myths (not in the Nippur catalogue) are listed in Table 13.2.

Much of the material in Sumerian Mythology is relevant in some way to an understanding of the development of Sumerian culture and religion; but clearly, in view of the large size of this literature, it is impossible to even summarise the major myths here. Our present focus is restricted to evidence relevant to the hierarchy of the Sumerian pantheon.

By the time the myths were written down, the polytheistic character of Mesopotamian religion was long established. Indeed, evidence from seals and tablets of the Protoliterate period shows that the patronage of each city by a different god was established 1000 years before the writing of most of the myths (section 14.1). For this reason we should expect that different myths, reflecting competing temple traditions, will be significantly contradictory. If we rely only on the myths themselves then it may be impossible to choose between competing traditions for the hierarchy of the pantheon. However, I argued above that we can use

156

biblical accounts to discover fragments of truth within the myths and hence to identify the True God in the pantheon and understand the process by which the pantheon was conceived.

Table 13.2 Some other important Sumerian myths

~~~~~~

Title of composition	English translation

~~~~~~

Enki myths

Title of composition	English translation
Enki and Sumer: the organisation of the earth	Kramer and Maier (1989) p. 38
Enki and the Journey from Eridu to Nippur	Kramer and Maier (1989) p.69
Enki and Inanna: Transfer of arts of civilisation	Kramer and Maier (1989) p. 57
Enki and Ninhursag: A Sumerian paradise myth	Ditto, p. 22; Jacobsen (1987) p. 181
Enki and Ninmah: The creation of man	Ditto, p. 31; Jacobsen (1987) p. 151

Dumuzi myths

Title of composition	English translation
Dumuzi and the wooing of Inanna	Jacobsen (1987) p. 3
The marriage of Dumuzi and Inanna	Jacobsen (1987) p. 19
The death of Dumuzi	Jacobsen (1987) p. 28

Other myths

Title of composition	English translation
Enlil and Ninlil: The birth of the moon god	Jacobsen (1987) p. 167
The journey of the moon god (Nanna) to Nippur	Kramer (1944) p. 47
The deeds and exploits of Ninurta	Jacobsen (1987) p. 233
The Flood story	Jacobsen (1987) p. 145
Disputation between bird and fish	Kramer and Maire (1989) p. 86

~~~~~~

Older translations listed in Kramer (1963, p. 171).

13.2 Myths of An and Enlil

There are only a few accounts of creation in Sumerian mythology, but these provide a very important guide to the identity of the supreme god or gods of the pantheon. Concerning the origin of the gods themselves, the first line of the 'Dispute between Cattle and Grain' claims that An was the father of the gods (Kramer, 1963, p. 220):

157

After on the mountain of heaven and earth,
An had caused the Anunnaki to be born...

Apart from this claim, the god An rarely plays an active role in the Sumerian myths. However, one case where An and Enlil act as co-equals in the act of creation is found in the Sumerian epic 'Gilgamesh, Enkidu and the Nether World (Kramer, 1979, p. 23). The main focus of the epic is the story of how Enkidu went to the world of the dead in a failed attempt to retrieve two wooden cult objects belonging to Gilgamesh, king of Uruk. These objects had been made by Gilgamesh from a magical 'huluppu tree' that had been planted at Uruk by the goddess Inanna. The section of the epic which describes Enkidu's trip to the underworld was later incorporated as the final tablet in the Epic of Gilgamesh. In that context, it provides a lesson that only the spirit of a man can return from the world of the dead, thus ending the pursuit of eternal life by Gilgamesh. However, the prologue to the Sumerian story, not included in the later epic, describes the creation of the world as a background to the origin of the huluppu tree. This prologue begins with the standard introduction 'On a faraway day' and proceeds to explain the creation as follows:

In ancient days when everything vital had been nurtured,
When bread had been tasted in the shrines of the land,
When bread had been baked in the ovens of the land-
When heaven had been moved away from earth,
When earth had been separated from heaven,
When the name of man had been fixed-
When An had carried off heaven,
When Enlil had carried off earth,
When Ereshkigal (goddess of the underworld)
        had been carried off to the underworld as its prize
When he (Enki) had set sail for the underworld...
Against Enki it hurled the big ones (stones)...
                                [Modified from Kramer, 1979]

This story seems to be saying that the creation of the universe began when heaven and earth were separated from one another, and that the gods An and Enlil then took dominion over these realms. It also presents the third member of the 'Cosmic Triad', Enki, in a battle against the forces of chaos, represented by the stone-throwing 'kur'. The latter word usually means mountain, but it can also mean the underworld, probably on the basis that the mountainous wasteland regions around Mesopotamia are connected to the underworld (Kramer, 1979, p. 24). The episode of the battle between Enki and the forces of chaos is not completed because the story moves on to its main focus, which is the huluppu tree. However, Enki was evidently the victor of the battle because he is sometimes referred to as 'En-kur' (Kramer, 1979, p. 25).

A myth which throws more light on the separation of the heavens and the earth is the 'Creation of the Pickaxe'. This begins in the following way:

> *The Lord whose decisions are unalterable*
> *Enlil, who brings up the seed of the land from the earth*
> *(Took care) to move away Heaven from Earth*
> *(Took care) to move away Earth from Heaven*
> [Kramer, 1944, p. 40]

This picture of Enlil as creator is supported by the oldest Sumerian myth presently known, called the Archaic Barton Cylinder after its first publisher. The cylinder is thought by the style of its script to date from around 2500 BC (Fig. 13.1). The Barton Cylinder claims that the separation of Heaven and Earth occurred when the first stroke of lightning occurred in Nippur, Enlil's cosmic mountain (Alster, 1976). The primitiveness of the script has not yet allowed this material to be fully translated.

This is an appropriate point to review two aspects of the character of Enlil which seem to find important parallels in the first chapter of Genesis. The first of these is his name, which cannot easily be captured in the English language. However, the best translation of the Sumerian word 'lil' seems to be the Hebrew word pronounced '*ruach*', approximated in English by the words 'gentle wind', 'spirit' or 'breath'. This aspect of Enlil's character is parallelled in Genesis 1:2:

> *Now the earth was total chaos, and darkness covered the deep,*
> *and the Wind of God hovered over the waters.*
> [Wenham, 1987, p. 2]

The other aspect of Enlil's character that may also be seen in Genesis 1 is his role just discussed in separating the Heavens and the Earth. This is parallelled in Genesis 1:3-10, where God's creative acts cause the separation between the realms of the cosmos. Hence, when we combine these characteristics, I suggest that Enlil, the second god of the Sumerian 'Cosmic Triad', preserves some of the attributes of the Spirit of God active in creation.

159

Fig. 13.1 The Archaic Barton Cylinder, shown in the orientation in which it would have been held to read the archaic cuneiform script. University Museum, Philadelphia.

13.3 Myths of Enki

The role of Enki in battling against primaeval forces of chaos was described above in the myth of Gilgamesh, Enkidu and the Nether World. However, there are several other important myths which can help us to understand something about the role of Enki in creation. One of the most important of the Myths of Enki is the story of 'Enki and Ninmah', which describes the creation of mankind in a manner similar to the Atrahasis Epic. This implies a common source for the two works, but it is not clear whether the version in Atrahasis derives from Enki and Ninmah, or whether both stories were separately derived from a common earlier source.

In the Sumerian myth 'Enki and Ninmah', the gods are wailing because of their hard work, whereupon Nammu, the mother of the gods, goes to Enki and tells him to create servants for the gods to do their work for them. Enki gives instructions that clay from the Apsu should be kneaded and nipped off, whereupon the mother goddess Nammu can give it form, presumably in her womb. To celebrate his creation, Enki gives a feast for the gods. However, as Enki and Ninmah become intoxicated with much beer, the feast degenerates into a drunken revel. Enki and Ninmah then engage in a contest in which one creates a disabled person and the other has to find employment for him. Enki wins the contest because he can decree a fate for all of the deformed creations of Ninmah, whereas she cannot find a role for the pitiful specimen of humanity created by Enki, which is so sick that it cannot even eat.

Despite its badly corrupted ending, this myth contains two important elements seen in Genesis. One is the creation of man from the 'dust of the ground' (ie clay) seen in Genesis Ch 2. The other is the concept of the 'rest of the gods' from their labours, which may have links to God's day of rest after six days of creation in Genesis Ch 1 (Lambert, 1965, p. 298).

Another important myth of Enki is the 'Organisation of the Earth and its Cultural Processes' (Kramer, 1944, p. 59). As the title indicates, this story describes how Enki organises the land of Sumer in successive realms. In the agricultural zone he plows the fields, provides all kinds of seeds, and provides houses for shelter. In the wild lands of the steppe he creates vegetation and wild beasts. In the countryside he builds sheepfolds and creates their herds. Enki also fixes borders between these different realms and provides clothing for mankind. However, Enki's 'daughter', Inanna, complains bitterly to Enki that he has neglected her-

161

the 'woman' amongst the great gods- by not giving her divine functions or offices over the earth (Kramer and Maier, 1989, p. 54). In reply, Enki lists many powers and functions that are indeed exercised by Inanna, such as her control over the strength of young men (in love and war?), her rule over the shepherd (Dumuzi?) and her power to lay waste and destroy. Finally, the myth ends with blessings pronounced over Inanna.

This myth presents Enki as the creator of the land of Sumer in a way that resembles the creation story of Genesis Ch 2. However, it is also important in showing how the upstart goddess Inanna achieved promotion to the highest rank in the pantheon. This promotion doubtless stemmed from the dominance of the economy of Uruk at the end of the Fourth Millennium, when the Temple precinct of Eanna became an immense storehouse of wealth. Having achieved this dominant economic position, the priests of Inanna demand to know why their goddess is not recognised as equal with the other great gods of the pantheon. Hence, we can infer that this myth and its sequel 'Enki and Inanna: the transfer of the arts of civilisation' were written to achieve and justify this promotion of Inanna to the highest rank in the pantheon.

Just as the myths sought to elevate Inanna to the highest level in the pantheon by presenting her as a disenfranchised woman amongst the great gods, they also sought to bring the great gods Enlil and Enki down to a human level by presenting them as lewd womanisers. So the myth of Enki and Ninhursag describes how Enki seduced the mother goddess Ninhursaga, their 'daughter' Nimmu, grand-daughter Ninkurra and great-grand-daughter Uttu. Similarly, the myth of Enlil and Ninlil describes a series of seductions of Ninlil by the 'young' Enlil, after which he is punished by the council of the gods with banishment from the town.

Although these myths reflect the corrupt morals of ritual prostitution, we must not fall into the trap of throwing out all of Mesopotamian literature or disbelieving all Mesopotamian theology as a result. If we do that then we will be rejecting valuable evidence about the historical transmission of God's first revelation to mankind. Instead, we must be discerning in order to recognise the threads of truth which are concealed in the tangled web of Mesopotamian literature, and hence to see how the Sumerians understood the character of the True God.

A myth of Enki that reveals important insights into the Sumerian cosmic hierarchy is the 'Journey of Enki from Eridu to Nippur', an example of a genre of myths involving journeys of gods from one city to another. Other examples are the journey of the moon god (Nanna) to

162

Nippur, and the visit of Inanna to Enki at Eridu, previously discussed in section 7.2. These myths were probably recited when the statue of the god was literally carried from one city to another. Since all of the cities of Mesopotamia were connected by river or canal, the gods always travelled by barge. The cylinder seal shown in Fig. 13.2 probably represents such a visit. In such situations we can be sure that the junior god or goddess went to visit the more senior god of the pantheon.

Fig. 13.2 Impression from an Akkadian-age cylinder seal showing the god Enki travelling by barge to visit another deity. Height 2.7 cm. Musee du Louvre.

The 'Journey of Enki from Eridu to Nippur' begins by describing how Enki built his temple, the 'Sea House', on the shores of the Apsu like a 'mountain floated upon the waters', as portrayed on cylinder seals (Fig. 13.3).

> *In those days, once the fates had been decreed*
> *after the year hegal, heaven-born, had broken through the earth*
> *spreading through the land like plants and herbs*
> *King Enki, Lord of the Apsu,*
> *Enki, lord who decrees the fates*
> *built, of silver and lapis lazuli blended as one, his house:*
> *its silver and lapis lazuli luminous as the day,*
> *the shrine sent joy through the Apsu.*
>
> [Kramer and Maier, 1989, p. 69]

Fig. 13.3 Cylinder seal impression showing the Sea House of Enki floating upon the waters of the Apsu. University Museum, Pennsylvania.

Despite the effusiveness of this praise of Enki, the myth recognises the supremacy of Enlil, because Enki must journey to Nippur to receive the blessing of Enlil, his 'father', as soon has he has built the Sea House. Hence, the myth provides powerful evidence that Enlil was indeed the head of the pantheon at the time when it was composed. Nevertheless, when Enki prepares a banquet at Nippur to honour the great gods, he seats An in the highest place, with Enlil next to An. This supports the theory that An had once occupied a place even higher than Enlil in the Mesopotamian pantheon.

We can infer that when the Sea House was newly built, the Temple of Enlil at Nippur was already in existence, otherwise it would not have been necessary to go to Nippur to receive Enlil's blessing. This suggests that the myth may have been written to mark the consecration of a new temple at Eridu during Early Dynastic times, when the cult of Nippur was long established. However, archaeological evidence suggests that the history of temples at Eridu goes back beyond 5000 BC, a full 1500 years earlier than the oldest buildings found at Nippur (Lloyd, 1978, p. 36). In the meantime it appears that the cult of Eridu had lapsed, so Eridu's claim to priority had been lost to Nippur. In the meantime, also, sea-level had risen, so that Eridu, once situated on a freshwater lake, was close to the seashore.

CHAPTER 14

THE ORIGIN OF THE PANTHEON

In the preceding three chapters we have made a detailed examination of evidence about the nature of the Mesopotamian pantheon and its chief gods. Written evidence covering the thousand year period from about 2600 to 1600 BC supports the view of most Sumerologists that Enlil was the 'executive' head of the pantheon, but that An may have predated Enlil as 'father of the Gods'. In his authoritative treatise on Mesopotamian religion *'Treasures of Darkness'*, Jacobsen (1976) summed up these roles by equating An with *authority* and Enlil with *force*. He viewed these roles within a pantheon of 'the gods as rulers', reflecting the struggles between a collection of competing city states for supremacy over the Mesopotamian plain. Therefore, in seeking to understand the origin of the pantheon, it may be useful first to examine the relationships between Mesopotamian cities and their gods.

14.1 Cities and gods

Most of the principal gods of the Mesopotamian pantheon were also the patron gods of individual cities:

> An and Inanna, god and goddess of Uruk
> Enlil, god of Nippur
> Enki, god of Eridu
> Nintur (=Ninhursag), goddess of Kesh
> Nanna (the moon god) of Ur
> Utu (the sun god) of Larsa
> Ningursu (=Ninurta), god of Girsu (province of Lagash)

Evidence for the relationships between cities and their gods comes from a lexical list that was reproduced over a long period of time, the archaic city list. This list was preserved in a nearly constant form for five hundred years, from the Protoliterate period (ca. 3100 BC) to the

Early Dynastic period (ca. 2600 BC), as illustrated by the two versions (a and b) shown in the middle of Fig. 14.1. The order of the cities in the list is also consistent with cylinder seals of Protoliterate age found in a temple administration building at Jemdet Nasr (Moorey, 1976, p. 103), except that the cylinder seal reverses Nippur and Larsa, placing the latter second after Ur (Fig. 14.1, top). This seal reveals the apparent origins of some of the inscribed signs. For example, the sign for Uruk, consisting of an ornamented temple platform, seems to correspond to a platform with successive levels on the seal, one of the earliest representations of a ziggurat. Finally, a comparison between the prehistoric cylinder seals / tablets and the much later literary texts shows that the patronage of particular cities by their gods remained constant throughout the known history of Mesopotamia- with the exception of the ascendancy of Inanna at Uruk.

The significance of the city list for understanding the Mesopotamian pantheon is that the signs for several of the cities are intimately connected to the names of the patron gods of those cities. This is shown in Fig. 14.1 by a comparison of the cuneiform signs of the first four cities and gods. In the case of Nippur, the signs for the city and the god are identical, except that the eight pointed star (*dingir*) is added in front of the city name to denote the god. In some other cases the city is indicated by the sign of the god accompanied by a pictogram of a temple on a mound. Thus Ur is designated by a temple with a standard, while Larsa is indicated by a temple surmounted by the rising sun. Uruk, on the other hand, is shown by an ornamented temple mound without any other sign, as if to say that this was the archetypal temple mountain. Furthermore, the absence of the standard of Inanna from the sign for Uruk suggests that her ascendancy occurred *after* the temple mountain at Uruk had been established.

As noted previously, the order of the entries in the standard list of professions represents a hierarchy, with the high-priest/king as the first in the list. If we apply this rationale to the city list, it implies that in Protoliterate times the most important cities were Ur, Nippur, Larsa and Uruk. Furthermore, since approximately the same order is found in records from Uruk, Jemdet Nasr and Abu Salabikh, this order cannot be attributed to local bias. This order is surprising, since we would expect the first city in the list to be Eridu, the oldest city of Sumer according to both archaeological and literary evidence, with a 2000 year tradition of temple building and worship at the time when the city list was composed. However, Eridu actually occupies only the 15th place on the city list.

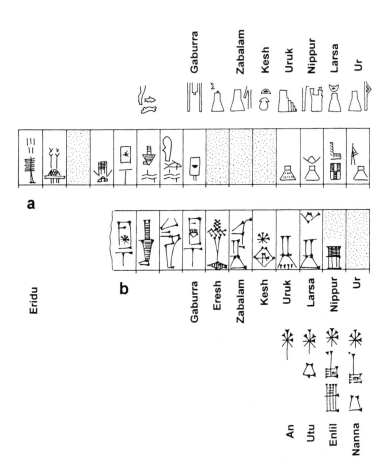

Fig. 14.1 The beginning of the standard list of Sumerian cities: a) from the Protoliterate level at Uruk, after Green (1977); b) from ED II at Tell Abu Salabikh, after Biggs (1974, pl. 10), compared with an ancient cylinder seal impression (top) after Matthews (1993, p. 37) and with the cuneiform signs for some gods (bottom). Stipple denotes damaged areas.

So, despite the fact that the Protoliterate period represents the dawn of written history, the earliest historical evidence suggests that it represented the *end* of a long period of religious and social development that stretched far back into prehistory. It is this period which we will now examine.

14.2 The gods of fertility

Most archaeologists and anthropologists interpret the religion of prehistory as a human reaction to the divine powers or *numina* seen in a variety of natural phenomena (Otto, 1923, p. 7). The earliest evidence for this phenomenon comes from figurines of women with exaggerated features that symbolise their fertility. For example, they may be shown as extremely pregnant or with extremely large breasts (Fig. 14.2). Such figurines date back to ca. 26,000 BC, in the middle of the Paleolithic period, and are found scattered over much of Europe (Baring and Cashford, 1991, p. 2).

It has been suggested that in the Neolithic period (beginning at 10,000 BC) the numinous power of female fertility began to evolve into the person of the Mother Goddess (e.g. Saggs, 1995, p. 34). For example, in the Sumerian pantheon, she was represented by Ninhursaga, also known as Nintur or Mami. However, the concept of a Mother Goddess is totally alien to the Bible, even though God is occasionally *compared* in the Bible to a Mother who cares for her offspring (e.g. Matthew 23:37). Therefore, examination of the cult of the Mother Goddess is not likely to shed much light on the revelation of the God of the Bible.

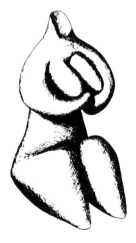

Fig. 14.2
Female figurine from northern Mesopotamia, interpreted as an embodiment of the numinous power of fertility. Clay. British Museum.

169

An important male fertility cult in the early pantheon of Mesopotamia was the cult of Dumuzi, called Tammuz in Akkadian. This cult had different aspects according to the context, representing alternatively the numinous power of fertility in the freshwater lagoon, in the date palm, in the herd, or in the field of crops. An important aspect of the cult was the diminishing of fertility at the end of spring as the searing heat of the summer sun wilted the grass of the pasture. This was reflected in the death of Dumuzi, who was then re-born in the spring of the following year as the pasture returned to life. This aspect of the cult is referred to as the 'dying god of fertility' (Jacobsen, 1976, p. 23-73).

Jacobsen argued that a transition occurred at the end of the prehistoric period, from revering the gods as numinous powers of nature to recognising their dominion as divine rulers over the heavens and the earth. This change apparently involved a gradual process of anthropomorphism of the gods whereby their representations changed from animal to human likeness. Thus, the essence of Dumuzi evolved from the life force in the womb of the pasture animal into the likeness of the shepherd, while the death of Dumuzi evolved from the withering of the pasture under summer's sun to the murder of the shepherd by brigands from the mountain wilderness (Jacobsen, 1961). With the personification of the fertility cult at the end of the Fourth Millennium, Dumuzi became the Fisherman, the Shepherd or the Farmer (Jacobsen, 1976, p. 43). Gradually these roles became merged, and the focus of the cult changed from the fertility of nature to the gathering of produce into the great temple store-rooms.

Jacobsen (1963) suggested that the ascendancy of the gods as rulers over Mesopotamian society began around 3000 BC and reflected a shift in the concerns of the people from the imminent threat of starvation to a fear of the ravages of war. Around this time (the Early Dynastic period), the office of King was first distinguished from that of the High Priest. Hence, Kramer (1956, p. 77) and Jacobsen (1963) suggested that the image of the human king was projected onto the divine level as the gods were recast into human form as divine rulers.

However, when we examine this 'kingship' theory for the evolution of Mesopotamian religion from the archaeological context of the Fourth and Third millennia, we find major problems. For example, the monumental architecture of the Uruk period points to a temple institution that had already reached a mature institutional stage, long before the threat of war had led to the institution of kingship. This degree of institutionalization suggests that the three great gods of the Cosmic Triad were already 'divine rulers' long before the appearance of the earthly office of kingship. Similarly, as Jacobsen himself pointed out (1963b), the evolution of Dumuzi from a divine life-force into a human image must have begun long before the Early Dynastic period because the cult of Dumuzi is illustrated on the Uruk vase (from the Protoliterate period). This suggests that the personification of the fertility cult was actually achieved during the Uruk period by the cult of 'Sacred Marriage' between Inanna and Dumuzi.

This evolution of the Mesopotamian fertility cult is totally opposed to the biblical view of the True God. For example, when the cult of Dumuzi (Tammuz) is mentioned in the Bible (Ezekiel Ch 8), it is in order to condemn it as a 'detestable practice'. This occurs when the prophet Ezekiel has an out-of-body experience and is transported by the Spirit of God from exile in Babylon to the temple in Jerusalem. In a vision he sees women mourning for Tammuz, just as the death of Dumuzi is described in the Sumerian myths (e.g. Jacobsen, 1987, p. 28-55). Part of the vision is described as follows (Ezekiel 8:14):

> *Then he brought me to the entrance to the north gate of the house of the LORD, and I saw women sitting there, mourning for Tammuz. He said to me, "Do you see this, son of man? You will see things that are even more detestable than this."*

The things that were 'even more detestable' than the worship of Tammuz were the worship of the heavenly bodies, the sun, moon and stars (Ezekiel 8:16):

> *He brought me into the inner court of the house of the LORD, and there at the entrance to the temple, between the portico and the altar, were about twenty-five men. With their backs towards the temple of the LORD and their faces towards the east, they were bowing down to the sun in the east.*

Cylinder seals of Akkadian age provide evidence that the worship of the heavenly bodies also originated from the fertility cult (Frankfort, 1933). For example, the seal impression in Fig. 14.3 shows the sun god Utu in his 'boat of heaven' with agricultural symbols, including a plough and a goddess of the fields (Frankfort, 1933, p. 17). This suggests that veneration of the sun god originated as a cult of agricultural fertility.

Similarly, the moon god Nanna probably originated in another fertility cult, based on the role of the moon in marking the agricultural seasons. Finally, the goddess of the storehouse, Inanna, became associated with Venus, the evening star. By this process of association, fertility cults at the cities of Ur, Larsa, and Uruk probably evolved into a triad of astral gods, Nanna, Utu, and Inanna, which rivalled the Cosmic Triad of An, Enlil and Enki. The success of the 'Astral Triad' is demonstrated by their position on a common type of Second Millennium boundary stone, the 'kudurru'. These stones bear the emblems of the gods in a hierarchical order, with the Astral Triad at the top, followed by the Cosmic Triad and then other important deities such as Murduk (Fig. 16.2). However, the *early* ascendancy of the Astral Triad, to rival the Cosmic Triad, is demonstrated by the prominent place of Ur, Larsa and Uruk in the Protoliterate city list, reflecting the early proliferation of the Sumerian pantheon.

Fig. 14.3. Impression of an Akkadian cylinder seal, showing the sun god in his 'boat of heaven' associated with symbols of agricultural fertility.

14.3 The god of Heaven

The difficulty faced by a secular historian in understanding the origins and evolution of the Mesopotamian pantheon is well illustrated in a paper by Jacobsen (1994) entitled 'The historian and the Sumerian gods', where he made the following observation (p. 146):

The evidence comes out of a very different world, one in which people tended to understand what happened to them as caused by supernatural agencies, gods, and demons, rather than as the outcome of rational causes.

However, it must be emphasised that although this was a 'very different world' in the eyes of Jacobsen (a secular historian) the viewpoint he describes is exactly that of the Bible. The Bible maintains, from cover to cover, that what happens to people is caused by supernatural agencies, but it maintains that a Supreme God is set over and above all other supernatural agencies. Therefore, I suggest that the only way of correctly understanding the origins of the Mesopotamian pantheon is to view it through a biblical frame of reference.

The essence of the Genesis account is that the True God revealed himself to a man at the dawn of Mesopotamian civilisation, and that this revelation was preserved, even through the great Flood, ultimately to be passed on to Abram. I suggest, therefore, that the point of True Revelation was the point at which human worship was *redirected* from a reverence for numina in the natural world to a relationship with a personal God. This corresponds to the transition from the General Revelation of God in nature to the Special Revelation of God described in the Bible, and was brought about when God communicated something of his divine character directly to a man in a personal encounter.

This view of divine revelation is supported by evidence from Sumerian written records, which imply that the cult of An, the God of Heaven and 'Father of the gods', evolved from a *personal* to an *impersonal* character with time, in the opposite way in fact to that proposed by secular historians. The evidence for this evolutionary trend comes from the pictographic representation of the name of An, which reaches back to the very earliest stages of Sumerian writing, in the Late Uruk period, nearly 3500 BC.

The Sumerian pictogram which is pronounced *'An'* is an eight pointed star. In the earliest period (Uruk, level 4), the pictogram has significant variety (Fig. 14.4), but by the Protoliterate period (Uruk level 3) it had more-or-less adopted the fixed form of the later cuneiform sign, made by four strokes and meaning 'heaven' or 'sky' (Green and Nissen, 1987, p. 175). However, by this time the meaning of the sign had also widened. As well as 'an' meaning 'heaven', the sign also became an ideogram with the general meaning of 'god', pronounced *'dingir'*. This suggests that long before the appearance of writing, the word An probably meant 'God of Heaven'. In Late Uruk times the star was adopted as the sign for the God of Heaven, but in the Protoliterate age the meaning of the sign broadened into a generic word for god. This change was probably associated with the 'promotion' of Inanna from the goddess of the store-house to the consort of the God of Heaven, becoming the Queen of Heaven (section 11.2). By Early Dynastic times, the sign 'dingir' was used as a 'determinative' for god-an indication that a certain name was a divine name. Finally, in the Akkadian language, the star sign was exclusively used as a divine determinative (pronounced *'ilu'*), while the name of the heavenly god changed to *'Anu'*, written as An-na.

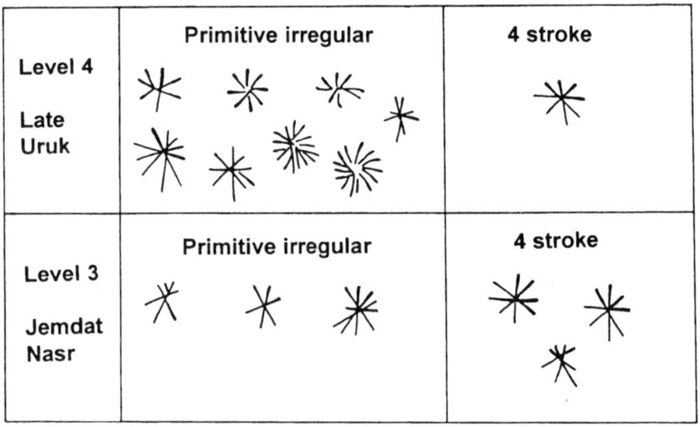

Fig. 14.4 Variety of forms of the sign for 'An' in Uruk
levels 4 and 3. After Green and Nissen, (1987, p. 175).

Evidence in support of the evolution of the sign for An is found in a parallel example from a time nearly 2000 years later. At the time of the patriarchs, the God of Abraham Isaac and Jacob revealed himself by the name 'El Shaddai', a name that is very similar to the early Canaanite name for the father god, 'El'. However, over time, the meaning of El broadened so that it gave rise to the word 'elohim', used in the Bible as a general word for god.

This broadening in the meaning of a divine name is analogous to the broadening of the meaning of a trade-mark into a generic name for a type of product. For example, in North America and Britain, the brand names 'Scotch tape' and 'Sellotape' respectively have broadened in meaning to refer to any kind of transparent adhesive tape. This broadening is detrimental to the owner of a trade-mark because it erodes the distinctiveness of the brand. In the commercial field, the owner of a brand name may try to combat the loss of distinctiveness by aggressively asserting the identity of his product. However, when the distinctiveness of the divine name became broadened to the point where it was no longer distinctive, God revealed himself under a new name. At the time of Moses, when the meaning of the name 'El' had been corrupted by broadening in meaning, God revealed himself by the new name 'I AM' or 'Yahweh', spelled in Hebrew as 'YHWH'. In the same way, I suggest that when the identity of 'An' (God of Heaven) was subverted by the cult of Inanna (Queen of Heaven), the True God revealed himself by a new name, Enlil, the Lord, Breath of God.

14.4 The god of Nippur

During the Early Dynastic period a new development was occurring in Mesopotamian civilisation that was touched upon above. This was the separation of 'Church' and 'State', or to be more exact, the separation of the office of High Priest from that of King. Evidence from archaeology and from Sumerian mythology suggests that before the Early Dynastic period, the Temple was the pre-eminent institution governing each city; for example the Eanna Complex of Uruk. However, at the beginning of ED II, Royal government is first visible as an institution distinct from the temple.

Evidence for this transition comes from Kish, where the earliest ruins are found of a Royal Palace separate from the temple. This so-called 'Palace A' dates from around the middle of the Early Dynastic period, possibly ED II, as it was found to contain one of the earliest inscribed stone tablets (Gibson, 1972, p. 118). The plan shown in Fig. 14.5 is quite distinct from that of temples, and one of its notable features is the double enclosing wall, with a particularly thick outer wall. This was presumably designed to provide protection for the Royal Household from the possibility of the palace being stormed. The interior of the palace consists of numerous rooms arranged around a central courtyard, accessed through a complex series of passages and rooms. This arrangement was probably designed to impress and disorientate visiting delegations, in order to give a psychological advantage to the king.

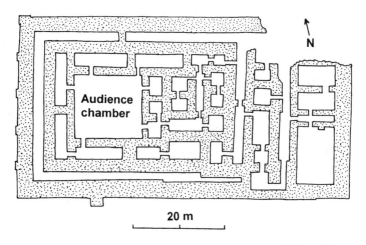

Fig. 14.5 Plan of Palace A at Kish. After Moorey (1978, p. 57).

The establishment of Royal Kingship at Kish which was separate from the temple was accompanied by another very important development during the ED II period; the building of a temple at Nippur that became a focus of worship for more than one city. Just as the Kingship of Kish came to symbolise secular dominion over the whole Mesopotamian plain, the Priesthood of Nippur symbolised spiritual dominion over the whole plain.

Excavations of the temple precinct of Nippur are supported by a map inscribed on a clay tablet, dating from around 1900 BC. The resulting reconstruction (Fig. 14.6) suggests that the temple platform (The Ekur) was accessible from the river Euphrates by means of a canal through the middle of the city. The name of Enlil is associated with Nippur from the earliest written records, since the sign for Nippur is literally 'place of Enlil'. The oldest known remains of the temple of Enlil date to the Early Dynastic II period and are preceded by the earliest remains of the temple of Inanna, of Early Uruk age. However, earlier remains of a cult of Enlil may underlie the Ekur, where little excavation has been possible (Gibson, 1992, p. 38). It is also possible that early temple structures under the Inanna temple were originally dedicated to An, the God of Heaven, and only later taken over by the cult of Inanna.

The fact that the founding of the temple of Enlil at Nippur coincided with the ascendancy of the kingdom of Kish over Sumer suggests that economic and/or military power was responsible for this change,

176

which broke the previous dominance of Uruk at the end of the Early Dynastic I period. It was suggested above that this crisis may have been caused by a change in the course of the Euphrates River (section 7.3), and that it was the event which gave rise to the story behind the Tower of Babel account. It is therefore important to re-examine the latter story to see if more details can be understood about the events behind the story.

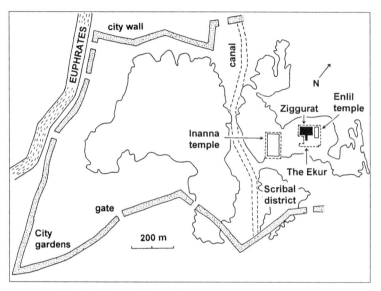

Fig. 14.6 Map of Nippur based on modern excavation and an ancient map. Higher ground is identified by the 12 m contour line. Modified after Roaf (1990).

In section 9.1 it was already argued that the judgement of Babel was against idolatry, and in the light of the historical and archaeological evidence outlined above we can deduce that this idolatry probably involved the elevation of Inanna to become Queen of Heaven. Hence, when Gen 11:4 describes the aim of the builders to 'make a name for themselves', we can assume that these were the priests of Inanna who were aiming to build their own power in the name of Inanna. This draws our attention to the cryptic observation made by God in Gen 11:6:

"If as one people speaking the same language they have begun to do this, then nothing they plan to do will be impossible for them."

177

These words seem to grossly exaggerate mankind's invincibility: merely speaking the same language does not really mean that mankind can do anything he wants. However, we need to look at this verse from the point of view of what the 'people' were actually trying to do, which was to replace the revelation of the True God with the cult of the false god Inanna. The economic power of the temple of Inanna at Uruk (the Eanna Complex) was so great that indeed they might have succeeded in eradicating the knowledge of God from the Earth if they had not been thwarted. For example, the cult of Inanna did spread over the whole land of Mesopotamia, and later, the cult of Ishtar and Ashtoroth spread over the whole Middle East.

The apparent vulnerability of God's revelation can be demonstrated by comparison with the much later events involving King Herod's murder of the babes of Bethlehem. If Herod had succeeded in killing Jesus as a baby then he would have thwarted God's plan. However, the fragility of God's plan is more apparent than real. God uses other agencies to thwart the plan of the enemy, and in the case of the Queen of Heaven it appears that it was the agency of nature, involving the River Euphrates. God had previously used this river to bring the great Flood of judgement against the idolatry of 'sacred marriage'. Now he apparently used the changing course of the river to bring a long-term drought on Uruk. This was a more subtle judgement than the Flood because the cult of Inanna continued to flourish and spread, but the decline of Uruk marked the beginning of a long period of retrenchment for the Sumerian people. By allowing the Semitic king of Kish to establish the temple of Enlil at Nippur as the new centre of worship for the whole land of Mesopotamia, God gave the True Revelation to the Semitic peoples to safeguard for future generations.

CHAPTER 15

THE NIPPUR PRIESTHOOD

The ascendancy of the temple of Enlil at Nippur during the Third Millennium can be demonstrated through two lines of evidence. The first consists of contemporary Royal Inscriptions dating from 2500 to 2000 BC, which show how individual kings reverenced Enlil as the supreme god of the Mesopotamian pantheon (section 12.1). The second line of evidence is a historical record made at the end of the dynastic period of Sumerian civilisation. This record is the Tummal chronicle, dating from the beginning of the Isin Dynasty (ca. 2000 BC), which summarises in a formulaic manner the history of the Nippur temple from 2700 to 2000 BC. Several partially complete copies of the chronicle are known, of which one was found in a scribal school house of Isin-Larsa age in the city of Ur. This shows that the chronicle was a popular subject for school exercises (Sollberger, 1962).

15.1 The history of the Nippur temple

The Tummal chronicle has six 'cycles', each of which describes the building of the temple by a certain king, its rise to pre-eminence under the king's son and its subsequent fall into ruin, before it was renewed in the next cycle (Poebel, 1914; Kramer, 1963, p. 47). The kings of these cycles are shown in Table 15.1, along with their city of origin and the dynastic period in which they reigned.

We should not attribute precise historical accuracy to the Tummal chronicle any more than the Sumerian King List. For example, the myth of 'Gilgamesh and Agga', describing the conflict between these two kings, suggests them to be contemporaneous, while a post-Sumerian royal hymn suggests that En-me-baragesi and Gilgamesh were contemporaries (Hallo and Simpson, 1971/98 p. 42). In addition, different versions of the chronicle actually place Gilgamesh and Mesanne-padda in the reverse order (Sollberger, 1962). Hence it appears that the events of the first three cycles of the chronicle were more or less contemporary at about 2700 BC, whereas the last three cycles are each separated by 200 - 300 years (Table 15.2). This shows that the historical coverage of the Tummal chronicle is very uneven. However, given this uneven coverage, it is nevertheless encouraging that the father-son relationships match those of the Sumerian King List. Furthermore, several of the kings are also known from royal inscriptions of their own time, to which the writers of the later Tummal chronicle may not have had direct access (the inscriptions were probably buried in the interim).

Table 15.1 Summary of the Tummal chronicle

Cycle	King	King's son	City of origin	Period
0	En-me-baragesi	Agga	Kish	ED II
1	Mesanne-padda	Meskiag-nunna	Ur	ED II
2	Gilgamesh	Ur-lugal	Uruk	ED II
3	Nanna	Meskiag-Nanna	Ur?	ED III?
4	Ur-Nammu	Shulgi	Ur	Ur III
5	Ishbi-Erra		Isin	Isin

It is particularly interesting that the Temple of Enlil at Nippur was founded by En-me-baragesi, a king of Kish and therefore of Semitic race. This shows that when political domination over the Mesopotamian plain first passed from Uruk to Kish, and hence from Sumerians to Semites, the latter adopted the Sumerian gods as their own. As argued by Jacobsen (1939b), this shows that there was no racial animosity between the two groups. During the ensuing conflict between Kish and Uruk under Agga and Gilgamesh, the rivalry was strictly between rival city states as political units, and not between Semites and Sumerians as enemy races.

After the period of the rival city states, the first king to decisively conquer the whole of the Mesopotamian plain was a Sumerian from Umma, Lugal-zagesi. When he had defeated Uruk, Lugal-zagesi set up his kingship there. It is notable that he also took the title 'King of the Land', specifically implying rulership over the area of Nippur. He expressed gratitude to Enlil by making offerings to him at the temple of Nippur and set up a statue of himself in the temple of Enlil at Nippur. However, despite Lugal-zagesi's Sumerian origin, his statue bears an inscription in Akkadian (Jacobsen, 1939b).

180

Table 15.2 Dynasties from ED III to Old Babylonian times

~~~~~~

Dynasty	King	Start of reign	
Umma	LUGAL-ZAGESI		
Akkad	SARGON	2370	
	|2		
	NARAM-SIN		
	|1		
Gutian invasion		2230	
Lagash	Gudea		
Uruk	Utahegel		
Ur III	UR-NAMMU	2113	
	SHULGI	2095	
	|2		
	IBBI-SIN	2029	
Isin	ISHBI-ERRA	2017	
	|5		(Loss of Ur to Larsa, ca. 1910)
	AMAR-SIN	1895	
	|3		
Larsa	NUR-ADAD	1865	
	|5		
	RIM-SIN I	1822	
Babylon	HAMMURABI	1792	(Conquest of Larsa, 1763)
	|3		
	Ammi-saduqa	1646	
	Samsu-ditana	1625	

~~~~~~

Dates back to Ur-Nammu are tied to the Middle timescale.
Dates for the Akkadian empire from Postgate (1992, p. 39).
Kings recognised by Nippur are capitalised (Hallo & Simpson, 1971, p. 94)
|x signifies number of intervening reigns not named here

15.2 Nippur and the empire of Akkad

Lugal-zagesi's domination of Mesopotamia was short-lived, and was overturned by Sargon, King of Akkad, in about 2370 BC (Table 15.2). While Lugal-zagesi was in the process of conquering Sumer, Sargon was the cup-bearer to Ur-Zababa, king of Kish. After the defeat of Kish by Lugal-zagesi, Sargon escaped and founded the new city of Akkad. However, after only twenty years he was able to capture Uruk, destroy its walls, and then defeat a combined army of Uruk's allies. These events are described at the beginning of a lament called the 'Curse of Akkad', which will be discussed below. Subsequently, Sargon subdued the principal Sumerian cities of the time (Ur and Umma), along with Susa in the east. He also conquered lands as far as Mari to the northwest. We know about these events because Sargon erected stelae and inscribed statues of himself in the temple of Nippur. The originals have not been found but the texts were later transcribed onto clay tablets which were found in the Library of Nippur. (e.g. Bermant and Weitzman, 1979, p. 40; Buccellati, 1993, p. 58).

Fig. 15.1
The Stele of Naram-Sin, carved from a 2m-high block of sandstone. The long vertical columns contain the inscription in Akkadian, while the Sumerian translation, almost lost to erosion, is in a block on the left. Musee du Louvre.

The empire of Akkad reached its greatest extent under the rule of Sargon's grand-son, Naram-Sin. His successful action against the Lullubi tribesmen of Iran is commemorated on the Stele of Naram-Sin (Fig. 15.1). This shows the king leading his army up wooded mountains and treading the enemy underfoot. Significantly it shows the king with the horned helmet of divinity, consistent with a contemporary inscription from the hill country of northern Iraq, in which Naram-Sin claims that the city of Akkad requested him to be its patron god (Postgate, 1992, p. 267).

It might be expected that the assumption of the title of god by Naram-Sin would provoke divine retribution. Retribution against Akkad is indeed described in a lament dating from the Third Dynasty of Ur, called 'The Curse of Akkad' (Cooper, 1983; Jacobsen, 1987). However, this document does not condemn Naram-Sin's claim to divinity but rather his demolition of Enlil's temple at Nippur (known as the Ekur). Because of the importance of the Curse of Akkad in understanding the institution of the Nippur temple, we will examine some excerpts (Jacobsen, 1987, p. 360).

The account begins by describing how Enlil had given the lordship over Sumer to Sargon of Akkad, comparing his triumph over Kish and Uruk to the killing of two great beasts. It then goes on to describe how work was begun on building a temple to Inanna at Akkad, called the Ulmash:

> *When Enlil's frowning brow had killed Kish, as it were the Bull*
> *   of Heaven,*
> *had cut the house of Uruk down into the dust as one would a*
> *   great ox,*
> *and Enlil then and there had given Sargon, king of Akkad,*
> *   lordship and kingship from south to north-*
> *In those days holy Inanna was building Akkad's temple close to*
> *   be her august home,*
> *To set up the throne in Ulmash...*
>
> [modified after Jacobsen, 1987, p. 360]

The account continues by describing how the riches of the empire flowing into Akkad were so great that the storehouses of Inanna had to be built larger and larger to accommodate them. However, the glowing reports are brought to a shuddering halt in line 57:

> *Upon this fell- as an ominous silence- the matter of Ekur...*

Exactly what this 'matter' was is not made clear. Jacobsen (1987) suggested that Naram Sin, king of Akkad, had sought to build a new temple for Enlil at Nippur, which would have entailed first demolishing the old temple. However, whatever it was that Naram Sin wanted to do, it was forbidden by omens. (These omens were usually obtained by examining the configuration of the guts of sacrificial animals, especially the shape of the liver). Naram Sin apparently persisted in his plan for seven years, attempting to get a favourable omen for his undertaking, but finally his patience ran out (line 99) and he did the unthinkable: he falsified the omen and then gathered his army to demolish the temple of Enlil at Nippur. This was done in such a violent way that it was likened to the sack of a city. Furthermore, he burned the sacred wooden statues of the temple precinct, cut down its sacred trees, and carried off the temple treasures to Akkad, melting down the silver, reshaping its jewels and hammering its copper vessels into scrap (line 140).

The violent character of the description suggests strongly that this was not a demolition for the purpose of rebuilding, but was a deliberate desecration of Enlil's temple. For example, if the temple was to have been rebuilt, great care would have been taken during the work to preserve the sacredness of the furnishings of the temple, which were the very household property of the god. Instead, the Holy of Holies, 'the house knowing not daylight' (line 129), was exposed to public view in front of the whole nation, representing the ultimate sacrilege. Based on this description of the demolition, I suggest that Naram Sin never intended to rebuild Enlil's temple at Nippur, but rather intended to glorify the temple of Inanna in Akkad at the expense of Enlil. In punishment, Enlil allowed Mesopotamia to be devastated by barbaric 'hordes' from the eastern mountains, the Gutians.

When we compare this account with other historical records, we find some disagreement about the timing of these events. For example, a later chronicle (Saggs, 1995, p. 75) attests to an invasion during Naram-Sin's own reign, but Akkad was evidently reduced only gradually to ruin because Naram-Sin's son reigned over a remnant of the former state. Nevertheless, the city was ultimately destroyed by the Gutians and is the only ancient capital not to have been rediscovered in modern times.

The description of the Cursing of Akkad seems in many ways to parallel the fall of Jerusalem described in the biblical accounts of 2nd Kings and 2nd Chronicles. In both cases their kings sinned against the Supreme God, elevating other deities at his expense. In both cases divine retribution was attributed to invading barbarians, but also in both cases the actual punishment was partially delayed, and the final devastation occurred under later kings. In both cases the pattern of unfolding events is described through a theological lens: Invasion is an effect which is linked to the king's sin as the original cause. In contrast, a secular historian, Saggs (1995) describes the 'Cursing of Akkad' as follows:

This was manifestly propaganda, behind which one may see the hand of the priesthood of Nippur, intent that all rulers should recognise the need to show favour to their temple. There are elements of history in the poem, insofar as it gives a fair picture of Akkad's widespread commercial empire and its consequent prosperity, but in detail it is tendentiously distorted. In particular it has telescoped events...

This is probably a reasonable assessment of the 'Curse of Akkad' from a secular point of view, but exactly the same kind of viewpoint (selective and often telescoped) is taken in many biblical accounts. Whether or not one feels that such a viewpoint is justified depends on whether or not one believes it to be true. If Enlil was indeed the True God, and the priesthood of Nippur his servants, then the demand that all rulers should show favour to his temple would be perfectly justified.

Despite these similarities between Mesopotamian and biblical history, there also seems to be a major difference between the acceptable worship of the True God by the Sumerians and by the Israelites. By the time of God's revelation to Moses, the command to have no other gods but the Lord was a cornerstone of the Law. However, the Sumerians were inveterate polytheists, and it seems to have been sufficient for Enlil to be worshipped as the Supreme God. Given this acknowledgement by the king, the worship of many other gods was tolerated. Indeed, even at Nippur itself there were several temples in addition to the Ekur of Enlil. These included the Tummal of Enlil's 'wife' Ninlil (after which the Tummal chronicle is named), and even a temple to Inanna.

15.3 Nippur and the Sumerian revival

The period of Gutian domination was a time of great upheaval in Mesopotamia, summed up in the Sumerian King List by the phrase *'Who was king? Who was not king?'* (Saggs, 1995, p. 80), and a statement that 21 kings reigned within a period of 91 years. During this time Lagash had a certain amount of autonomy, probably because it was accustomed to dealing with the mountain people from the east and was therefore most willing to 'collaborate' with the invaders. In this period the most prominent ruler of Lagash was Gudea, immortalised in numerous statues.

An important historical record from this period is the Stele of Gudea, which consists of a limestone panel sculptured in relief (Fig. 15.2). It shows Gudea being led by a 'personal god' into the presence of a greater god who is seated on a throne (but largely missing). The feature of this sculpture which is most interesting is the form of dress of the different persons involved. Gudea has the shaven head and clean-shaven features typical of a Sumerian, and is wearing a bordered Sumerian mantle. In contrast, the gods (with horned helmets) have their hair in bundles at the back and have long beards, in the Semitic style. They are also wearing a typical Semitic garment, consisting of a long plaid which is repeatedly wrapped round the body with the end thrown over the shoulder. The significance of the racial affinity of the worshipper and the gods is that Gudea, a Sumerian, is worshipping gods which were originally Sumerian, but over the passage of time have become recognised as Semitic. This must be due to the fact that Enlil, the chief god of the Third Millennium pantheon, had his temple in Nippur, which had now long been under the influence of the Semitic Akkadians.

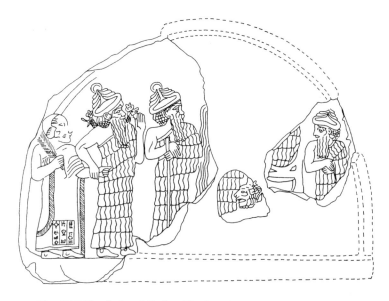

Fig. 15.2 The Stele of Gudea. Vorderasiatisches Museum, Berlin.

Gudea is also commemorated in the longest surviving Sumerian literary work, the 'Cylinders of Gudea', written about 2150 BC (Jacobsen, 1987, p. 387). The two extant cylinders (A and B) comprise the middle and end of an original three-part poem entitled 'The House of Ningirsu' (Fig. 10.5). At the beginning of the extant part, Enlil gives permission for Gudea, ruler of Girsu, to build a new temple for the city god Ningirsu. Gudea seeks further enlightenment from Ningursu regarding the style of the temple to be built. After receiving this enlightenment in a dream and testing it with an omen, Gudea begins the work of building, which is described in great detail. The third cylinder describes the installation of Ningirsu and his wife (daughter of An), followed by the offering of sacrifices and the establishment of temple offices.

The Gutian inter-regnum was brought to an end by king Utahegel of Uruk, but his power was shortly usurped by one of his governors, Ur-Nammu, who established the Third Dynasty of Ur in about 2115 BC. He took for the first time the title 'King of Sumer and Akkad' and established a dynasty that was to last for 100 years, ushering in a great revival of Sumerian culture. Ur-Nammu began a major temple building program throughout Mesopotamia, which included the rebuilding of Enlil's Ekur in Nippur and the Great Ziggurat of Ur (Fig. 8.1). A stele of Ur-Nammu, found in Ur, shows Ur-Nammu, in Sumerian dress, approaching the moon god Nanna and his consort (Fig. 15.3). Both gods are shown in Semitic dress, as previously seen on the Stele of Gudea. Thus, even under the 'Sumerian Revival' the gods had now become permanently identified as Semitic, under the leadership of Enlil. Thus, it is easy to see how, in later times, the Sumerian origin of the Mesopotamian pantheon might have been overlooked.

The Sumerian revival reached its height during the reign of Ur-nammu's son Shulgi, who seems to have emulated Naram-Sin of Akkad, taking the title 'King of the Four Quarters (of the world)' and having himself deified. This was indicated by adding the prefix '*Dingir*' (= god) in front of his name. Shulgi built powerful defences round Mesopotamia to protect his empire from external attack, but within Sumer and Akkad he presented himself as a man of peace and culture. He made sure that the temples of Nippur were well supplied with offerings by re-surveying the temple lands and building royal cattle pens at nearby Puzrish-Dagan (Fig. 6.3). He established a schedule of monthly offerings which the major Sumerian and Akkadian cities (now provinces) were responsible for supplying to the Nippur temples and their priesthood.

Fig. 15.3 View of part of the stele of Ur-Nammu showing the king pouring drink offerings to the moon god (right) and his consort (left). Each frieze is about 50 cm high. University Museum, Philadelphia.

Shulgi had been trained as a scribe when he was young, and he founded scribal schools at Nippur and Ur where Sumerian grammar was systematised and compiled into word lists and canonical phrase lists (Hallo & Simpson, 1971/98 p. 79). Shulgi probably encouraged the development of the written language in order to more adequately express literary works, since many of the extant Sumerian myths are thought to have been first written down at this time.

During the early years of the Ur III dynasty the Gutians continued to be a threat, but during its latter years a new threat appeared from the northwest in the form of a group of Semitic invaders, the Amorites. Under this onslaught, the last ruler of Ur, Ibbi-Sin, gradually lost control of the rest of the Mesopotamian plain. At this time, Ur was heavily dependent on food supplies from the north, probably due to a drying regional climate which caused salination of the soil and hence decreased food production. When supplies from the north were cut off there were food shortages and hyper-inflation. These must have hampered the defence of the empire against invaders and in the end Ur fell to the Elamites and other peoples from the East around 2005 BC.

15.4 Nippur in the Isin/Larsa period

During the declining years of Ur, the city of Isin rose to prominence under Ishbi-Erra, who recaptured Ur from the Elamites, allowing a last flowering of Sumerian culture. Despite their Amorite origins, the kings of Isin were very anxious to portray themselves as the true successors of the past glories of Sumerian civilisation. This is indicated by the extension of the Sumerian King List and the writing of the Tummal chronicle during this period, both of which were intended to show the continuity of the Isin dynasty with those that had gone before. It was also at this time that the 'Lament for the Fall of Ur' was written. The kings of Isin maintained the undivided loyalty of nearby Nippur, so they were regarded by the Nippur priesthood as the rightful inheritors of the Kingship of the Land. However, Isin did not have complete control of the Mesopotamian plain, and Larsa in the south rose to prominence at about the same time. These two cities generally maintained friendly relations, but Larsa gradually grew in importance, and in about 1910 BC gained control of Ur. A hundred years later Larsa finally overcame Isin, but was in turn conquered shortly afterwards by Hammurabi of Babylon.

Through all of the changes during the 250 year period after the fall of Ur, the Nippur priesthood somehow survived, so that it could pass on its traditions and records to the Old Babylonian period, from which our copies of the Sumerian myths actually date. Looking back over the history of this priesthood, we can see that it maintained the worship of Enlil as the Supreme God for a thousand years from the Early Dynastic period to the Old Babylonian period. In this role, the Nippur priesthood bears comparison with the Roman Catholic Church, which preserved Christianity for a thousand years from the fall of the Roman Empire until the reformation. In both cases, I suggest, God used an institutional priesthood at a religious centre to maintain his True Revelation through the comings and goings of many secular kingships.

CHAPTER 16

THE ECLIPSE OF ENLIL

Three great Babylonian literary compositions, the Epic of Creation, Epic of Atrahasis and Epic of Gilgamesh are generally regarded as the greatest written works of Mesopotamian civilisation. This is a fair judgement from a literary point of view. However, from the point of view of biblical history, these epics date from after the eclipse of Sumerian civilisation, and almost certainly from after the departure of Abram from Mesopotamia. Therefore they tell us not so much about Early Mesopotamian religion as about the evolution of religious thought *after* the Sumerian period. They are reviewed here in order to see this evolution, which can also throw light on the way in which religious thought evolved amongst the west Semitic peoples, including the Israelites.

In Akkadian cuneiform, the names of Enlil and Enki were written with the same signs as in Sumerian, although these names were now pronounced as 'Ellil' and 'Ea' respectively. As noted above, the name of the god An (pronounced *'Anu'*) is written in Akkadian cuneiform as An-na. This was probably done in order to avoid confusion, since the sign for An had become the generic sign for 'god' pronounced as *'ilu'* in Akkadian. In order to reflect the Akkadian language of these sources, we will now use the Akkadian versions of the divine names.

16.1 The Atrahasis Epic

As noted in section 6.2, the Atrahasis Epic claims to have been written in Akkadian by Nur-Aya at Sippar during the Old Babylonian period. The epic purports to tell the story of the earliest history of man, but it contains much evidence of having originated in an institutional society under the control of the monarchy and the temple.

The labour in which we supposedly find the lesser gods involved at the beginning of the epic is the back-breaking work of canal building, carried out under the direction of a high official. This has all the marks of a repressive monarchy. Meanwhile, in speaking of Ellil, the gods exclaim:

"let us carry Ellil, the counsellor of gods, the warrior, from his dwelling"

Subsequently, when the gods revolt during the night, it is reported:

Ekur (the ziggurat) *was surrounded, Ellil had not realised. Yet Kalkal* (the temple guard) *was attentive, and had it closed, he held the lock and watched the gate.*

Immediately, Ellil is roused by his vizier:

"My lord, your house is surrounded, a rabble is running round your door!"

When Ellil is finally roused, he calls for weapons so that the vizier can stand guard in front of him to protect him. The picture here is of a temple institution containing a helpless idol which must be carried about and which must be watched over and guarded by the temple priesthood and temple guards.

Despite the apparent helplessness of Ellil in the face of a riot, he is evidently capable, later in the epic, of bringing about the disaster of the great Flood. Therefore, his portrayal here is not as a powerless idol but an unmerciful and unreachable power over nature. In contrast, Ea is the benefactor and saviour of mankind. Thus, Ea disclaims all responsibility for the flood (Table 2, column 7):

"The flood you mention to me- What is it? I don't even know! Could I give birth to a flood?"
[quotes from the Flood Story in Atrahasis, translated by Dalley]

Having been forbidden by Ellil to warn Atrahasis about the flood, Ea then proceeds to warn him indirectly, through the medium of the whispering reed hut. Meanwhile, the comment is made (immediately prior to the flood):

Ellil performed a bad deed to the people.

After the flood; when Ellil sees that Atrahasis has escaped death in a boat, he is furious:

"We, the great Anunna, all of us, agreed together on oath! No form of life should have escaped! How did any man survive the catastrophe?"

In reply, An suggests to Ellil that it must have been Ea:

"He made sure that the reed hut disclosed the order."

To this, Ea defiantly admits:

"I did it in defiance of you! I made sure life was preserved."

In conclusion, the Atrahasis Epic illustrates a trend towards presenting Ellil as a god who is remote from human concerns and not capable of meeting human needs. He is apparently not capable of controlling his own family (the lesser gods). From these he must be protected by armed force. He is also not capable of controlling mankind, whose noise becomes so great that Ellil cannot sleep. However, in response to this disturbance, Ellil is evidently capable of causing natural disaster (the Flood). Then, from a god who is theoretically supreme, but not really in full control, to a god who is apparently indifferent to human suffering, it is but a short step for one of his 'offspring' to usurp his power and declare themselves the Supreme God in his place.

16.2 The Code of Hammurabi

The Code of Hammurabi (Fig. 16.1) gives us the political background for the waning of Ellil's authority as the Supreme God of Mesopotamia. Thus, when Hammurabi made Babylon the capital of Mesopotamia in 1760 BC, he sought to promote the city god of Babylon, named Marduk, to the level of one of the chief gods of the Mesopotamian pantheon.

The Code of Hammurabi, written in Akkadian on a 2.3 m high diorite stele, establishes a large body of Case Law, prescribing verdicts and punishments for specific injuries and infractions of the law. However, the code begins with a prologue that presents its legal authority as a set of statutes handed down by the gods. The process of divine dispensation is illustrated in a large sculptured relief which shows Hammurabi receiving laws from the sun god, Shamash, whose identity is shown by the rays of light spreading out from his shoulders (Fig. 16.1). The role of Shamash as the god of justice was based on the premise that those who felt they were being treated unjustly would look up to the sun and appeal for help: "Oh Shamash!".

Fig. 16.1 The Stele of Hammurabi: a) general view; b) close up view of the top showing Hammurabi receiving laws from the sun god Shamash. Musee du Louvre.

In the course of citing his divine authority to rule, Hammurabi claims that Ellil, the lord of heaven and earth, had voluntarily delegated his authority, expressed as the 'Ellil functions over all mankind' to Marduk, the god of Babylon:

When lofty Anu, king of the Anunnaki, and Ellil, lord of heaven and earth, the determiner of the destinies of the land, determined for Marduk, the first born of Ea, the Ellil functions over all mankind, made him great among the Igigi, called Babylon by its exalted name, made it supreme in the world, established for him in its midst an enduring kingship, whose foundations are as firm as heaven and earth- at that time Anu and Ellil named me to promote the welfare of the people, me, Hammurabi, the devout, god-fearing prince, to cause justice to prevail in the land, to destroy the wicked and evil,

193

that the strong might not oppress the weak, to rise the sun (of justice) *over the black-headed people...*

[Meek, 1955].

The Stele of Hammurabi survived several invasions of Babylon over the next 600 years but was finally carried off to Susa by the Elamites, following a successful invasion in ca. 1150 BC (Finegan, 1979, p. 78). The statue of Marduk was also carried off to Elam at this time, as in fact it had also been carried off to Assyria a few decades earlier. However, when Nebuchadnezzar I invaded Elam in about 1100 BC, he recovered the statue of Marduk and returned it to Babylon. It appears that Nebuchadnezzar took this opportunity, of the return of Marduk's image, to cement Marduk's supremacy over the Babylonian pantheon. The Epic of Creation is the declaration of that supremacy (Lambert, 1992).

16.3 The Epic of Creation

The Babylonian Epic of creation is usually referred to by its first two words 'Enuma Elish' ('When Above...'). It describes how Marduk, the god of Babylon, achieved supremacy over the Babylonian pantheon in a cosmic battle of the gods. The epic was written in Akkadian, and all available versions date from the First Millennium and show little variation. Lambert (1992) attributed the epic to the reign of Nebuchadnezzar I around 1100 BC, and in fact the epic may have marked the re-installation of Marduk's image in the temple at Babylon after its return from captivity in Susa. According to a tablet of ritual instructions for the New Year Festival in Babylon, the Creation Epic was to be recited on the fourth day of that Festival (Dalley, 1991, p. 231). Consistent with this purpose, the Epic is intended to impress the listener with its cosmic perspective.

The Enuma Elish begins by describing a genealogy of the gods (Table 16.1). From the union of the two primaeval bodies of water, Apsu, the father of the gods, and Tiamat, the mother, a lineage was derived which included their grandson Anu and great grandson Ea (Enki in Sumerian). The latter generation, we are told, made so much noise that Apsu plotted with his vizier (Mummu) to kill them. However, Ea the wise heard about the plot and cast a spell on Apsu to put him to sleep. After killing Apsu, Ea *'set up his dwelling on top of Apsu'* and named this dwelling Apsu, thus usurping Apsu's position. Ea's lover was Damkina, and she gave birth to Marduk, destined to become Bel, the new Lord of the gods.

Table 16.1 Genealogy of the Gods in the Enuma Elish

~~~~~~

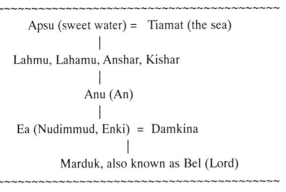

Apsu (sweet water) = Tiamat (the sea)
|
Lahmu, Lahamu, Anshar, Kishar
|
Anu (An)
|
Ea (Nudimmud, Enki) = Damkina
|
Marduk, also known as Bel (Lord)

~~~~~~

Dalley (1991, p. 228); Sandars (a paraphrase: 1971 p. 73)

After Marduk's birth, Anu (his grandfather) created four winds and gave them to Marduk to let him play. The winds made a flood-wave that stirred up Tiamat (the sea) so that she heaved restlessly day and night. The gods could not rest, so they plotted with Tiamat to avenge the murder of Apsu. However, Ea heard that Tiamat was preparing for war and held a council with Anshar, Anu and the Igigi gods. They called on Marduk, who agreed to fight Tiamat. Eventually the two came face to face and Tiamat was killed and sliced in two. Marduk put half of her body up to roof the sky and arranged the lower half of her corpse so that the seas could not escape. He set up constellations of stars to mark out the divisions of the year, and the moon to mark out the days of the month.

In the Enuma Elish, Ellil has almost disappeared from our notice. He does not appear in the genealogy of the gods, whose descent now goes through Anu and Ea to Marduk (see Table 16.1). However, Ellil's name is still mentioned indirectly when Marduk is credited with the foundation of cult centres for Anu, Ellil and Ea. This reference provides unwitting evidence that these three deities were the original supreme gods of the Mesopotamian pantheon, also referred to as the 'Cosmic Triad'.

The Cosmic Triad is found grouped together throughout the Second Millennium on a particular design of stele that was first used by the Kassites (after the Old Babylonian period). Fig. 16.2 shows a typical example of this design, in which the gods are grouped into horizontal registers. At the top are the signs for the astral deities, Ishtar, Sin and Shamash. These are followed in the second register by three altars bearing horns, representing the triad Anu, Ellil and Ea. However, it is interesting to note that these three gods are not represented by any other symbol[8]. The third register contains the altars of Marduk on the left and Nabu, god of writing in the middle. That on the right may show an umbilical cord, representing the mother goddess. The fourth register contains the gods of war, while the bottom two registers contain other gods and demons. A large serpent (not visible in Fig. 16.2) climbs up the edge of the stele and over its top.

Fig. 16.2
Limestone stele from the time of Nebuchadnezzar I, show-ing sacred emblems of the gods of Mesopotamia. Height 56 cm. British Museum.

In the original publication of the Enuma Elish, King (1902, p. 77, 267) translated the name Ellil as the 'older Bel', a name which means Lord and refers to the head of a pantheon (Dalley, 1991, p. 318). The title Bel is also given to Marduk, thus signifying that Marduk sup-planted Ellil as the head of the Mesopotamian pantheon, as noted above. The most frequent references to Anu, Ellil and Ea concern their cult centres, which are described in passing as part of the creation by

196

Marduk. This implies that recognition of Ellil as one of the great gods was a relic of older beliefs that had not quite disappeared at that time. On one occasion, Ellil is referred to in passing as 'father' (Dalley, 1991, p. 273). However, on another occasion, Anu, Ellil and Ea each present Marduk with gifts, indicating their subservience to Marduk under the Babylonian world order. This process would shortly be completed when Ellil was ousted from his own temple by Simbar-Shipak, who ruled a century after Nebuchadnezzar I.

16.4 The votive inscription of Simbar-Shipak

Votive objects were presented in the temple as offerings from the worshipper. Often these were small statues, intended as substitutes for the worshipper himself, to represent him in constant prayer before his god. Fig. 16.3 shows a typical example of such a statuette, from the Early Dynastic III period at Lagash. On the back of the statuette is an inscription which gives the name of the worshipper as Dudu, and his profession as a scribe.

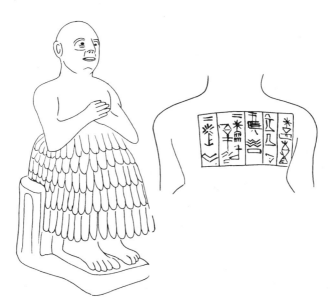

Fig. 16.3 Statuette of the scribe Dudu from EDIII Lagash, prob-ably intended as a votive object. The inscription (reading from right to left) is translated as: *'To the god Ningirsu, Dudu the scribe, two Imduguds has presented'*. Iraq Museum, Baghdad.

Votive inscriptions are an important class of documents because they describe the worshipper (often the king) responsible for the offering and the god to whom the offering is made. These dedicatory inscriptions therefore provide evidence of the evolution of the Mesopotamian pantheon over time. An important votive inscription of king Simbar-Shipak (1025-1008 BC) describes the restoration and reinstallation in the Ekur temple at Nippur of a throne of Ellil first manufactured by Nebuchadnezzar I a hundred years earlier (1124-1103 BC). The inscription shows how Marduk finally ousted Ellil from his own temple (Hurowitz, 1997).

The inscription begins by describing the exalted rank and universal domain of the god Ellil, and continues by proclaiming his authority over all of the other gods. The inscription then describes the manufacture and installation of the throne. It goes on to request that when Marduk sits on the throne, he might guarantee the destiny of Simbar-Shipak. The inscription ends by describing Marduk as *'Great Lord, exceedingly great Ellil of the gods'* (Hurowitz, 1997). Hence, it appears that when he restored Ellil's throne at Nippur, Simbar-Shipak took this opportunity to complete the ascendancy of Marduk by seating Marduk on Ellil's own throne.

The complete eclipse of Ellil by the end of the Second Millennium marks the culmination of a long process of apostasy. This was accompanied by greater and greater reliance amongst the Babylonians on divination as a means of attempting to discern the future course of events and to avoid adverse circumstances. As noted by Saggs (1978), Babylonian divination was largely non-deistic (ie not associated directly with the gods) even though it came under the overall umbrella of Babylonian religion. This is exemplified by the appearance of 'omen tables' in the Old Babylonian period, which link portents and their results in a largely arbitrary fashion. A few examples are quoted here from various Akkadian omen tables (Saggs, 1978, p. 135):

> *If water is poured out at the door of a man's house and it looks like a snake, he will experience evil*
> *If a wild bull is seen in front of the (city) gate, the enemy will attack the city*
> *If a man is covered in warts,*
> *he will have food to eat (even) in a famine*
> *When Mars again returns from the head of Leo and touches*

Cancer and Gemini, this is the interpretation: 'End of the reign of the king of Amurru'
When Jupiter stands behind the moon, this is its interpretation: 'There will be hostilities in the country'

Such methods of divination were regarded as abominations under the Law of Moses (Lev 18:9-13), and by the time of the prophet Isaiah (ca. 700 BC), Babylon itself would become a symbol in the Bible of everything that is offensive to God. Thus, in Isaiah 13:19, the following judgement is prophesied against it:

Babylon, the jewel of kingdoms, the glory of the Babylonian's pride will be overthrown by God like Sodom and Gomorrah. She will never be inhabited or lived in through all generations...

This judgement finally reaches its climax in the book of Revelation (Ch 17:3-5):

The angel carried me away in the Spirit into a desert. There I saw a woman sitting on a scarlet beast that was covered with blasphemous names and had seven heads and ten horns. The woman was dressed in purple and scarlet, and was glittering with gold, precious stones and pearls. She held a golden cup in her hand, filled with abominable things and the filth of her adulteries. This title was written on her forehead:

MYSTERY
BABYLON THE GREAT
THE MOTHER OF PROSTITUTES
AND OF THE ABOMINATIONS OF THE EARTH

I have argued that during the Third Millennium, God had a plan to preserve the honour of his name in Mesopotamia, by means of the temple priesthood of Nippur. However, the rise to power of Babylon and the elevation of its god Marduk are historical watersheds. With the call of Abram, God refocuses his purposes. His message will now be carried into a new land by a single man. From the human point of view, the Old Babylonian empire will pass into the Kassite, Assyrian, and Babylonian empires, but spiritually, enlightenment will leave Mesopotamia until the Jewish exile more than 1200 years later.

CHAPTER 17

THE HISTORICAL CONTEXT OF ABRAM

In order to understand how Abram inherited aspects of Mesopotamian culture and religion and carried them to a new land, it is important to be able to put the Patriarchal age into the context of Middle Eastern history. This requires us to estimate the period when Abram lived, based on the biblical account of the succession from Abram, through Moses, to the Israelite monarchy. The Bible gives a time frame for this succession based on genealogical information. However, the Bible also gives other evidence which can be tied to historical chronologies. Both of these lines of evidence will be examined in an attempt to date the Patriarchal age and the subsequent sojourn of the Israelites in Egypt.

17.1 The biblical genealogies

Biblical chronology dates the birth of Abram exactly 1200 years before the founding of the Temple of Solomon, which occurred in about 970 BC (e.g. Thiele, 1977, p. 31). The period of 1200 years is itself divided up into three periods, based on two critical migrations. Measuring back from the time of the monarchy, we note that according to 1st Kings 6:1, 480 years elapsed between the Israelite 'Exodus' from Egypt and the founding of the Temple of Solomon, which would place the Exodus in 1450 BC. Then, according to Exodus 12:40, exactly 430 years elapsed between Jacob's arrival in Egypt and the Exodus from Egypt, which would place Jacob's arrival in 1880 BC. In addition, 290 years elapsed between the birth of Abram and Jacob's migration to Egypt, based on the genealogies of the Patriarchs in Genesis. This would place the birth of Abram in 2170 BC, at the very beginning of the Third dynasty of Ur. However, whenever we find a perfect number such as 1200 used in the Bible we can expect that it may have a schematic rather than a historical meaning, and this would also apply to the three time intervals which together make up the total of 1200 years.

We will first examine the most recent of these three periods, which is the 480 year span between the Exodus and the founding of the Temple of Solomon, recorded in 1st Kings 6:1. This figure was probably derived from the genealogy of Levi, which contains twelve generations between Moses' brother, Aaron, and the priest Azariah, who served in the Temple of Solomon (1st Chron 6:3-10). Since the Israelites were forced to remain 40 years in the desert until a whole generation had died, this may have given rise to the idea that 40 years was the typical length of a generation (Finegan, 1979, p. 432). Hence, 12 generations of 40 years could have led to a schematic figure of 480 years between the Exodus and the founding of the Temple.

When we examine the length of the Sojourn in Egypt from a biblical perspective, we also find evidence for a schematic rather than literal meaning. Thus, when God makes his covenant with Abram after his meeting with Melchizedek (Gen Ch 15), he tells Abram that his descendants will be oppressed in a foreign land for 400 years (Gen 15:13), but in the fourth generation they will return to Canaan. The apparent contradiction between a period of 400 years and of 4 generations is suggestive that the time period described may be symbolic. However, each of these statements is supported by other biblical texts. On the one hand, the numerical figure of 400 years (obviously a round number) is supported by the statement in Exodus 12:40-41:

Now the length of time the Israelite people lived in Egypt was 430 years. At the end of the 430 years, to the very day, all the Lord's divisions left Egypt.

On the other hand, the four generation period in Egypt is supported by the family genealogy of Levi (son of Jacob) in 1st Chron 6:1-3:

The sons of Levi: Gershon, Kohath and Merari.
The sons of Kohath: Amram, Izhar, Hebron and Uzziel.
The children of Amram: Aaron, Moses and Miriam.

If we assume that a generation lasts 30 or 40 years then four generations appear to be much shorter than 400 years. However, we must remember that the length of the Sojourn in Egypt was foretold to Abram, who, according to Genesis, was 100 years old when Isaac was born. Thus, by the standards of Abram, 400 years was indeed four generations, and so the two parts of the prediction are consistent. Hundreds of years later, when the genealogy of Levi was compiled, the author obviously did not want to contradict God's promise that the sojourn would be of four generations, so he compiled a schematic genealogy whose primary function was to affirm the unbroken succession of the Levitical line. The real genealogy between Levi and Moses was undoubtedly much longer, to allow the Israelites to increase in number from a single family to a nation.

Another comment on the length of the sojourn comes from the apostle Paul in Acts 13:20. In his sermon to the Jews of Pisidian Antioch (in modern Turkey), Paul recounts that the sojourn in Egypt, together with the 40 years of wandering in the desert and the initial conquest of Canaan took 'about 450 years', suggesting that he was following the round number of 400 years for the Egyptian sojourn foretold to Abram. What is particularly interesting is that Paul uses this round number in preference to the claim in Exodus that the sojourn lasted '*430 years, to the very day*' (as quoted above). This suggests that the expression 'to the very day' is also intended to be symbolic, and thus to highlight the perfection of God's plan of rescue, rather than to specify the exact duration of the sojourn.

Finally, when we consider the length of the Patriarchal age, we move into a period of scarce written records, when schematic genealogies become even more likely. This can be seen by an examination of some of the numbers given in Genesis. Thus, Sarna (1966, p. 83) pointed out that the 75 years that Abram lived with his father Terah in Mesopotamia is matched by the 75 years that he lived with his son Isaac in Canaan. Similarly, the 17 years that Joseph lived with Jacob in Canaan is matched by the 17 years that Jacob lived with Joseph in Egypt. These patterns suggest that the life-spans of the Patriarchs are not intended as chronological records but as theological statements: the use of special numbers and the creation of number symmetry implies evidence of the divine plan behind historical events, rather than a haphazard train of events. We will return to a reconsideration of the Patriarchal genealogies after considering archaeological evidence for the date of the Egyptian sojourn.

17.2 The Egyptian Sojourn

In contrast to the schematic, non-literal nature of many biblical genealogies, much evidence collected over the past century suggests that the Bible describes events, places and people with great historical accuracy. Hence, we will now attempt to use the biblical account of events, placed in the context of Egyptian history, to determine independent dates for the Egyptian sojourn.

Egyptian history was first compiled by a priest named Manetho who wrote an account for Alexander the Great shortly after his conquest. Although this account is only preserved in fragments, we also have three ancient king lists from about the time of Rameses II ('Rameses the Great'). Two of these king lists are inscribed in hieroglyphics on temple walls at Abydos and Saqqara, located near the royal cities of Thebes and Memphis (Fig. 17.1). The third source, called the Turin Canon of Kings, is written in hieratic script on papyrus and now resides in the Turin Museum (e.g. Finegan, 1979, p. 184).

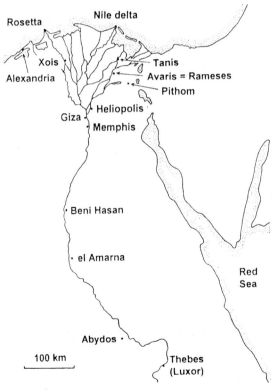

Fig. 17.1 Map of Egypt showing significant localities, including the centres of kingship for different dynasties.

Fig. 17.2 The Stele of Merneptah (ca. 1210 BC) which contains a reference to the defeat of the people of Israel in the penultimate line of the inscription. Only 3 lines out of 28 are shown to save space. Cairo Museum.

Manetho divided Egyptian history into 30 dynasties, later revised to 31, and these are now grouped into 6 eras of strong central rule and 3 intermediate periods. The three main eras of central rule comprise the Old, Middle and New kingdoms, while the intermediate periods represent times when Egypt was either divided amongst several rulers or was under the control of foreign kings. These periods are compared with the major episodes of Mesopotamian history in Table 17.1. The Old Kingdom, which was the period of great pyramid building, overlapped with the Early Dynastic and Akkadian periods. After this time, periods of stability in Egypt tended to occur during periods of turmoil in Mesopotamia, and vice versa, as the tides of war and peace ebbed and flowed across the Middle East. As a historical note, the New Kingdom included the well known boy king Tut-ank-amun (18th dynasty) and the famous monument builder Rameses II (19th dynasty).

The only mention of the Israelites in any known Egyptian inscription comes from the Victory Hymn of Merneptah, successor to Rameses

II, which is carved on a 2.3 m high granite monolith (Fig. 17.2) found in the funerary temple of Merneptah. After describing Merneptah's victory over a Libyan invasion (in about 1220 BC), the text continues with a general celebration of victory over all of Egypt's enemies in Canaan, including the Israelites. This shows conclusively that the Israelites were already in Canaan by this time, and therefore places the latest possible time for the Exodus at the start of the reign of Rameses II.

Table 17.1 Mesopotamian and Egyptian Periods, 3000 - 1000 BC

Years B.C.	Name of Period in Mesopotamia	Name of Period in Egypt	Year B.C.	Dynasty numbers
1000	Neo-Assyrian	3rd Intermediate		21-24
		~~1070		
	~~			
	Kassite	New Kingdom		18-20
	~~			
1500	Dark Age			
	~~	~~~~~~~~~~~~~~~~~1550		
	Babylon I	2nd Intermediate		13-17
	~~	~~~~~~~~~~~~~~~~~1790		
	Larsa	Middle Kingdom		12
2000	Isin	~~~~~~~~~~~~~~~~~1990		
	Ur III	1st Intermediate		7 - 11
	Gutian	~~~~~~~~~~~~~~~~~2180		
	Akkadian			
	~~			
2500	Early Dynastic III	Old Kingdom		3 - 6
	Early Dynastic II			
		~~2690		
	Early Dynastic I			
3000	~~~~~~~~~~~~~~~	Early Dynastic		1 - 2
	Protoliterate			

Dates of Egyptian dynasties from Finegan (1979).

There are two principal pieces of biblical evidence which are used to support the early 19th dynasty of the New Kingdom (around the time of Rameses II) as the time of the persecution of the Israelites and their Exodus from Egypt. Firstly, Exodus 1:11 says that during their slavery the Israelites built Pithom and Rameses as store cities for Pharaoh. These cities were located in the NE delta, near the region of Goshen that was inhabited by the Israelites, and the city of Rameses was named after Rameses II. Secondly, Exodus 2:5 describes how Pharaoh's daughter found the baby Moses in the River Nile when she went to bathe. This account demonstrates that the Royal Family had a palace in the delta area near Goshen at the time of Moses' birth, which is consistent with the 19th dynasty, but not the 18th dynasty, whose kings ruled from Thebes or Amarna in the south (Fig. 17.1). Hence it is often suggested that the persecution may have begun under Rameses I and continued through the reign of Seti, followed by the Exodus early in the reign of Rameses II.

A date around 1280 for the Exodus implies that the Israelites arrived in Canaan around 1240 BC, after 40 years wandering in the desert. A problem with this date for the arrival of the Israelites in the Promised Land is that it does not tie in with estimated dates of destruction of the Canaanite cities Jericho and Hazor. This has caused some authors, such as Bimson (1978) to propose that the Exodus occurred in 1440 BC, as implied by biblical genealogies. However, recent dates for the major destruction level in Jericho suggest that this may have occurred even earlier, around 1590 BC (Bruins and van der Plicht, 1996).

To some extent, this uncertainty about the date of the Exodus is irrelevant to our attempts to date the entry of Jacob into Egypt, because the duration of the sojourn is itself unknown. Therefore, a better way to date the Patriarchal age is to examine the historical/cultural clues in the Joseph story in order to place this directly in its correct historical period.

One of the important pieces of evidence in the Joseph story is the account in Gen 37:28 of how he was sold into slavery by his brothers for 20 pieces of silver. Kitchen (1995) has compared this price with the progressively increasing price of slaves through the Third and Second Millennia to estimate the approximate date of the patriarchal age (Fig. 17.3). Kitchen cited evidence for a price of 10 shekels of silver during the Ur III dynasty, 20 shekels during the reign of Hammurabi, 30 shekels from Ugarit around 1400 BC, and 50 shekels during the Assyrian Empire. The price of 20 shekels during the reign of Hammurabi is testified by three sections of the Code of Hammurabi, as well as records from

Mari at this time. The agreement between this number and the price of Joseph's sale (Gen 37:28) supports an early Second Millennium date for this event.

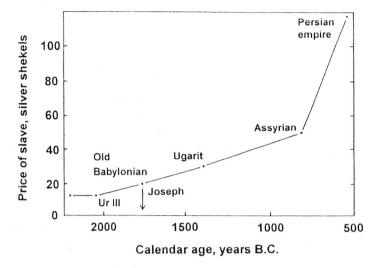

Fig. 17.3 Increasing price of slaves during the Second Millennium compared with the price of 20 shekels of silver for which Joseph was sold by his brothers. After Kitchen (1995).

The first half of the Second Millennium is divided into two major periods of Egyptian history, the Middle Kingdom and the Second Intermediate period (Table 17.1). The Middle Kingdom began in 1990 BC when Amun-emhet I gained supremacy over all Egypt and founded the 12th dynasty at Itj-towy, near Memphis, ushering in a golden age of Egyptian prosperity. This was a period of great stability, lasting nearly 200 years, when the kingship was passed securely from father to son by means of a system of co-regency, instituted by Amun-emhet I. In this system, the son was installed as King while his father was still on the throne, thus ensuring an orderly succession.

The succession of the 12th dynasty finally failed in about 1800 BC, and was followed by a less stable period, the Second Intermediate period, when many kings reigned in quick succession. During this period rival dynasties ruled from Thebes in the South and Xois in the western Nile delta. However, towards the end of this period there is evidence that the eastern Nile delta was under the control of Semitic kings, and by about 1730 BC (Hassan and Robinson, 1987) they had captured Memphis. These kings were referred to in later times as the 'Hyksos', a name whose origin is disputed but is probably derived from the expression 'chief of foreign lands' (Finegan, 1979, p. 253). They controlled Egypt for nearly 200 years (as the 15th and 16th dynasties) from a capital named Avaris in the eastern delta. The 17th dynasty marked the decline of Hyksos rule, during which time a rival dynasty of Theban kings was established in the south. The Hyksos were then finally expelled from Egypt in about 1550 BC.

A second source of evidence to date Joseph's entry into Egypt is provided by evidence for the migration of other Semitic peoples into Egypt during the early Second Millennium. This history of migration is described in the 'Prophecy of Neferti', preserved in the 18th dynasty 'Leningrad Papyrus'. This describes Amun-emhet as the deliverer of Egypt from the turmoil of the First Intermediate Period. As well as achieving military victories he stemmed the immigration of a plague of Semitic nomads from Sinai:

> *The Asiatics will fall to his sword, and the Libyans will fall to his flame...There will be built the Wall of the Ruler... and the Asiatics will not be permitted to come down into Egypt that they might beg for water in the customary manner, in order to let their beasts drink. And justice will come into its place, while wrongdoing is driven out.*

> [Finegan, 1979, p. 238]

The Wall of the Ruler was a line of fortresses across the NE frontier of Egypt, built by Amun-emhet to '*oppose the Asiatics and crush the Sand-Crossers*', according to the Story of Sinuhe, told about one of Amun-emhet's younger children. Notwithstanding this wall, there is evidence that Semitic immigration into Egypt continued, and by 1870 BC (under Sesostris III, great great grandson of Amun-emhet) fairly peaceful relations seem to have existed between the Egyptians and the Semitic peoples of Sinai and Canaan. This is demonstrated by the large numbers of Semitic names which appear in records of this time as permanent inhabitants of Egypt. For example, the Brooklyn Papyrus (Cornfeld, 1961, p. 99) lists 77 servants of an Egyptian household, of which 45 are men, women and children of Semitic race, probably sold as slaves. In addition, a painted wall relief from an early 19th century tomb has two friezes depicting Western Asiatic nomads, possibly

Amorite shepherds and metal-workers, arriving in Egypt (Fig. 17.4). It is possible that Joseph became the steward of Potiphar, and later the vizier of all Egypt, during this period of racial harmony.

Fig. 17.4 Egyptian tomb relief of the Middle Kingdom at Beni Hasan showing the arrival of Western Asiatic nomads in Egypt.

Another period when it would have been relatively easy for a person of Semitic race to have risen to prominence in the court was the Hyksos period. However, two aspects of the Joseph story argue against such a date. One of these is the reference to the death of Joseph, which describes how he was mummified in the tradition of Egyptian kings, rather than in the tradition of the Semitic Hyksos kings (Gen 50:26). The second reference describes the purchase of the land of Egypt by Pharaoh, as a result of the seven years' famine (Genesis 47:20):

> *The Egyptians, one and all, sold their fields, because the famine was too severe for them. The land became Pharaoh's, and Joseph reduced the people to servitude, from one end of Egypt to the other.*

This text would not make sense in reference to the later Hyksos period, when Egypt was already under foreign domination. However, it fits perfectly to the reign of Sesostris III (also known as Senwosret III), who reigned from ca. 1875-1855 BC, when historical evidence records a marked centralisation of power in the hands of Pharaoh (Hallo and Simpson, 1971/98, p. 246; Wilson, 1985, p. 67).

A final piece of evidence supporting the reign of Sesostris III as the time of Joseph's residence in Egypt is an inscription from the tenth year of Sesostris III, recording an unusually high water level in the River Nile (Wilson, 1985, p. 67). This may have been associated with the seven years of plenty in Egypt, which preceded the regional drought which led to the seven years famine. Therefore, I suggest in conclusion that the best date for Jacob's entry into Egypt is about 1860 BC.

17.3 The Patriarchal age

In order to use biblical evidence to determine the duration of the Patriarchal age, the best starting point is again the story of Joseph. In contrast to the schematic nature of the chronological information about the life-spans of Abram and Isaac, we can derive more precise chronological information from the stories of Jacob's exile in Padan Aram and Joseph's exile in Egypt (Table 17.2).

Thus, we can determine that Joseph was 39 years old when his father came down to Egypt at the end of the second year of the seven years of famine. Similarly, we know that Joseph was born after Jacob had served Laban for 14 years. Hence, we can see that Jacob went down to Egypt 53 years after he stole Esau's blessing and fled to Padan Aram. However, in a conversation with Pharaoh (Gen 47:9), Jacob claims that he is 130 years when he enters Egypt, which implies that he received the blessing from Isaac when he (Jacob) was 77 years old. This is not consistent with the picture we get in Gen Ch 27 - 29 of Jacob and Esau as relatively young men competing to receive Isaac's prophetic blessing.

In order to obtain a realistic chronological estimate for the length of the patriarchal era we must apply God's pronouncement in Genesis 6:3 that man shall have a lifespan of not more than 120 years. If we then specify that the life-spans of Abram, Isaac, Jacob and Joseph are 120, 120, 110 and 110 years respectively, we obtain the results in the third column of figures in Table 17.2. Since Abram seems to have been on his deathbed when he arranged Isaac's marriage (Gen 24:1-3), we assume that Isaac married at the age of 20 but did not have children for 20 years, since Rebekah was barren (Gen 25:21). We assume that the life of Isaac was in three equal parts, with the birth of his sons at age 40 and his blessing of them at age 80 (when he was nearly blind). Finally, we know that Jacob entered Egypt 53 years later (when he would be age 93) and lived another 17 years in Egypt to die at age 110, regarded by the Egyptians as the 'perfect lifespan'. Although this calculation is obviously formulaic, I believe that it gives a credible estimate of 233 years for the patriarchal age. This would place the birth of Abram at around

2100 BC, suggesting that Abram was probably born during the Third Dynasty of Ur.

Table 17.2 Events in the lives of the Patriarchs based on literal or schematic readings of Genesis

Event described	Literal reading life	total	Schematic reading life	total	Genesis reference
Birth of Abram	0	0	0	0	
Departure from Haran	75		75		12:4
Birth of Isaac	100	100	100	100	21:5
Death of Abram	175		120		25:7
Birth of Isaac	0	100	0	100	
Marriage to Rebekah	40	140	20	120	25:20
Birth of Jacob	60	160	40	140	25:26
Blessing of Jacob	137	237	80	180	27:41-3
Death of Isaac	180		120		35:28
Birth of Jacob	0	160	0	140	
Journey to Padan Aram	77	237	40	180	31:41
Birth of Joseph after 14 years	91	251	54	194	30:25
Jacob enters Egypt	130	290	93	233	47:9
Death of Jacob	147		110		47:28
Birth of Joseph	0	251	0	194	30:25
Joseph's dreams	17		17		37:2
Joseph becomes vizier	30		30		41:46
Joseph meets Jacob in Egypt	39	290	39	233	45:6,11
Death of Joseph	110		110		50:22

Uncertainties in both the Egyptian and Mesopotamian time-scales (e.g. Rose, 1994; Reade, 2001) make it problematical to look for an exact cross reference point between them. However, biblical evidence can be used to test the historical context of Abram determined above, which would place him in Canaan around 2000 BC. This evidence comes from the account in Genesis Ch 14, describing Abram's rescue of Lot after his capture by Kedorlaomer, king of Elam (Kitchen, 1995).

Genesis 14 describes a war between two groups of allied kings, involving four kings of Mesopotamia and five kings of Canaan. This pattern of alliances fits particularly well with the period between the Ur III empire and the first dynasty of Babylon, as recorded in the Mari archives:

There is no king who is strong on his own: Hammurabi of Babylon has a following of 10 or 15 kings, Rim-Sin of Larsa the same, Ibal-pi-El of Eshnunna the same, Amut-pi-El of Qatna the same, and Yarim-Lim of Yamhad has a following of 20 kings...

[Postgate, 1992, p. 46]

In particular, the mention in Genesis 14:9 that one of the kings of the Mesopotamian alliance was king of Elam is consistent with the Isin-Larsa period, when the lack of a strong empire in Mesopotamia would have allowed essentially free movement for a small army to cross from Susa in the east to Canaan in the west (e.g. Fig. 19.2).

Further support for the timing of this event in the early Second Millennium BC comes from the description in Genesis 14:3 of the site of the battle: *'All these kings joined forces in the Valley of Siddim (the Salt Sea)'*. Frumkin and Elitzur (2001) argued that the reference to the Valley of Siddim came from the original account by Abram, whereas the reference to the Salt Sea was a later editorial note, added to explain to the reader of Genesis that the original site of the battle had since been flooded by the Dead Sea.

Since the Dead Sea is a closed basin, its water level is controlled by a balance between river input and evaporation (as described for Lake Van in section 8.1). However, the Dead Sea consists of a very deep northern basin and a very shallow southern basin. Therefore, changes in water level have caused the southern half to experience some periods of dryness and some periods of flooding over human history. These variations have been recorded in nearby caves, cut into solid rock salt. Radiocarbon dating of timber trapped at different levels in these caves allowed Frumkin (1997) to reconstruct past variations in water level relative to the lake bed of the southern basin (Fig. 17.5). These results show that the southern part of the Dead Sea has only been dry for three intervals in the Holocene period; once around 5000 BC, once around 2000 BC, and once at the present day. Hence, a date around 2000 BC for Abram's life in Canaan is consistent with the period when the southern basin was dry land.

This interpretation is supported by the description in Gen 14:10 of the retreat of the kings of Sodom and Gomorrah after the battle:

Now the valley of Siddim was full of tar pits, and when the kings of Sodom and Gomorrah fled, some of the men fell into them and the rest fled to the hills.

212

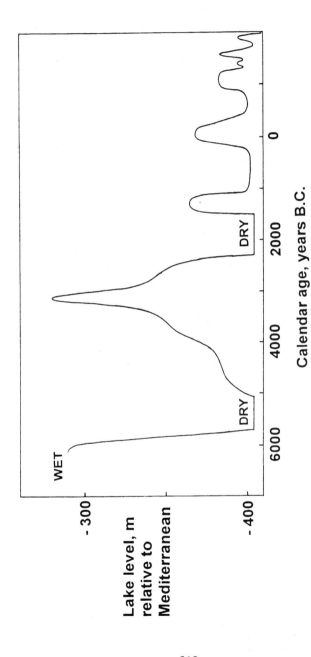

Fig. 17.5 Past water levels in the southern part of the Dead Sea, quoted relative to the Mediterranean. During periods marked 'dry', the south basin is thought to have dried completely. After Frumkin et al. (1991) and Frumkin (1997).

Frumkin and Elitzur (2001) argued that the correct translation of 'tar pits' was actually 'slime pits', referring to circular collapse structures which often form near the shore of the Dead Sea and which contain a semi-liquid saline slurry. Hence this represents additional evidence that the battle of Genesis 14 occurred while the southern basin of the Dead Sea was dry land.

This evidence for a dry climatic period at the end of the Third Millennium in Israel is consistent with historical evidence from Mesopotamia. The evidence indicates that the supply of water for irrigation was critically limited during the later years of the Ur III empire. This allowed saline groundwater to rise near the surface of the low-lying fields of southern Mesopotamia, causing salination of the soil, an environmental disaster. The resulting food shortages are recorded in the bureaucratic records of the Ur III empire and were probably largely responsible for its collapse, which was brought to completion by the invasion of Amorites from the north and Elamites from the east.

As an inhabitant of Ur during its declining years, it would have been natural for Terah and his family to migrate to Haran. This city in northern Mesopotamia would have been less affected than Ur by the drought, yet it shared with Ur the veneration of the moon god, Sin. Hence, Terah and Abram were probably part of a wave of migration fleeing the food shortages which heralded the fall of Ur. Indeed, the first appearance of God to Abram may actually have involved a warning to flee the coming destruction. We will now examine how this appearance may have occurred.

CHAPTER 18

THE CALL OF ABRAHAM

The last chapter of the book of Joshua describes the renewal of the Mosaic covenant between the Israelite people and the LORD, the God of Israel. In his final speech to the people (Ch 24:2-3), Joshua speaks God's words as follows:

> *"Long ago, your forefathers, including Terah the father of Abraham and Nahor, lived beyond the River and worshipped other gods. But I took your father Abraham from the land beyond the River and led him throughout Canaan and gave him many descendants."*

These words show that Abram grew up in Mesopotamia in a polytheist environment where even his own father did not recognise the LORD as the only true god. How then did Abram discover the True God, and how did he discover the history of God's dealings with the earlier patriarchs, including Adam and Noah?

Some of these questions were tackled by Woolley (1936) in his book '*Abraham*'. Having excavated the Mesopotamian city of Ur over a period of many years, Woolley was in a good position to look for any possible archaeological evidence that might throw light on the origins of Abram and his faith in the LORD. The most important evidence, from Ur and elsewhere, is that which points to the worship of Family Gods around the time of Abram (ca. 2000 BC). This evidence comes from illustrations on cylinder seals of the time, along with inferences we can make from household architecture and furniture of this period.

18.1 The Family God

A prevalent theme in many cylinder seal illustrations from the end of the Third Millennium, beginning during the Akkadian Dynasty around 2300 BC, is the so-called 'introduction scene' (Figs. 18.1, 23.1). These scenes show the introduction of the worshipper to one of the major gods by a minor god who is his advocate. The divinity of this advocate is indicated by the horned hat, the universal mark of divine status. Of particular interest in Fig. 18.1 is the fact that the worshipper and the advocate appear to be in Sumerian dress, whereas the great god is in Semitic dress. He rests one foot on a platform between two mountains, possibly representing his temple mountain, and is backed by a sacred tree. It is inferred from such scenes that the 'Great Gods' of the Mesopotamian pantheon, including the patron gods of each city, had grown so remote from the individual worshipper that the divine advocate was necessary to make an introduction (Nissen, 1988, p. 177-178).

Fig. 18.1 Akkadian cylinder seal impression showing the owner of the seal, Lugal-Ushumgal, bearing a sacrifice and being led into the presence of a great god, on the right, by the personal or household god. Musee du Louvre.

The names of family gods may be determined from the inscriptions on some seals, as well as the Greeting Formulae used to begin and end letters (van der Toorn, 1996). Some family gods were minor deities, perhaps of local character, that are not known outside this sphere. For example, King Shulgi built a temple at Ur for the minor goddess Nimintabba, and archaeological evidence from the neighbourhood surrounding this temple shows evidence of devotion to her as a family goddess (van der Toorn, 1996, p. 83). Other personal gods were popular in certain professions. For example, Nisaba and Nabium, god and goddess of writing, were often adopted as personal gods by scribes. Since the profession of a scribe was probably passed down in the family, the worship of the family god was doubtless passed down as well.

Sometimes the great gods of the pantheon were worshipped as family gods, but investigations by Charpin (1980) suggested that the personal god was usually distinct from the city god. Thus, for the small town of Kutalla, 15 km from Larsa, oaths were made in the names of Sin and Shamash (city god of Larsa), but personal devotion was addressed to other gods. Similarly, the following seal inscription shows that a priest of the sun god Shamash nevertheless worshipped Marduk as his personal god (van der Toorn, 1996, p. 67):

Shalim-palih-Marduk, son of Sin-gamil
shangum priest of Shamash
servant of Marduk

In the case of kings, because they were the rulers of the nation, they might claim the national god or gods as their personal god. Thus, Hammurabi referred to Marduk as his personal god, even through records show that his family god was Sin (van der Toorn, 1996, p. 86). On the other hand, Inanna (Ishtar), goddess of love and war and patron goddess of Uruk, is not known on seals as a personal goddess. This can be explained by the fact that Ninshubar, the vizier of Ishtar, was a popular choice of personal god because he could intercede to Ishtar on behalf of the worshipper. The sky god An (Anu) is also unknown as a personal god, and Shamash and Enlil are very rare.

Excavations by Woolley of the residential district of Ur from the Larsa period throw some more light on the worship of the family gods who are believed to have been the divine advocates. These family gods were evidently worshipped in domestic shrines or 'family chapels' which were found in several of the larger houses (Fig. 18.2). The shrine occupied one of the rooms of the house, usually at the back and probably open to the sky. At the end of the room a low platform formed the altar, on which small offering cups and dishes were sometimes found *in situ* by the excavators. In the middle of the altar was a hearth for burning incense and behind this a square groove in the wall acted as a chimney. In one corner of the room there was a raised platform, usually covered in plaster mouldings in imitation of wood panelling. This platform formed a shew-table on which offerings of food and drink were placed. Evidence of rod sockets in one such table suggested to Woolley that the table might have had curtains that would be drawn across except during the presentation of the offering. Finally, a recess beside the altar might lead into a small store-room that formed a family archive.

Fig. 18.2 View of a Family Chapel from the Larsa period (ca. 1900 BC) showing a hearth for incense burning, along with an offering table to the left and a store room for tablets on the right. The lower wall is of baked bricks and the upper part un-baked. From a photo by Woolley (1954, facing p. 188).

In some household shrines of this type, baked clay plaques or cult statues have been found (e.g. Fig. 18.3). Some of these figurines are probably votive offerings- figures which represent the person of the worshipper in order that figuratively they may be present continually before the god to petition for the protection that the god can give. However, other figures have horns, which are an indication of divinity. These figures must be 'household gods', or *teraphim* as they are called in the biblical story of Jacob's escape from Laban (Gen 31:34). In this story, Rachel stole Laban's household gods during the escape of Jacob's family from Padan Aram. When Laban pursued Jacob in order to recover the gods, Jacob denied having removed them. He invited Laban to search his possessions in order to find them, but Rachel hid the gods in a sack and sat upon them, claiming that she could not rise to greet him because of her monthly period. This gives us an idea of the relatively small size of these figures.

Another aspect of the story of Jacob's escape throws further light on the role of household gods in the patriarchal family. In order to cement a non-aggression pact with Jacob, Laban asks Jacob to swear an oath to observe the agreement (Gen 31:53). Laban says, *"May the God of Abraham and the God of Nahor, the God of their father* (Terah), *judge*

218

between us." Abram and Nahor were brothers, and the latter was Laban's grandfather. Therefore, Laban is suggesting that a single god was recognised by the whole extended family, beginning with their common ancestor Terah. However, Woolley argued that this god cannot have been the moon god, Nanna, who was the patron god of Ur and Haran. Abram had abandoned this god when he left Mesopotamia, so the name of Nanna would not have been binding on Jacob. Instead, Laban must be thinking of a god who was recognised by both Laban and Jacob, and thus a Family God.

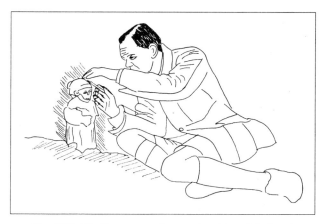

Fig. 18.3 Woolley excavating a clay 'teraphim' god from Ur. From a photo in Magnusson (1977).

Woolley concluded from this evidence that the god who called Abram to leave his own country and travel to the land of promise was the Family God of Terah, who became elevated in Abram's understanding to the supreme god of the earth. However, it is not in the natural order for a god to be *'instantly promoted'* from a minor deity to the Supreme Lord of the Earth. Even in the case of Marduk, who supplanted Ellil as a result of the military conquest of Mesopotamia by Babylon, this process of usurpation took hundreds of years to complete. Instead, I suggest that God's revelation to Abram took the opposite form, by which the Supreme God Enlil (Ellil in Akkadian) revealed to Abram that He (the Supreme God) could also be the Family God of Abram. Laban was evidently not able to distinguish the god of Abraham, Isaac and Jacob from his own household god, but Jacob draws a distinction (Gen 31:53), and swears instead in the name of the *'Fear of Isaac'*.

219

18.2 The Holy God

God is both kind and stern in his character (Rom 11:22). Therefore, the kindness of the Family God is balanced by the severity of the Holy God. The latter aspect of God's character is expressed in the name 'Fear of Isaacc' and is also seen in Exodus Ch 19, when God appears on Mount Sinai. At that time the people were told (v. 12):

> *Be careful that you do not go up to the mountain or touch the foot of it. Whoever touches the mountain shall surely be put to death.*

Following God's appearance at Sinai, the tabernacle was established as a sacred place that was devoted to God. The holiness of this place was demonstrated by the deaths of Aaron's sons when they offered unauthorised incense before the Lord: they were themselves consumed by fire (Leviticus, Ch 10).

An examination of Sumerian literature (Wilson, 1994) shows that the Sumerians had a similar concept of the holiness of their temples, as places that were the realm of the gods. This concept was described by the word ku_3, such as in the phrase: *'e-kur ki-tush-ku$_3$ an en-lil-la'*, which was translated by Wilson (1994, p. 5) as:

> *The Ekur, the holy dwelling place of An (and) Enlil*

Furthermore, in Sumerian, the word 'holy' (ku_3) is distinct from the word 'pure' (*sikil*) which means 'ritually clean' but does not directly imply the presence of a god. Hence, sikil is used where the sense is to purify a person or an object in order to present them to god.

The Akkadian word *'ellu'* is often used to translate Sumerian ku_3 (holy), but it is also used to simply mean that something is clean, even in describing clean laundry (Wilson, 1994, p. 67). Wilson concluded from a detailed study of the use of these words that, unlike the Sumerians, the Semitic peoples of Mesopotamia did not have a clear concept of holiness, in the sense of the unapproachability of the gods. Hence, Wilson deduced that before the Semitic peoples encountered Sumerian religion, Akkadian religion was mainly focussed on purification from uncleanness (evil spirits) rather than an encounter with the divine person. This inference is significant in deducing the origins of Abram's faith.

It was noted above (section 9.3) that the names of Shem's descendants imply a transition from Sumerian to Semitic cultural background.

In other words, this is a schematic line of descent that actually represents the passing of Sumerian culture and religion to the Semitic immigrants of Mesopotamia. By the time of Abram, the Sumerians had largely died out as a distinct race, as they had been completely assimilated by the dominant Semitic immigrants. However, the evidence described above, from philology, supports the biblical genealogy of Shem in suggesting that the concept of the Holy God was passed from the Sumerians to the Semitic peoples, and thus from Noah to Abram.

18.3 The stages of revelation

The evidence from the biblical text suggests that God's revelation to Abram occurred in progressive stages. As quoted in Gen 12:1, God's dealings with Abram started with the command *"Leave your country, your people and your father's household"*. Many scholars have argued that this command came to Abram in Haran, but in his defence before the Sanhedrin (Acts 7:2), Stephen claims that God revealed himself to Abram in Mesopotamia, *before* he lived in Haran:

> *The God of Glory appeared to our father Abraham while he was still in Mesopotamia, before he lived in Haran; "Leave your country and your people," God said, "and go to the land I will show you." So he left the land of the Chaldeans and settled in Haran. After the death of his father, God sent him to this land where you are now living.*

This speech is particularly interesting because it was made before the greatest Hebrew theologians of the day. Given the gravity of the situation, it seems unlikely that Stephen would have wanted to compromise his message by an erroneous summary of biblical history. Indeed, the impression we get from the account in Acts Ch 7 is that the Sanhedrin listened in rapt attention until Stephen accused them of murdering God's Messiah. Therefore, this account of Abram's call was probably universally accepted at the time.

Another aspect of Abram's call which Stephen tells us about is the fact that God *appeared* to Abram. This leads us to ask what kind of appearance this was, and how God communicated his command to Abram. The principal means of receiving instructions from the gods in ancient Mesopotamia was by means of dreams and visions. For example, the Cylinders of Gudea (section 15.3) report that Gudea, king of

Lagash, had a vision of Ningirsu, god of the city of Girsu, in the following form:

> In the dream there was a man - as huge as the sky! As huge as
>   the earth!
> He was (like) a god according to his head,
> Like the thunderbird according to his arms,
> Like a flood according to his lower parts;
> To (his) right and left lay lions.
>
> [Wilson, 1996, p. 26]

However, most of the gods of the Mesopotamian pantheon were only aspects of the natural world that had been 'deified' by the human imagination. Thus, Ningirsu was expected to appear in a dream as the 'thunderbird' and the 'flood wave' since the thunderstorm and the accompanying flood of the Tigris were the aspects of nature that were deified as Ningirsu.

Genesis also records instances where God also used dreams to communicate to people. For example, when Jacob had his dream at Bethel of a stairway stretching to heaven, God stood above him and said *"I am the LORD, the God of your father Abraham and the God of Isaac."* In this case, God introduced himself to Jacob both as the 'LORD' and as the 'God of his father'. The meaning of the divine name 'the LORD' will be discussed later. However, in the meantime we may ask how God introduced himself to Abram, whose own father worshipped the moon god. The manner of the first encounter is not described, but according to Gen 15:1, the word of the LORD came to Abram in Canaan in the form of a vision, in which God said (15:7): *"I am the LORD, who brought you out of Ur of the Chaldeans to give you this land..."*

In this case the introduction is based on what the LORD *did* in bringing Abram safely from Ur to Canaan. Therefore, we may deduce that when the LORD first introduced himself to Abram, he probably did so by identifying himself with things that Abram already knew about the character of God, probably in the person of the LORD of the Mesopotamian pantheon, Enlil.

In later encounters, God's revelation reaches a new level of intimacy when he takes on what appears to be human form. Genesis Ch 16 describes such an encounter between Hagar, Sarah's slave girl, and the 'angel of the LORD' (16:11). However, when Hagar later describes the incident, she says *"You are the 'God who sees me', for I have now seen the 'One who sees me"*. In this incident, Hagar identifies the 'Angel of the LORD' with the person of God himself. This identification is confirmed in Abram's next encounter with God (Gen 17:1). In this encounter, God reveals himself to Abram as 'El Shaddai' and gives Abram the new name of Abraham. Significantly, Abraham falls face down in the presence of God (Gen 17:3), which suggests a new level of experience of God's presence. God will appear to Abraham again in human form when he comes with two angels as the 'three visitors' to predict the imminent birth of a son to Abraham and Sarah.

The appearance of God to Abram in bodily human from, after centuries of nominal religious practice in Mesopotamia, marks a totally new phase in the working out of God's plan. This was accompanied by the first of several promises to Abram, giving the inheritance of the Land to Abram's descendants. In gratitude, Abram is described for the first time as building an altar and calling on the name of the LORD. This ritual of altar building echoes the acceptable sacrifice of Abel (Gen 4:4), while the act of calling on the name of the LORD echoes the first time when 'men began to call on the name of the LORD' after the birth of Seth (Gen 4:26).These references emphasise that God's plan had returned to a new beginning. Just as God's revelation to humanity began with one man, and was preserved through one man during the Flood, so the revelation would be carried to the people of Israel through the one man, Abraham.

CHAPTER 19

THE SEMITIC PANTHEON

The Bible says that Abraham obeyed the call of the LORD to go to a new land, but in this new land he lived amongst Semitic peoples who worshipped different gods from the gods of Mesopotamia. To what extent then did these peoples influence Abraham's concept of the character of the LORD his God? To answer this question we must explore the identity of the God of Abraham in the context of the gods of the Semitic peoples.

One of the commonest practices of the Middle East is the custom by which people are either named after a god or adopt the name of a god as part of their own name. This practice is very important in determining the identity of the gods who were worshipped by ancient peoples, because of the common occurrence of names in a wide variety of ancient documents. Cross (1973) applied this approach to the problem of identifying the god of the patriarchs Abraham, Isaac and Jacob.

When we examine the Genesis account, we see no names based on YHWH, the name by which God revealed himself to Moses, which is translated by most English Bibles as 'LORD'. However, we do see several compound names based on the divine name El, which also means 'Lord'. Examples are: Ishma-el (The Lord hears, Gen 16:11); Beth-el (The House of the Lord, Gen 28:19); Isra-el (He struggles with the Lord, Gen 32:28) and Peni-el (Face of the Lord, Gen 32:30). Subsequently, we see the double and triple use of El in two instances: El Beth-el (The Lord of the House of the Lord, Gen 35:7) and El El-ohe Isra-el (The Lord, the Lord of him who struggles with the Lord, Gen 33:20). God also specifically revealed himself to Abram as El Shaddai (normally translated 'God Almighty') when he inaugurated the covenant of circumcision (Gen 17:1).

The importance of the name El in the history of God's people is amply demonstrated by the fact that, via the patriarch Jacob, they adopted this very name of God as the name of their nation: Isra-el. But what is the origin of the name El by which God revealed himself to Abram, Isaac and Jacob? Cross (1973) believed that El was adopted by Abraham from the peoples which the Bible calls Canaanites or Amorites, who were 'living in the land' to which God had sent Abraham. We have no written records of these peoples from the time of Abraham, but we do have a detailed record of their beliefs from a few hundred years later, during the time when God's people were sojourning in the land of Egypt. These detailed records, from around 1400 BC, come from the ancient city of Ugarit.

19.1 The gods of Ugarit and Canaan

Ugarit, located near the Mediterranean coast in northern Syria, was discovered in 1929 when excavation was begun on a tell called Ras Shamra. Almost immediately, two large temples were uncovered which were later found to be dedicated to the gods Baal and Dagan. Nearby, several clay tablets were found, some of which identified the site as ancient Ugarit, a city already known from the 'Amarna letters' of mid Second Millennium Egypt. Subsequent excavation of Ras Shamra revealed a fortress and a royal palace containing extensive archives, mostly dating from the golden age of Ugarit, around 1400 to 1100 BC. Ugarit was never the centre of an empire, but rather was a small independent kingdom located between the larger and more powerful Egyptian and Hittite empires. However, Ugarit provides a detailed view of the religious environment of northern Canaan at about the time when the Israelites were settling in southern Canaan after the exodus from Egypt.

Baal was the chief god of the Ugaritic pantheon. He was also the god of the thunderstorm, and is often shown on stelae brandishing a mace and a thunderbolt (Fig. 19.1a). Baal was the subject of a major Ugaritic epic written around 1400 BC, normally referred to as the Baal Cycle. This epic consists of six tablets, of which the first two describe Baal's battle against the sea god (Yamm), the middle two describe Baal's palace, and the last two describe Baal's battle against the god of the underworld, Mot, who is the personification of death. When challenged by Mot, Baal voluntarily gives himself up to death, but his sister god Anath kills Mot and grinds him to pieces. Anath goes off with the sun god in search of Baal, and after a long gap we find Baal restored to life. Seven years later Baal is again challenged by Mot, but El, the father of the gods, rules that Mot must submit to Baal, who then takes the throne as king of the gods.

Fig. 19.1 Ugaritic stelae from Ras Shamra. a) the storm god Baal with mace and thunderbolt. Height 1.4 m, Musee du Louvre. b) the god El seated on his throne. Height 0.5 m. National Archaeological Museum, Aleppo (Halab), Syria.

The Baal Cycle can be interpreted (e.g. Caquot and Sznycer, 1980) as an aetiological myth, a story that explains facts of nature. Thus, Baal, as the thunder god, represents the fertility brought by rain. However, in order to bring fruitfulness to the dry ground, Baal must disappear into the earth (the domain of death). From the earth, the water is gathered by Anath, the goddess of springs, who brings forth streams from the ground. Finally, Baal is rejuvenated by the sun, whose heat gathers water from the earth to form clouds again. In these clouds, Baal fights against his other, anonymous brothers, causing thunder.

In the Baal Cycle, Baal himself is often referred to as 'son of Dagan', which is natural, because Dagan's name means 'cloudy' or 'rainy' in Aramaic (Smith 1994, p. 91). Furthermore, a fragment of writing from northern Mesopotamia also presents Addu (=Baal) as the son of Dagan (Roberts, 1972). On the other hand, the Baal Cycle also refers to El as the 'father of the gods'. El was also recognised as the creator of the world and the human race (de Moor, 1980), but he was perceived as a distant god who did not intervene directly in human affairs. This is consistent with the only known illustration of El, which shows him seated on a throne in the manner of a king (Fig. 19.1b). This portrayal contrasts with that of Baal as a warrior brandishing a club.

The inconsistency in Ugaritic mythology over the paternity of Baal shows that Baal is the adopted son of El rather than his 'true son'. Thus, Baal is the local god of Ugarit who has been grafted onto the general West Semitic pantheon with El at its head, but his name 'son of Dagan' betrays his true origin. The local origin of Baal, compared to El, is illustrated by the contrasting 'homes' of the two gods. El dwelt at a distant place in the middle of the waters that surrounded the inhabited world (Caquot and Sznycer, 1980, p. 13), just as Enlil dwelt at the distant meeting point between water and sky. In contrast, Baal had his residence on cloud-covered Mount Sapan (Zaphan), a mere 40 km north of Ugarit.

The ascendancy of Baal at Ugarit points to a process similar to that which happened at Babylon: the distant father-figure of the gods, Ellil in Mesopotamia and El at Ugarit, was eclipsed in importance by his more vigorous offspring, Marduk at Babylon and Baal at Ugarit. This process probably reflected the political independence gained by Ugarit under the dynasty of Niqmaddu Stolz (Smith, 1994, p. 91), just as the rise of Marduk over the Mesopotamian pantheon accompanied the rise of Babylon under Hammurabi. However, unlike Marduk's eclipse of Ellil, Baal never completely replaced El, perhaps because Ugarit never rose to the status of an empire but was always overshadowed by its more powerful neighbours.

Based on the premise that Abraham knew God as El, and based on the prominence of El in the Ugaritic pantheon, many scholars have followed Cross (1973) in believing that Abraham must have adopted his god El from the people who were living in Canaan when he arrived. But in Genesis the Canaanite 'cities of the plain' are object lessons in wickedness, already under the judgment of God (Gen 19:25), so it is hardly credible that Abraham could have inherited his faith in El from these people. A more reasonable alternative is that *both* Abraham and the peoples of Canaan learned of the creator god El from the peoples of Mesopotamia. In order to examine this possibility it is necessary to compare the expressions of Semitic and Sumerian religion as they developed in the Third Millennium, hundreds of years before Abraham lived.

227

19.2 The gods of Ebla

An important view of the Semitic pantheon around the middle of the Third Millennium (2500 BC) is provided by the ancient city of Ebla, located 300 km N of Damascus in northern Syria. Ebla is known from several Mesopotamian inscriptions, including those of Sargon the Great and his grandson Naram-Sin, who both claimed lordship over Ebla. The successful campaign of Sargon was recorded on temple stelae at Nippur, of which later Akkadian copies have been found. One of these reads as follows:

Sargon, the king, bowed down to the god Dagan in Tuttul.
He (Dagan) gave to him (Sargon) the Upper Land:
Mari, Iarmuti and Ebla as far as the Cedar Forest and the Silver
*   Mountains.*
5400 men daily eat in the presence of Sargon,
the king to whom the god Enlil gave no rival.

[Frayne, 1993, p. 28]

The location of Ebla was unknown when, in 1964, excavation was begun by Matthiae on one of the largest Syrian mounds, Tell Mardikh. Ten years later the excavators came upon a royal palace with an archive containing an immense collection of over 15,000 tablets. These tablets showed beyond doubt that Tell Mardikh was the ancient city of Ebla, and also represented the earliest major find of cuneiform documents written in a Semitic language. This language, named Eblaite, was previously unknown, but its decipherment by Pettinato was assisted by the discovery of several Sumerian-Eblaite dictionaries amongst the tablet collection. The style of cuneiform on the tablets suggested them to be very early, around 2500 BC, equivalent to the pre-Sargonid period in Mesopotamia. The tablets show that Ebla built an empire which reached as far as Mari on the upper reaches of the Euphrates (Fig. 19.2). This was a strategic error on the part of Ebla because it posed a threat to the civilisation of Lower Mesopotamia. The evidence suggests that Sargon may first have attacked Ebla in order to reduce its influence, but it was finally destroyed by his more powerful grandson Naram Sin. This is recorded on the Stele of Naram Sin (Fig. 15.2) as follows:

Never since the creation of mankind has any king among kings
taken Armanum and Ebla....

228

Thanks to the might of Dagan, who exalts his majesty, Naram-Sin the strong conquered Armanum and Ebla and, from the bank of the Euphrates to Ulisum, struck down the peoples whom Dagan delivered into his hands...

[from Matthiae, 1977, p. 177]

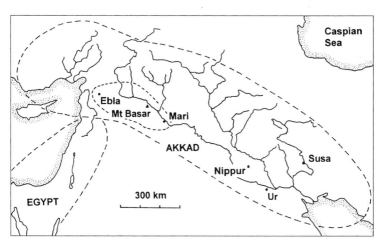

Fig. 19.2 Map of the Middle East showing the area under the control of Ebla before its defeat by Akkad (small dashed enclosure). Large dashed enclosures show the area of influence of the Old Kingdom of Egypt, and the maximum area of influence of the Empire of Akkad. Rivers are shown in the modern courses. Revised from Hallo and Simpson (1971/98, p. 60).

After the palace and its archives were sacked (probably by Naram Sin, although this cannot be proven) no further traces of the Eblaite language have been found. The city of Ebla was rebuilt, but after this time all written material is in Akkadian cuneiform.

Tablets from the mid Third Millennium archive suggest that Ebla was a secular society in its form of government, with a pantheon that was markedly polytheist (Pettinato, 1979, 1991). The Eblaite tablets confirm the evidence from the stelae of Sargon and Naram-Sin that the god Dagan was the head of the Eblaite pantheon. At Ebla the phrase 'Lord of the Land' is used of Dagan in the same way that in Sumer it is used of Enlil (Matthiae, 1977, p. 187). The bilingual vocabularies give the Eblaite equivalents to many Sumerian gods. For example, the Sumerian goddess Inanna is called Ash-tar in Eblaite, closely related to the Akkadian Ishtar. However, Dagan is not equated with Enlil. Instead

229

the Eblaites simply used the phonetic pronunciation Il-ilu (Pettinato, 1979, p. 251) meaning the god Il, which equates to El-lil in Akkadian. This evidence shows that the Eblaites recognised Dagan and Ellil as distinct deities, although they became synonymous in the Second Millennium (Pettinato, 1979, p. 250). If one was to look at the situation from the point of view of Ellil as the Supreme God, this means that Dagan gradually usurped Ellil's place.

One of the other prominent gods of the Eblaite pantheon was A-da (=Adad, Hadad or Hadda, meaning thunderer). This god may later be recognised as Baal, head of the Ugaritic pantheon (Steiglitz, 1987, p. 85), as discussed above. Another god of the Eblaite pantheon is named Ya, Yau, or Yaw. It was suggested at an early stage in the excavations that this might be the same god as Yahweh, but in fact the similarity of the two names can only be a coincidence. There is no basis for connecting the Ya of Ebla at 2500 BC with the Yahweh who revealed himself to Moses around 1300 BC. The latter revelation and its relationship to the Genesis narrative will be discussed further below.

The fact that Ebla was administered as a secular society shows that it was not in the theocentric tradition of Sumer and Israel. In both of the latter cases, God was recognised as the ruler of the land, and the earthly leader (ensi in Sumer) was merely his chief executive. A modern multiculturalist would see the Eblaite approach to religion as a strength of their society, whereas a worshipper of the True God would see the Eblaites as agnostics: those who don't really know who or what they worship.

19.3 The gods of the Hurrians

The Hurrians were a non Semitic people who took control of the foothills north of Mesopotamia and south of the Armenian mountains during the late Third Millennium. Since Haran was within the territory of the Hurrians it has been suggested by some scholars that Abram was influenced by these peoples. For example, Speiser (1963) observed that the story of Abram passing off his wife as his sister (Gen 12:13) had parallels with traditions described on clay tablets from the Hurrian city of Nuzi in the far eastern area of Hurrian territory. However, it is not the purpose of the present study to examine the Nuzi tablets, which have been widely discussed, but to see whether Abram might have been influenced by aspects of Hurrian theology.

The Hurrian view of the gods is portrayed in an important group of myths which were passed down from the Hurrians to the Hittites, their successors in the northern region of the Fertile Crescent. This group of myths, described as the Kumarbi Cycle, describes a battle between two groups of gods, headed by Kumarbi, god of the underworld, and Tessub, god of heaven, for kingship over the gods (Hoffner, 1990, p. 38). Other gods, including Ellil, Ea, and some so-called 'primeval deities' are essentially neutral in this battle, although Ea (Enki) is sometimes abetting Kumarbi. This presumably reflects Enki's connections to the underworld in his capacity as god of the underground springs.

The first of the myths, the Song of Kumarbi, begins by describing how Anu, the God of Heaven, deposed an earlier god, named Alalu, from the kingship over the gods. However, Alalu's son, Kumarbi dragged Anu down from the sky. He bit off Anu's sexual organs and swallowed them, only to find himself giving birth to Anu's own offspring, including Tessub and the deified River Tigris. The subsequent myths describe how Kumarbi seeks to use various of his own offspring to depose Tessub from the kingship.

It seems clear from these myths that the Hurrians obtained a large chunk of their pantheon directly from Mesopotamia. Probably the battle reflects a competition for supremacy between imported Mesopotamian theology and local gods of the Hurrian region. The fact that Ellil is neutral in the battle seems to suggest that he was a respected deity but did not have a major impact on the Hurrian consciousness. Hence, it seems clear that Abram's veneration of the god El was not significantly influenced by Hurrian religion.

19.4 The gods of the Amorites

The peoples called the Amorites in the Bible, or Amurru in cuneiform sources, were nomads who inhabited the highland region between Ebla and Mount Basar, upstream from Mari on the River Euphrates (Fig. 19.1, Hallo and Simpson, 1971/98, p. 60). They are first mentioned in cuneiform sources during the last years of the Akkadian empire and they begin to appear frequently in Mesopotamian records during the period of anarchy before the Ur III empire. Consistent with their nomadic way of life, the Amorites were shepherds and herders. When they entered Mesopotamia, some were assimilated into the life of the cities while others maintained a distinct identity.

Amorite immigration into Mesopotamia continued throughout the Ur III empire and was accompanied by increasing threats of armed invasion. During the last two reigns of the Ur dynasty, a defensive 'Amorite Wall' was built across the narrowest section of the Mesopotamian plain between the Tigris and Euphrates, but these barriers did not keep the Amorites out for long. As the empire collapsed, Amorite rulers took control of many of the city states of Mesopotamia, including Isin, Larsa and Babylon. Hammurabi was descended from one such immigrant family. Thus the Amorites finally took control of Mesopotamia, but in the process were assimilated into its civilisation.

The gods worshipped by the Amorites are revealed from contracts of the Old Babylonian period, which often carry seals bearing the name of the personal god of the seal's owner. A collection of such material from Yale (Finkelstein, 1972) reveals the identities of some of the most popular gods of the Amorites (Table 19.1). The provenance of the material is uncertain, but is probably mostly from the area around Babylon (Kish, Dilbat and Sippar). Examination of Table 19.1 shows that the most popular gods in this area were the moon god, Sin, and the patron god of the Amorites, Amurru. (The name An-Martu is the Sumerian form of Amurru, e.g. van der Toorn, 1996, p. 90). In this region, other major gods of the Amorites: Adad, Dagan and Marduk were relatively less popular as personal gods.

Table 19.1 Deities named on Old Babylonian seals.

Name of god	Number of seals	Name of god	Number of seals
Sin	23	Neirigal	5
Amurru	19	Adad	4
Nin.si.anna	9	Ea (Enki)	2
Nabium	7	Dagan	1
Lugal-gu-duea	6	Marduk	1
An-Martu	6	Shamash	1
Kabta	5		

Names underlined signify Sumerian script. Not all minor gods are included.

The god Amurru has a characteristic appearance on cylinder seals of the Old Babylonian period (Kupper, 1961). He always carries a shepherd's crook (Fig. 19.3) and often has his foot on an animal of the herd-either sheep, goat or gazelle. Sometimes he has the horned headdress of divinity but often he has a cylindrical hat. The combination of this hat with a bordered long jacket makes his outfit resemble the Morning Suit popular at English weddings. This form of attire is quite different from the layered gown that Mesopotamian gods wear (section 15.3).

Fig. 19.3. Cylinder seal impressions showing the god Amurru in two of his guises. After Kupper (1961, Figs. 30 and 10).

The Myth of Amurru describes the arrival of the God Amurru in Mesopotamia for the purpose of marrying the daughter of Numushda, the patron god of the city of Kazallu in NW Mesopotamia. A commonly quoted excerpt from this myth (Buccellati, 1966, p. 92) describes the Amorites in derogatory terms as follows:

> *A tent dweller... who digs up truffles from the hills but does not know how to kneel; who eats raw meat; who has no house during the days of his life, and is not buried on the day of his death.*

The comment that the Amorites '*do not know how to kneel*' is significant. It supports the conclusions of the study on the Holy God (section 18.2), suggesting that the Amorites did not have the same reverence for the gods as the Sumerians, and largely inherited their pantheon from the Sumerians. For example, iconographic and literary evidence suggests that the god Amurru himself was essentially an invention of the Sumerians, designed to personify the character of the Amorite peoples in order to fit them into the Mesopotamian world-view (Kupper, 1961, p. 88; Haldar, 1971, p. 69). Hence, the Myth of Amurru was probably composed not later than the Ur III period in order to incorporate Amurru into the Mesopotamian pantheon (Kupper, 1961, p. 75; Postgate, 1992, p. 271). Van der Toorn (1996), following Cross (1973, p. 57) identified the god Amurru with the god El of west Semitic peoples such as the Canaanites. However, since the god Amurru (An-Martu) was essentially an invention of the Sumerians, this does not represent a credible origin for the Supreme God El worshipped by Abram.

An important Amorite settlement of the Ur III empire, Puzrish Dagan (modern Drehem) was established by King Shulgi near Nippur. This town housed royal stock pens and acted as a clearing centre for sacrificial offerings from throughout the empire, which were intended for Enlil's temple at Nippur and for the temples of other major gods of the Mesopotamian pantheon. Detailed records were kept of all transactions, and these reveal the involvement of Amorites in the supply of animals. Given the Semitic affinity of Abram that is claimed in the Table of Nations (section 9.3) it is quite likely that Abram's ancestors entered Mesopotamia around this time and adopted the Sumerian way of life. They may even have been engaged at Drehem as stock breeders, before moving to Ur. If Abram himself spent his first years in Drehem then he could have learned about the god Enlil from the priests of Nippur. Therefore, despite Abraham's Amorite racial affinity, I would argue that his understanding of God originated from his experience of Mesopotamian worship, later developed and matured by the personal revelations which are described in Genesis.

CHAPTER 20

MESOPOTAMIAN SOURCES IN GENESIS

If Abram began his Faith Pilgrimage in Mesopotamia, to what extent did he bring with him a Mesopotamian account of the Creation, the Fall, the Flood, and the Tower of Babel? In studying the structure and origin of the Book of Genesis there are two useful lines of evidence. One is to look at Genesis in comparison with some of the important Mesopotamian myths; the other is to look at evidence from the internal structure and composition of Genesis itself.

In 1872, George Smith of the British Museum read an influential paper to the Society of Biblical Archaeology in which he claimed to have found fragments of cuneiform tablets from Nineveh describing the Creation and the Flood. In 1876 he published his groundbreaking book *'The Chaldean Account of Genesis'* containing short translated excerpts from several tablets, including parts of what we now recognise as the Atrahasis Epic and the Epic of Creation. At this early stage, when the cuneiform texts were fragmentary, there appeared to be strong similarities with Genesis. As the cuneiform texts have become more complete, the divergence in style between the Babylonian and biblical texts has become more obvious. Nevertheless, there remain many passages with strong parallels. As a result, most scholars have assumed that Genesis originated after the Babylonian epics, either as a "cleaned up" version (e.g. Driver, 1904; Bloesch, 1994, p. 259-260,) or as a "polemic" written in opposition to the Babylonian epics (e.g. Hasel, 1974).

20.1 The Atrahasis Epic

Kikawada and Quinn (1985) resurrected the case for a close relationship between Genesis and Atrahasis, arguing that Genesis was written as a polemic against Atrahasis but following the same structure as the epic. Examination of the text of Atrahasis shows that it has a very clearly developed repetitive structure. The epic begins with the story of man's creation but then describes four attempts by Enlil to wipe out mankind because of the excessive noise that he was making as a result of over-population. These threats to man's existence (culminating in the Flood) are averted by Enki in response to the intercessions of Atrahasis. Thereafter, the problem of over-population is finally resolved by a reduction in female fertility and by the institution of human mortality by the gods.

Kikawada and Quinn argued that there was a strong parallel between the various threats to man's survival in Genesis and the threats against mankind in the Atrahasis. However, they complicated the comparison between the two texts by including the Tower of Babel story (Gen Ch 11) in the analysis, arguing that this represented the resolution to the four preceding threat-escape cycles. In fact, it is quite clear that Genesis Ch 9 is the resolution to the preceding chapters. Starting at Gen 8:21, this describes God's covenant with Noah, in which God promises never again to cut off all life by the waters of a Flood. The fact that this promise is unconditional is amply demonstrated by the second half of Chapter 9, which describes Noah's fall into drunkenness. So Ch 9 is the real resolution of Ch 1 - 8, where God 'comes to terms' with man's sin and declares that despite the continuation of the same sins that provoked his judgement, he will not again destroy the world by Flood. Hence, this is the basis for the comparison between Atrahasis and Genesis in Table 20.1.

Having removed Genesis Ch 11 from the comparison, we can now examine the series of threats which represent the strongest parallels between Atrahasis and Genesis. The general concept of threat and escape is indeed seen in the stories of Adam, Cain and Noah; however, the creation stories (Genesis Ch 1 - 2) do not fit well with Atrahasis. In addition, the suggestion that the taunt of Lamech (Gen 4:23-24) is a threat on the same par as the others seems highly suspect. However, the biggest problem for the model of Kikawada and Quinn is that there is no overt emphasis on three threats in Genesis, whereas the similarity of the threats in the Atrahasis Epic is strongly driven home by exaggerated repetition. If Genesis was indeed written as a polemic against Atrahasis then we would expect the repetition of threats in Genesis to be of comparable prominence to those in Atrahasis, in order that the reader could discern the focus of the polemic.

Despite the lack of support for Genesis as a polemic against Atrahasis, there are distinct similarities in detail between the two stories.

This suggests that the two epic stories may come from a common early Mesopotamian source. However, the more exaggerated repetitive style in Atrahasis, compared with Genesis, suggests that Atrahasis underwent more modification from this early source than Genesis. Nevertheless, there are some important points of similarity between the two accounts.

Table 20.1. Comparison of the structure of Atrahasis and Genesis Ch 1-9

Atrahasis	Genesis
Creation Story	
Distribution of work amongst the gods	Creation of the Heavens and the Earth
Revolt of the lesser gods	Creation of man (Gen 1:27)
Creation of man	Creation of man (Gen 2:7)
First Threat	
Man's overpopulation causes excessive noise	Sin of Adam and Eve
Enlil commands a plague	Banishment from the Garden
Enki helps Atrahasis to bribe gods to stop plague	Death is postponed
Second Threat- part 1	
Man's overpopulation causes excessive noise	Sin of Cain
Drought commanded by Enlil brings famine	Banishment of Cain
Enki helps Atrahasis to bribe gods to stop drought	Cain marked to save his life
Second Threat- part 2	
Man's overpopulation causes excessive noise	Sin of Lamech
Drought commanded by Enlil brings famine	?
Enki helps Atrahasis to bribe gods to stop drought	Boast of Lamech
Third Threat	
Man's overpopulation causes excessive noise	Sin of Mankind
Enlil sends the Flood	God sends the Flood
Enki saves Atrahasis by telling him to build boat	God saves Noah by telling him to build Ark
Resolution	
Enlil and Enki agree on means of 'birth control'	God reconciles himself to human sinfulness

The first point of similarity is the emphasis on human multiplication before the Flood in both stories. In Atrahasis, each threat cycle begins with the statement that human multiplication had created excessive noise that disturbed the repose of Enlil, provoking retribution. Similarly, Genesis 6 contains two statements about multiplication, in verses 1 and 5 respectively (translated by Hendel, 1987):

When mankind began to multiply on the face of the earth...
Yahweh saw that the evil of mankind multiplied on the earth.

Several commentators have suggested that this theme of multiplication is inherited in Genesis from Atrahasis (e.g. Millard, 1967). However, there is no suggestion in Genesis that the multiplication of the *population* was a cause for the Flood, only the multiplication of sin. Therefore, it seems more likely that Atrahasis inherited the multiplication theme from an early Mesopotamian source similar to Genesis and then exaggerated this theme for dramatic effect.

The second point of similarity is the decree of mortality for mankind as a result of his multiplication (of population or of sin). In Atrahasis, this occurs at the end of the Flood Story, where Enki and Enlil agree on measures to control human population. This includes at least infant mortality (e.g. Dalley, 1991, p. 35), but other lines of the text are damaged. However, Lambert (1980) suggested that the missing part probably contained a decree on the general mortality of mankind. This suggestion was based on comparison with the end of tablet 10 of the Gilgamesh Epic (immediately preceding the Flood Story on tablet 11), where human mortality is decreed by a council of the gods. Genesis here resembles Gilgamesh, in that the decree (Gen 6:3) comes immediately before the Flood Story:

Then the LORD said, "My Spirit will not contend with man for ever, for he is mortal, his days will be a hundred and twenty years."

The exact order of the material in Genesis and the different epics may well have been modified as both Mesopotamian and biblical editors compiled multiple sources into the finished text. However, the sense of the material in biblical and Mesopotamian stories remains similar.

A final point of comparison between Genesis and Atrahasis is the period of 600 years leading up to the Flood. In Atrahasis the passing of 600 years precedes each threat, and is used to exaggerate the cyclicity of the narrative. This exaggeration is missing in Genesis, but the age of Noah at the time of the Flood is noted to be 600 years, a fact that will be discussed further in section 22.3. Hence, it is concluded that Genesis and Atrahasis do share several common features, but these were not due to borrowing from Atrahasis to Genesis. Instead, both epics probably derive from a lost Sumerian source, but Genesis underwent less modification from this source than Atrahasis.

20.2 The Epic of Creation

Enuma Elish is the Babylonian Epic of Creation, and is both the nearest to Genesis in its aim to explain the creation of the world, yet furthest from Genesis in its degree of theological corruption. It starts with a beautiful poem that seems to resemble Genesis 1:1-2:

When above heaven was not named
And the earth beneath did not yet bear a name
And the primeval Apsu, who begat them,
And chaos, Tiamat, the mother of them both-
Their waters were mingled together

[King, 1902, p. 2]

However, Enuma Elish proceeds to describe the origin of the gods by a kind of spontaneous genesis, thereafter degenerating gradually into a gruesome battle of the gods.

Lambert (1986) has presented detailed evidence (reviewed by Clifford, 1994, p. 85) that Enuma Elish was derived from an earlier Akkadian work, the Myth of Anzu. This is consistent with the relatively late date of appearance of Enuma Elish, around 1100 BC. The Myth of Anzu is itself found in a rather fragmentary Old Babylonian version (OBV), and a more complete 'Standard Version' from the Assyrian period.

This myth describes how the bird-like monster Anzu (Fig. 20.1) steals the 'Tablet of Destinies' from the gods, thus rendering the gods powerless. Several of the gods are approached with a request to attack Anzu and regain the Tablet, but despite the great rewards offered, they all decline. Finally, Enki approaches the goddess Mami and asks for the services of her son. In the OBV this is the god Ningirsu, patron god of Girsu in southern Mesopotamia. However, in the Standard Version, Ningirsu has been replaced by the Ninurta, patron god of Nimrud in northern Mesopotamia. These are both gods of the storm cloud, so they make worthy adversaries for Anzu (Imdugud in Sumerian), who is also in fact a god of the storm cloud.

Fig. 20.1 Copper relief of the bird-like monster Anzu, called Imdugud in Sumerian. Height 1 m. British Museum.

Having agreed to his commission, Ningirsu attacks Anzu with bow and arrow, but using the Tablet of Destinies, Anzu can deflect the arrow. Nevertheless, the attack is renewed on the advice of Enki, and Ningirsu finally wears out Anzu with a whirlwind and tears off his feathers. While Anzu is thus distracted, Ningirsu shoots him through the heart with his bow and arrow, thus regaining the Tablet and receiving the acclaim of all the gods.

In Enuma Elish, the battle between the god Marduk and the sea monster Tiamat replaces the battle between Ningirsu/Ninurta and Anzu. However, according to Lambert (1986), several vestiges of the older story betray the origin of Enuma Elish. This, and other evidence, shows that Enuma Elish is an eclectic work, put together from several sources for the purpose of glorifying Marduk in his achievement of supremacy over the Mesopotamian pantheon under Nebuchadnezzar I of Babylon. Hence, we can conclude that those passages of Enuma Elish which do resemble Genesis must go back to much earlier common sources. It is highly unlikely that there was any direct borrowing from Enuma Elish to Genesis.

An example of possible common source material between Enuma Elish and Genesis is the account of creation from Tiamat's sliced up corpse in Enuma Elish (at the end of tablet 4). The waters of Tiamat's corpse are separated into two parts. One half is placed above the sky and

240

its waters are held back with a bolt. The other half is placed under the sky to form the Earth. This is reminiscent of the separation of the waters in Genesis 1:7 into the waters above the sky and the waters under the sky. The common source for these two accounts was probably Sumerian but it has not yet been discovered during the excavation of ancient Mesopotamian sites.

20.3 The Flood stories

Ever since the work of George Smith it has been recognised that the Flood Story represents one of the closest parallels between biblical and Mesopotamian literature. Clearly, the more grossly polytheistic aspects of the Mesopotamian Flood Story are in contrast to Genesis, but on the other hand there are a large number of similarities between them, particularly in the description of events (Table 20.2). Some of these events, such as the sending out of birds to test for the abatement of the waters, are not vital to the overall direction of the story but are little pieces of descriptive detail. Their inclusion in both biblical and Mesopotamian accounts would be extraordinary if they were not from a common source.

Another crucial observation, made by Wenham (1978, 1987), is that the complete biblical account of the Flood has more correspondences with Mesopotamian versions than either of the hypothetical source documents 'J' and 'P' proposed in the Documentary Hypothesis. This is demonstrated in Table 20.2, and suggests that the Flood Story is derived direct from a Mesopotamian source, and not as a patchwork made up from the hypothetical documents J and P.

If the Genesis Flood Story has a common origin with the Mesopotamian stories, what is the relationship between them? In order to make detailed comparisons, we must distinguish between parts of the story that could be missing due to gaps ("?" in Table 20.2) and parts that are absent, even from complete sections ("N"). When this distinction is made, the evidence suggests that there is a progression of increasing attention to detail from the Sumerian Flood Story to Atrahasis to Gilgamesh, and that the last of these most resembles Genesis.

If we were to assume that the Flood Story was fictional, the increasing amount of detail in the three Mesopotamian versions would be attributed to gradual embroidery of the story during its long oral transmission (e.g. Teeple, 1978, p. 24; Ryan and Pitman, 1998). However, if we were to assume that the Flood Story in Genesis was an eye-witness

Table 20.2 Comparison of proposed biblical source documents with Mesopotamian documents

Event in the story	Genesis Source#	Mesopotamian* G	A	S
1. The Flood was caused by divine plan.	J	Y	Y	?
2. A reason is given for the Flood	P&J	N	Y	?
2. The hero was warned by divine revelation.	P	Y	Y	Y
3. The hero was instructed to build large boat of a given size.	P	Y	Y	?
4. The hero is attentive and obeys the divine command	P&J	Y	Y	?
5. Animals as well as people were loaded on the boat.	P&J	Y	N	?
6. The hero was instructed to enter the boat.	J	Y	Y	?
7. The door was closed	J	Y	Y	Y
8. The duration of the rain and flood-water rise is described.	P&J	Y	Y	N
9. The death of mankind is described.	P&J	Y	Y	Y
10. The end of the rain is described	P&J	Y	?	N
11. The grounding on a mountain is described.	P	Y	?	Y
12. The hero opens a window	J	Y	?	N
13. The duration of waiting for the waters to subside is described.	J	Y	?	N
14. The hero sends out birds to test for the abating of the Flood.	J	Y	?	N
15. The hero offers sacrifices of worship after he is delivered.	J	Y	Y	Y
16. Divine appreciation of the sacrifice is described.	J	Y	Y	?
17. The hero receives a divine blessing.	P	Y	?	Y

Biblical sources: J =Yahwist, P = Priestly source. Modified after Wenham (1978, 1987).
* Mesopotamian sources: G = Gilgamesh, A = Atrahasis, S = Sumerian Flood Story.

account of a real event, we would have to assume that the Flood Story in the Gilgamesh Epic was also largely accurate, as far as the course of events was concerned. This would imply that the three Mesopotamian versions do not form a sequence of increasing elaboration but represent different selections of material from a common source in order to fulfil three different purposes. Thus, the Sumerian version is a historical-theological account concerned with the survival of kingship after the Flood; Atrahasis is a theological account concerned with the relationships between gods and men and the solution to the problem of overpopulation; whereas Gilgamesh is intended as a thrilling story whose focus is the search for immortality. Since the Flood Story is not conclusively known as part of the Gilgamesh Epic until Assyrian times, this provides another example of the incompleteness of the earlier written record.

20.4 The Disputations

Disputations are a genre of Sumerian literature that appear to have been written for performance as entertainment at the royal court of the Ur III dynasty, but which were probably based on much older stories. Of the seven known disputations, two seem to have strong parallels with the story of Cain and Abel. In the 'Dispute between Cattle and Grain', Cain and Abel are replaced respectively by the goddess of grain (Ashnan) and the god of cattle (Lahar). Excerpts of the story are quoted from Kramer (1944):

> *After on the mountain of heaven and earth, An had caused the Anunnaki to be born...*
> *Because the name of Ashnan had not been born...*
> *there was no ewe...*
> *Because the name of .... Lahar the Anunnaki, the great gods, did not know...*
> *the grain of the pure living creatures did not exist..*
> *In those days, in the creation chamber of the gods... Lahar and Ashnan were fashioned.*
> *The produce of Lahar and Ashnan the Anunnaki... eat... and drink, but remain unsated;*
> *For the sake of the good things in the pure sheep-folds, Man was given breath.*

[from Kramer, 1944, p. 72]

According to the myth, Lahar and Ashnan were created to provide the Annunaki gods with food (in the form of offerings), but the gods were not 'sated' until man also was 'given breath'. Presumably the role of man was to present the produce of Lahar and Ashnan (cattle and grain) to the great gods in their temples:

> *At the pure word of Enki and Enlil, Lahar and Ashnan descended*
> *from the Dulkug* (heaven)
> *For Lahar they set up the sheepfold, plants and herbs they pre-*
> *sented to him;*
> *For Ashnan they established a house, plow and yoke they pre-*
> *sented to her.'*

[Kramer, 1944, p. 53]

The end of the myth describes how Lahar and Ashnan drank too much wine and began to quarrel about their relative merits until their dispute was stopped by Enlil and Enki, whereupon Ashnan (goddess of grain) was declared the victor.

A similar pattern is seen in the 'Dispute between Emesh and Enten' (Kramer, 1963, p. 218), except that in this case the contest is between two brothers. Enten seems to be an agriculturalist, concerned with irrigation of the land, whereas Emesh is perhaps nomadic. Both brothers bring thank offerings to Enlil at Nippur. Enten brings a variety of produce of the land, including animals, plants, wine and beer, whereas Emesh brings precious metals, stone, wood and fish. However, Enten, 'the faithful farmer of the gods' is pronounced the winner.

In both of these Sumerian disputations it appears that the winner is the settled farmer with his irrigated land, rather than the nomadic shepherd. This attitude must be expected from Sumerian civilisation, which valued the institutionalised way of life. It is also not surprising that this is the opposite of God's choice in the story of Cain and Abel, which is based on spiritual rather than outward physical attitudes. However, the strong similarities between the stories suggests that they represent another example of biblical and Sumerian accounts which came from a common source.

It is concluded from all of the above evidence that there was probably a pool of oral narrative material in early Mesopotamia which gave rise to written accounts found in both Sumerian and biblical literature. The divergence of these two traditions from their common source may well have occurred during the reign of Shulgi of the Ur III dynasty, when much of Sumerian literature was first written down. During this inscription exercise it is likely that the oral versions of the myths were 'improved' to suit current political tastes, and therefore departed from long-maintained traditions. However, if Abram received these ancient traditions directly from their oral sources, he could have preserved them in their original form for transmission to future generations, ultimately to be included in the written text of Genesis.

CHAPTER 21

THE INTERNAL STRUCTURE OF GENESIS

In seeking to understand the origins of the Book of Genesis, an important approach is to examine its internal structure in order to see what kind of sources may have given rise to the written text. However, in this investigation it is not necessary to look for hidden signs; the structure of the book is indicated in the very title, Genesis, which is the Greek translation of the Hebrew '*toledoth*'. This word is used 13 times in Genesis, usually in the formula '*this is the toledoth of x*', where x is the name of one of the patriarchs. This phrase separates major narrative sections of Genesis and is clearly critical to its structure, but the correct interpretation of the phrase has been difficult to discern.

21.1 The importance of toledoth formulae

The word *toledoth* is used 39 times in the Bible. This word is of such importance in understanding the structure of Genesis that a complete list of the biblical references is given in Table 21.1, including the context of all of the uses in Genesis. In the Authorised Version and the Revised Standard Version the word is almost invariably translated 'generations', but in the New International Version the translation is more variable as the NIV attempts to paraphrase the meaning. Thus, in Genesis and Numbers it is generally translated as 'account', in Exodus as 'records', and in Ruth as 'family line'. Finally, in 1st Chronicles the word is translated variously as 'genealogy', 'genealogical record' or 'family genealogy'.

It has generally been assumed by biblical scholars that the *toledoth* formula introduces a new narrative section which is often, but not always a genealogy. However, Wiseman (1936) proposed that the *toledoth* formula was instead a colophon, which is a title placed at the end of a work. Most Mesopotamian tablets (both Sumerian and Akkadian)

Table 21.1 Occurrences of the word *toledoth* in the Bible

~~~~~~

Genesis (13 cases)

2:4	This is the *toledoth* of the Heavens and the Earth
5:1	This is the written *toledoth* of Adam
6:9	This is the *toledoth* of Noah
10:1	This is the *toledoth* of Shem, Ham and Japheth
10:32	These are the clans of Noah's sons according to their *toledoth*
11:10	This is the *toledoth* of Shem
11:27	This is the *toledoth* of Terah
25:12	This is the *toledoth* of Abraham's son Ishmael
25:13	These are the ... sons of Ishmael... according to their *toledoth*
25:19	This is the *toledoth* of Abraham's son Isaac
36:1	This is the *toledoth* of Esau
36:9	This is the *toledoth* of Esau
37:2	This is the *toledoth* of Jacob

Exodus (3 cases)

6:16	These were the names of the sons of Levi according to their *toledoth*
6:19	These were the clans of Levi according to their *toledoth*
28:9-10	Engrave... the names of the sons of Israel according to their *toledoth*

Numbers (13 cases)

1:20	From the descendants of Reuben... according to their *toledoth*
1:22-42	Eleven more corresponding examples from the other tribes
3:1	This is the *toledoth* of Aaron and Moses

Ruth (1 case)

4:18	This is the *toledoth* of Perez

1st Chronicles (9 cases)

1:28-29	The sons of Abraham: Isaac and Ishmael: this is their *toledoth*:
5:7	Their relatives by clans, listed according to their *toledoth*, are:
7:2	...these were fighting men listed in their *toledoth* (also 7:4, 7:9, 8:28, 9:9, 9:34)
26:31	Jerijah was their chief according to the *toledoth* of their families

~~~~~~

have a colophon at the end of the text rather than a title at the beginning. For example, the Atrahasis Epic ends with the following colophon, where each slash symbol indicates a new line on the tablet:

The End/ Third tablet/ 'When the gods instead of man'/
390 lines/ Total 1245/ For the three tablets/
Hand of Nur-Aya, junior scribe/
Month Ayyar [.... day]/ Year Ammi-saduqa was king/
A statue of himself [......]/[......]

[Dalley, 1991, p. 35]

According to the Wiseman theory, the *toledoth* formula in Genesis was inherited from written Mesopotamian texts on clay tablets. If we take Genesis 5:1 as an example, Wiseman interpreted the phrase '*This is the written toledoth of Adam*' to mean 'This is the account written by Adam', referring to the chapters which precede this formula, describing the Garden of Eden, the Fall of Man and the story of Cain and Abel. The theory of Wiseman is appealing because of the clear evidence for a Mesopotamian origin for the stories in the first few chapters of Genesis. Based on this origin for the stories, we might expect to see the Mesopotamian style of colophon used at the end of a set of tablets which recorded the history of each Patriarch. However, when examined in detail, the Wiseman theory has fatal flaws. These flaws are seen most clearly in the *toledoth* formulae of Ishmael and Esau (Garrett, 1991).

The *toledoth* formula of Ishmael is used twice in immediate succession (Gen 25:12 and 13). At this location these formulae come at the end of the story about Abraham, but immediately before the genealogy of Ishmael. The *toledoth* formula of Esau is also used twice, but here the two occurrences are eight verses apart (Gen 36: 1 and 9). The first formula comes at the end of the story about Jacob, but immediately before a short genealogy of Esau. The second formula then precedes a longer genealogy of Esau.

According to the Wiseman theory, this implies that Ishmael recorded the story of Abraham, and Esau recorded the story of Isaac. However, the Genesis account makes it clear that neither Ishmael nor Esau were the type of person interested in keeping a written account, and furthermore that they were not privy to the encounters described in Genesis between God and Abraham, or between God and Jacob. Finally, even if Ishmael and Esau had obtained such information, there is no logical way that they could have passed this information on to the descendants of Jacob. On the other hand, if we accept the fact that these *toledoth* formulae refer to the genealogies which follow them, the layout of the text is quite rational. For example, two separate genealogies of Esau are each introduced by a *toledoth* formula.

In contrast to Wiseman (1936), the data in Table 21.1 support the argument of Garrett (1991, p. 93) that *toledoth* refers specifically to a family genealogy and not to a more general kind of written account. In cases where the family genealogy is listed (such as the ten generation genealogy in Ruth Ch 4), the *toledoth* formula is usually used at the beginning of the genealogy. This is also the normal practice in Genesis, but there are three important exceptions. One of these involves the Table of Nations (the descendants of Shem, Ham and Japheth). In this case the *toledoth* formula is used at both the beginning and end of the genealogies (Gen 10:1 and 32). A second case involves the genealogy of Jacob's sons. In this instance, Garrett has shown that the *toledoth* formula (Gen 37:2) has become separated from its genealogy, which is found in Gen 46:8-27. This separation was caused by the insertion of the story of Joseph at this point.

The final special case involves the *toledoth* of the Heavens and the Earth. I will argue that this refers to a pseudo-genealogy describing the 'family history' of the Heavens and the Earth, which comprises Genesis chapter 1. However, the *toledoth* could not be included at the beginning of Chapter 1 because this would pre-empt the opening line *'In the beginning God created the heavens and the earth'*. A good reason why this *toledoth* formula goes with Chapter 1 is that it echoes Genesis 1:1 by repeating the phrase 'the Heavens and the Earth'. In contrast, the second creation story (beginning in Genesis 2:4b) reverses the word order and refers to 'the Earth and the Heavens'. These creation stories will be discussed in detail at a later point.

21.2 The identification of toledoth sources

If we accept the proposition that the *toledoth* formula is used exclusively to describe genealogical records then we can use it to identify specifically genealogical sources in Genesis and distinguish them from the sources that gave rise to the rest of the text. Following Garrett (1991), genealogical sources are identified as those with a *toledoth* formula that also include information such as names of descendants, age at the birth of the firstborn and age at death. A limited amount of relevant geographical information is also included in these sources, such as where some individuals lived and died and the lands inhabited by their descendants.

The result of this analysis is to distinguish eleven genealogical sources and perhaps ten sources that comprise stories (Table 21.2). These 21 or so distinct sources were combined by an editor, who may have been Moses, into the original version of the book of Genesis. This editor apparently tried to interfere as little as possible with his source material, believing it to be the inspired Word of God. Therefore, in order

Table 21.2 The Sources of Genesis

~~~~~~

1.1*	Genealogy of creation in six days
2.4b	Story of the Garden and the Fall
4.1	Story of Cain and Abel
5.1	Genealogy of Adam's family line (10 generations, linear)
6.1	Story of the Nephilim
6.9	Genealogy of Noah's family (1 generation, branched)
6.11	Story of the Flood
9.28	Completion of Noah's genealogy?
10.1#	Genealogies of Japheth, Ham and Shem (5 generations, branched)
11.1	Story of Babel
11.10	Genealogy of Shem's family line (10 generations, linear)
11.27	Genealogy of Terah (2 generations, branched)
12.1	Story of Abraham
25:12$	Genealogy of Ishmael's family (1 generation, branched)
25:19	Genealogy of Isaac (1 generation)
25:21	Story of Jacob and Esau
35:28	Completion of Isaac's genealogy?
36:1	Genealogy of Esau (1 generation, branched)
36:9	Genealogy of Esau (10 generations?, branched)
37:1	Genealogy of Jacob (title only)
37:2b	Story of Joseph
46:8	Main body of genealogy of Jacob's Family (3 generations, branched)
46:28	Story of Reunification of Jacob's Family
50:26	End of Genesis

~~~~~~

*Toledoth at the end
#Toledoth at the beginning and the end
$Toledoth twice at the beginning

to fit his text together into as near chronological order as possible, he sometimes interleaved his sources. Thus, as Garrett has argued, the family genealogy of Jacob was split from its title by the insertion of the story of Joseph. It is less clear, but probable, that the short genealogies of Noah and Isaac were also split by the insertion of the Flood Story and the story of Jacob and Esau respectively.

An important point to note from this analysis is that these sources are of variable length. The shortest sources are some genealogies comprising a single generation (such as the genealogies of Noah and Isaac). The longest sources are the stories of Abraham, Jacob and Joseph (comprising 9 - 13 chapters each). A short source, such as the genealogy of Isaac, is important, not so much for the information that it contains, but to preserve and emphasise the underlying pattern of the Book.

21.3 The toledoth of Noah

It was suggested above that the Toledoth of Noah might have been sandwiched on either side of the Flood Story when these two sources were combined. However, it seems likely that other toledoth fragments are in fact interleaved within the Flood Story (shown by italics in Table 21.3). If this is the case then the separation of these sources will give us a better understanding of their origins. This is particularly important for the Flood Story because it may help us to see more clearly its relationship with Mesopotamian accounts.

Examination of Table 21.3 shows that the parts of the Flood Story and the toledoth of Noah identified in this analysis can both be read as separate documents. In addition, two other points can be made about this division of sources:

1. The proposed toledoth fragments do not contain any of the information identified in section 20.1 as common between the biblical and Mesopotamian stories. In other words, this 'toledoth source' may have been interleaved at a later date with a complete Flood Story which had a source in common with the Mesopotamian stories.

2. The proposed toledoth fragments do not contain any of the numbers necessary for the Flood chiasmus (section 4.1). Nor do they contain any of the references to events of the Flood in terms of the lunar calendar of months and days.

The toledoth source, as proposed in Table 21.3, contains one reference to Noah's age before the Flood and one reference to his remaining life after the Flood. However, two other references to Noah's age, one

Table 21.3 Possible identification of toledoth and narrative sources in the biblical Flood Story

~~~~~~

6:9-10	*This is the account of Noah. Noah was a righteous man, blameless among the people of his time, and he walked with God. Noah had three sons: Shem, Ham and Japheth.*
6:11-7:5	Account of how God told Noah to construct the Ark in order to be saved from the Flood.
7:6-7	*Noah was six hundred years old when the floodwaters came on the earth. And Noah and his sons and his wife and his sons' wives entered the ark to escape the waters of the Flood.*
7:8-9:17	Account of Flood, including entry into the Ark, the advance and retreat of the waters, the exit from the Ark, the sacrifice of burnt offerings, and the new covenant between God and Noah.
9:18-19	*The sons of Noah who came out of the ark were Shem, Ham and Japheth. Ham was the father of Canaan. These were the three sons of Noah, and from them came the people who were scattered over the earth.*
9:20-27	Account of Noah's drunkenness and the cursing of Ham.
9:28-29	*After the flood Noah lived 350 years. Altogether, Noah lived 950 years, and then he died.*

~~~~~~

at the beginning of the Flood and one at the end, were omitted from the proposed toledoth source. The latter reference (Gen 8:13) reads as follows:

> *By the first day of the first month of Noah's six hundred and first year, the water had dried up from the earth. Noah then removed the covering from the ark and saw that the surface of the ground was dry.*

There are three reasons for this exclusion. Firstly, this section includes a reference to the removal of the covering of the Ark, which is also mentioned in the Mesopotamian stories, and is therefore believed to be part of the Flood narrative itself. Secondly, this section contains a reference to the lunar calendar of months and days, which is also believed to be part of the Flood Story itself. Finally, and most importantly, the Hebrew text does not actually mention Noah at this point. This reference was inserted as a gloss in the Greek Septuagint text of Genesis and was also included by the translators of the New International Version; but the Hebrew text says simply:

> *By the first day of the first month of the six hundred and first year, the water had dried up from the earth.*

There is a very similar statement at the beginning of the Flood Story (Gen 7:11-12):

> *In the six hundredth year of Noah's life, on the seventeenth day of the second month- on that day all the springs of the great deep burst forth, and the floodgates of the heavens were opened. And rain fell on the earth forty days and forty nights.*

This passage also cannot be included in the toledoth source because it contains a reference to the lunar calendar of months and days. In this case the reference to six hundred years *in the life of Noah* is found in the Hebrew text itself, but it was probably inserted as a gloss at an early stage in the evolution of the text.

In conclusion, therefore, I suggest that the references to the Flood beginning in the year 600 and ending in the year 601 were derived from an ancient Mesopotamian narrative source independently from the toledoth source. The significance of this suggestion will be considered in the next chapter (section 22.3).

CHAPTER 22

THE ORIGINS OF
TOLEDOTH SOURCES

Given the breakdown of Genesis into the two different source categories, as described above, one of the most critical questions to ask regarding these sources is when their texts were first written down. Wiseman (1936) argued that if the Sumerians recorded financial transactions in minute detail as early as 3000 BC, they would surely have recorded such momentous events as the creation of the Universe. This is a logical argument to the modern mind but one not supported by the evidence. The evidence in fact suggests that literary works such as the Flood Story were not written down until near the end of the Third Millennium BC, while the earliest genealogies date to a similar period. Since the closest non-biblical parallel to the *toledoth* genealogies of Seth and Shem is the Sumerian King List, we will examine this document in order to see how it was composed. Because the King List exists in a variety of versions, a study of these versions may help us to understand the composition and evolution of the Genesis toledoth sources.

22.1 The Sumerian King List

An examination of Sumerian literary sources suggests that the motive for compiling genealogies was generally to legitimise a later dynasty by linking it to an earlier heroic period. Thus, Rowton (1960) suggested that the King List was first compiled at the beginning of the Ur III dynasty in order to affirm the cultural continuity of this dynasty with the legendary kings of the Early Dynastic period, bridging over the periods of Akkadian and Gutian dominance in between. The king list was extended during the dynasty of Isin, again as an affirmation that the dynasty of Isin was following in the same great traditions of ancient Sumer.

Slightly different copies of the King List, dating from the Old Babylonian period, have been found in several Sumerian cities. The

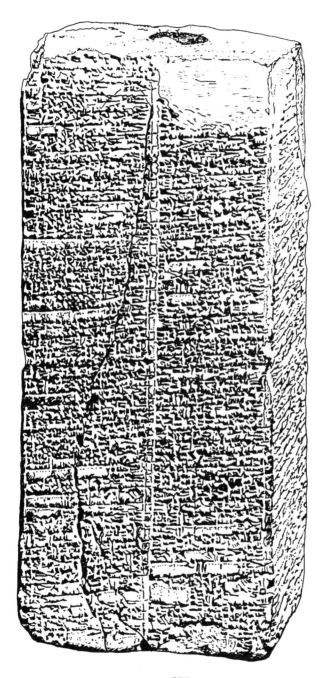

Fig. 22.1 View of the Weld-Blundell prism, the most complete version of the Sumerian King List. A hole visible in the end of the prism may have allowed it to be mounted horizontally for reading. Length 25 cm. Ashmolean Museum, Oxford.

'standard' version of the king list is the Weld-Blundell prism (WB444), shown in Fig.22.1 in the original orientation in which it was probably read (section 10.1). An interesting feature of the versions from Nippur is that they end with a summary which runs from the first dynasty of Kish to the first dynasty of Isin, but which omits the antediluvian section. The omission of this section from the summary suggests that the antediluvian kings were added during the Isin period as a 'prequel' (Hallo, 1963, p. 56).

Further evidence in support of this theory comes from some strange wording of the antediluvian section, which is different from the post-diluvian section (Finkelstein, 1963, p. 42). Thus, when kingship was passed from city X to city Y in the post-diluvian section, the following expression is used: *'X was smitten with weapons, its kingship was carried to Y'*. However, in the antediluvian section, a different expression is used, which may be translated literally as *'I will bring to an end city X, its kingship was carried to Y'*. Finkelstein suggested that the use of the first person in the future tense reflected a quote from a separate source in which a god, probably Enlil, was pronouncing judgement on each city. This expression was apparently imported verbatim into the King List.

Jacobsen (1939, p. 60) argued that the most probable source for the prequel of antediluvian material was the Sumerian Flood Story. In the Flood Story it is Enki who saves mankind, and in the King List it is Eridu, site of Enki's temple, that is the first city. Hence, it is suggested that the antediluvian section of the King List was composed in the style of the main list, using the information from the Sumerian Flood Story.

A comparison of the antediluvian cities cited in different versions of the King List (Table 22.1) supports the theory that the King List is based on material from earlier stories. The Weld-Blundell prism (WB 444) matches the Flood Story, but all other versions have minor variations. The version from Larsa adds this city to pander to local patriotism, while the University of California fragment (UCBC9, possibly from near Larsa) omits Larak, probably due to a scribal error, since this tablet appears to be a student exercise. The Nippur version mixes up the order of Bad-tibira and Larak, while that from the library of Ashur-banipal mixes up Larak and Sippar. Finally, Berossus omits Sippar and Shuruppak and replaces Eridu with Babylon. Finkelstein (1963) concluded that these variant traditions arose because scribes were writing from their memory of an orally transmitted story rather than copying verbatim an original written source.

Table 22.1. Comparison of the order of dominance of antediluvian cities in different sources

Flood Story	WB444	WB62(Larsa)	UCBC9-1819	Nippur3195	Ashur-banipal	Berossus
Eridu	Eridu (2)	Ha.a (2) Larsa (2)	Eridu (2)	[missing]	[missing] (2?)	Babylon (2)
Bad-tibira	Bad-tibira (3)	Bad-tibira (2)	Bad-tibira (3)	Larak (2)	Bad-tibira (3?)	Bad-tibira (5)
Larak	Larak (1)	Larak (1)		Bad-tibira (?)	Sippar (1)	Larak (3)
Sippar	Sippar (1)	Sippar (1)	Sippar (1)	[missing]	Larak (1)	
Shuruppak	Shuruppak (1)	Shuruppak (2)	Shuruppak (2?)	[missing]	Shuruppak 2)	
	8 kings	10 kings	7 or 8 kings	?	9 kings	10 kings

Sources: Finkelstein (1963), Lambert (1973).

257

22.2 The genealogies of Cain and Seth

Genesis provides internal evidence that the stories likewise preceded the genealogies in the date of their composition. This is based on a comparison of the three genealogies of Adam which are listed in Genesis Ch 4 and Ch 5. These are summarised in Table 22.2, where the genealogy involving Cain is listed in column 1, the short genealogy involving Seth is in column 2, and the long genealogy involving Seth is in column 3. It has long been observed that the genealogies in Genesis Ch 4 and Ch 5 (columns 1 and 3) are composed essentially of the same names, partially rearranged and with small variations in spelling (e.g. Vawter, 1977, p. 103). Most commentators agree that these genealogies came from the same source, and this seems extremely likely. Much speculation has been made as to how this came about, but an equally important question is *why* the material is presented in this way, with obvious duplication. It surely must have been done knowingly and deliberately.

The best explanation seems to be that the reader was intended to see a parallel between the righteous lineage of Seth and the unrighteous lineage of Cain. The unrighteous affinity of Cain's lineage is emphasised by the story of Lamech, who boasts to his wives that, like Cain, he has killed a man, and that, like Cain, he will get away with it. This is in complete contrast with the words of the righteous Lamech in Seth's lineage. He names his son Noah, meaning comfort, because *'he will comfort us in our labour and painful toil of our hands...'* (Gen 5:29). A similar comparison can be made between Lamech's three sons (Jubal, Jabal and Tubal) and Noah's three sons (Shem, Ham and Japheth). Lamech's three sons are the originators of three aspects of nomadic life (shepherding, musicianship and metallurgy, in Gen 4:20), whereas Noah's three sons are the forebears of the three divisions of the Table of Nations (Gen Ch 10).

As well as murder, the lineage of Cain is claimed as the origin of some of the hallmarks of Human Civilisation: The agricultural way of life (Gen 4:2) and the founding of cities (Gen 4:17), as well as the three aspects of nomadic life mentioned above. The unwelcome message, for those who glory in the achievements of Human Civilisation, is that in God's eyes, even the high points of man's achievement are intermingled with violence. Sumerian mythology recognised exactly this mixed character in human civilisation. For example, the myth of Inanna and Enki, which describes how the arts of civilisation were transferred from Eridu to Uruk, lists over 100 divine decrees which form the basis of Sumerian

Table 22.2 Genealogies of the Patriarchs, according to the Masoretic Text

1 Ch 4:17-22	2 Ch 4:25-26	3 Ch 5:3-32	4 Lifespan	5 Ch 11:10-26	6 Lifespan
Adam	Adam	Adam	930	Shem	600
|	Seth	Seth	912	Arphaxad	438
|	Enosh	Enosh	905	(Cainan)	?
Cain		Kenan	910	Shelah	433
Enoch		Mahalalel	895	Eber	464
Irad		Jared	962	Peleg	239
Mehujael		Enoch	365	Reu	239
Methusael		Methuselah	969	Serug	230
Lamech		Lamech	777	Nahor	148
		Noah	950	Terah	205
Jabal, Jubal, Tubal		Shem, Ham, Japheth		Abram, Nahor, Haran	

259

civilisation, but which contain both good and evil decrees. For example: truth and falsehood, straightforwardness and enmity, rejoicing and lamentation, the kindling flame and the consuming flame, exuberance and weariness, the shout of victory and the destruction of cities...

A major difference between the genealogies of Ch 4 and 5 is their style of presentation. The genealogy of Seth has a rigid formalism, and, most notably, there is specific mention in the toledoth that it was a written record. In contrast, Cain's genealogy lacks a toledoth formula and is presented in an anecdotal style that is typical of accounts handed down orally in story form. Such means of transmission are not necessarily any less reliable than the written word because the structure of the story acts as a memory aid and helps to maintain its integrity. In fact, an orally transmitted account is most likely to be modified at the moment when it is written down.

Putting all of the above evidence together, it seems very likely that the stories of Ch 4 existed before the toledoth of Ch 5, and that Ch 5 was in fact fashioned as a written theological treatise by combining and reworking the two genealogies of Ch 4. The reader should remember that Matthew did something similar when he fashioned his genealogy of Jesus into three sequences of fourteen generations. In order to do this he had to shorten the historical genealogies recorded in Kings and Chronicles, but this was justified by the spiritual meaning of the number 14, symbolising the perfection of God's plan of revelation.

22.3 The ages of the patriarchs

Another major difference between the genealogies of Genesis Ch 4 and 5 is the quotation in the latter of the age of each patriarch at the time of birth of his named son (presumed to be the firstborn, but not necessarily so) and the age of the patriarch at the time of death (Table 22.3, columns 2a and 2b). There has been much speculation about the meaning of these figures, which are obviously not natural life-spans. However, all arithmetic solutions to the enigma of the ages have raised as many problems as they have solved. For example, attempts to reduce the life-spans of the patriarchs to 'normal' durations have the effect of reducing their ages at the birth of their sons to abnormally low ages.

If we compare the three different versions of Genesis, the Hebrew Masoretic Text, the Samaritan Pentateuch, and the Greek Septuagint, it is generally agreed that the Hebrew text is the original from which the others have been derived. This is because the other two texts 'fix' perceived problems in the Hebrew text to make it more consistent. Thus, the Samaritan Pentateuch partially harmonises the ages of the patriarchs at the time when their sons were born by reducing the three highest ages to more reasonable numbers (bold italics in column 3a). This had the effect of lowering the calculated time from the Creation to the Flood, so the life-times of Methuselah and Lamech also had to be reduced so that they did not outlive the Flood (according to the Hebrew text, Methuselah died in the year of the Flood). On the other hand, the Greek Septuagint transla-tion of Genesis has harmonised the ages of the patriarchs when their sons were born by *increasing* the six lowest ages (bold italics in column 4a). This increases the apparent time from Creation to the Flood. Finally, one or two other changes in both texts probably resulted from scribal errors.

Given these considerations, it is generally argued that if we wish to try to recover the original intent of the writer of this genealogy, we must look at the Masoretic Text. However, if the names in the genealogy of Genesis Ch 5 are derived from the account in Ch 4 in order to compile a theological treatise, surely the ages in this genealogy are also theo-logical symbols. When we approach the ages from this point of view, we notice three things.

Firstly, we see that eight of the patriarchs, including Methuselah and Noah, have life-spans in the relatively narrow range 895 - 969. In other words, just short of a thousand years. Secondly, the 777 year lifes-pan of the righteous Lamech echoes the boast of the unrighteous Lamech and seems designed to draw out further the parallels and con-trasts between the two lineages. Finally, the 365 year span of Enoch (before he was taken by God) corresponds to the number of days in a year, which has often been taken to signify completeness. Furthermore, Enoch, who '*walked with God; then he was no more because God took him away*' nevertheless had the shortest earthly life-span of the ante-diluvian patriarchs. This implies some interesting things about the viewpoint of the author of this genealogy on the meaning of life.

The writer implies that when God took Enoch away, this was to be seen as a reward rather than a punishment. Therefore, we must infer that the writer thought that Enoch went to a 'better place' (Hebrews 11:40), perhaps resembling the Garden of Eden. All of the other righteous patri-archs, including Noah, died rather than being taken away; but if they were righteous then surely they also went to the 'better place'. Now Adam, we are told in Genesis Ch 3, had already experienced the Garden

261

Table 22.3   Antediluvian life-spans in different sources

1 Ch 5:3-32	2a* Masoretic	2b	3a Samaritan	3b	4a Septuagint	4b	5 Weld Blundell Prism	6
Adam	130	930	130	930	*230*	930	Alulim	28,800
Seth	105	912	105	912	*205*	912	Alalgar	36,000
Enosh	90	905	90	905	*190*	905	Enmenluanna	43,200
Kenan	70	910	70	910	*170*	910	Enmengalanna	28,800
Mahalalel	65	895	65	895	*165*	895	Dumuzi	36,000
Jared	162	962	*62*	847	162	962	Ensibzianna	28,800
Enoch	65	365	65	365	*165*	365	Enmeduranna	21,000
Methuselah	187	969	*67*	720	167	969	Ubartutu	18,600
Lamech	182	777	*53*	653	188	753		
Noah	500	950	500	950	500	950		
Time of Flood		1656		1307		2242		241,200

* a = age of patriarch at birth of named son, b = lifespan of patriarch.

262

of Eden, but had been expelled for his disobedience. If however, he had any expectation of returning to a 'Garden of Eden' after his death then his great lifetime on the earth might be not so much a blessing as a punishment. Thus, the experience of Enoch tells us that the writer of Genesis Ch 5 does not necessarily see longevity as a sign of God's favour (Hamilton, 1990, p. 257).

Considerable attention has been given by many authors to examining possible relationships between the ages of the biblical patriarchs and the reigns of the antediluvian Sumerian kings (Table 22.3). For example, Cassuto (1961) suggested that the writer of Genesis composed the toledoth as a polemic against the King List. He might have received the tradition of immense antediluvian ages but believed that a thousand years was a period of time reserved for the divine. Therefore, he might have allowed his patriarchs ages of just less than a thousand years, but reflecting the variations that he knew to be true of life in this world. However, I suggest that the direction of influence was more likely in the opposite direction: the large ages in the Genesis account reflect a common early Mesopotamian source that was also used in an exaggerated form in the King List to create reigns of astronomical length (e.g Bailey, 1993, p. 60-62).

While attempts to observe direct links between the biblical genealogies and the King List have generally proved fruitless, the close resemblances between the biblical and Mesopotamian Flood Stories have already been noted. Hence, this may be a more fruitful area to look for links between biblical and Mesopotamian chronological references.

It was suggested in section 21.3 that references to the year 600 and the year 601 for the beginning and end of the Flood were derived from an ancient narrative source independently from the toledoth source. In the Sumerian sexadecimal system the number 600 is often used to mean 'a large number', equivalent to the number 1000 used in biblical literature (e.g. Ps 90:4). Hence, the occurrence of the Flood in the Year 600 is indicative of an ancient Mesopotamian chronology. This link is supported by evidence from the Atrahasis Epic, which refers repeatedly to an anticipated period of 600 years:

600 years, less than 600 passed...

This phrase is repeated three times in the epic before each of the plagues which Enlil invoked to try to control the population: first disease, then famine, then more disease and famine together. Each of these plagues was averted because Enki (Ea) showed Atrahasis how to make the gods relent by offering sacrifices. Thirty six lines are missing at the beginning of the Flood Story; however, we may assume that these lines contained an announcement by Enlil of his plan to finally exterminate mankind by sending the Great Flood. This announcement was probably also introduced by the phrase: *'600 years, less than 600 passed'*.

Since the Flood represents the climax of the Atrahasis Epic, we can infer that in the epic, the 'long period' schematically represented by 600 years was the time between the creation of man and the Flood. Since parts of the Atrahais Epic and the biblical Flood Story appear to originate from a common source (section 20.1), the reference to the Flood subsiding in the year 601 may have been based on a schematic date for the Flood 600 years after the creation of man. It is important to emphasise that this would have been a schematic chronology: 600 years symbolises a long but unknown age between the Creation and the Flood. If the oral source of the biblical Flood Story contained a reference to the Flood occurring in the Year 600, this number may later have been incorporated into the toledoth of Noah as part of the schematic genealogy linking Adam to Abram.

Despite the schematic nature of this genealogy, a combination of biblical and archaeological evidence suggests that 600 years represents the correct order of magnitude for the period between Adam and Noah. This evidence comes from the story of Cain and Abel, whose agricultural setting is described in Genesis 4:2:

Abel kept flocks and Cain worked the soil.

Assuming that this reference is not an anachronism, we can compare it with the appearance of agriculture and animal husbandry in northern Mesopotamia (Moore et al., 2000, p. 478). This evidence suggests that plant cultivation began around 9000 BC, cereal and pulse agriculture began around 8000 BC, and sheep and goat husbandry began around 7000 BC. However, it was earlier estimated (section 8.1) that the Great Flood occurred between 5500 and 6000 BC. Therefore, if the historical context of Cain and Abel is accurate, less than 1500 years elapsed between Adam and Noah. Hence, we can see that the biblical account is self-consistent and also fits within the available archaeological constraints.

22.4 The genealogy of Shem

When we examine the genealogy of Shem (Genesis 11:10-26) it seems to be related to the genealogy of Seth because it has the same length and branching structure. This suggests that this genealogy too is schematic, a conclusion supported by the names themselves (Table 22.2). Thus, the top half, from Shem to Peleg, matches the corresponding part of the Table of Nations, argued in section 9.3 to be a schematic representation of the continuity of culture from the Sumerians to the Semitic peoples and then to the Hebrews. On the other hand, most of the names in the bottom half of the genealogy correspond to the names of cities in NW Mesopotamia; the area to which Abram migrated from Ur. These names include Serug, Nahor, Terah, and Haran (Albright, 1940, p. 236). Based on the amalgamation of these diverse sources in the genealogy of Shem, it seems very likely that the genealogy was composed after the Table of Nations, perhaps during the sojourn in Egypt, in imitation of the genealogy of Adam through Seth (Ch 5). If this explanation for the origin of the Shemite genealogy seems contrived, it should be remembered that Whitcomb and Morris (1961) regarded a literal interpretation of this genealogy to be 'astonishing, if not almost incredible' (Section 2.2).

Thus we conclude our examination of the famous genealogies of Seth and Shem by suggesting that they were both composed after the story material of Genesis to link together the testimony of three great men and their experience of God. By thus linking Adam, Noah and Abram, the genealogies portray the vista of God's plan as it unfolded through Mesopotamian history and link this primaeval history to the later unfolding of God's plan through Abraham and his descendants.

CHAPTER 23

THE NAMES OF GOD

More than 500 years after God appeared to Abraham, he revealed himself to Moses at the Burning Bush (Exodus 3:14). In that encounter, God also revealed his new name 'YHWH' (Yahweh), literally translated as 'I AM'. Later, after Moses' first rebuff by Pharaoh, God explained this revelation further (Exodus 6:3):

> *"I appeared to Abraham, to Isaac and to Jacob as El Shaddai, but by my name YHWH I did not make myself known to them."*

This claim that the Patriarchs did not know the name of YHWH presents a conundrum because YHWH is used widely in Genesis, both in narrative and dialogue. Therefore, various explanations have been offered in an attempt to get around this apparent contradiction, leading to some fundamentally different interpretations of the whole Pentateuch.

One approach is to argue that the syntax of Exodus 6:3 has been misunderstood. For example, the NIV gives an alternative reading as a footnote *"... by my name YHWH did I not let myself be known to them"*. This exactly reverses the sense of Exodus 6:3, but does not seem to be consistent with the sense of Exodus 3:14-15, where the name YHWH appears to be a new revelation to Moses. A different approach, but with similar objective, argues that Exodus 6:3 has the normal reading but should not be taken literally. Instead, we should understand that the patriarchs did know the name YHWH, but did not understand its full significance. The case against this and the previous approach comes from the absence of biblical personal names in Genesis compounded from YHWH, unlike those quoted in section 19.1 which are compounded from El. The third approach is the Documentary Hypothesis, by which Exodus 6:3 is translated normally, but all YHWH passages in Genesis are regarded as Mosaic or post-Mosaic. As noted in the introduction, the Documentary Hypothesis distinguishes separate sources in Genesis according to whether they use the word Elohim (normally translated God) or YHWH (normally translated LORD). Thus the sources J and E were conceived, but a Priestly editor (P) and a Deuteronomist editor (D) were also called for to "weave" the two proposed sources into one seamless whole (JEDP). Substantial input to the text as late as the Babylonian exile is often a component of this model.

Wiseman (1936) offered a radical solution to the problem of Exodus 6:3, claiming that Genesis was largely written in cuneiform by the Patriarchs but was transcribed and compiled (i.e. edited) by Moses. He suggested that during the transcription, Moses replaced an earlier divine name by YHWH. Wiseman speculated that this older name was El Shaddai; however, this name seems to have been a new revelation to Abraham at the giving of the covenant of circumcision, and not known before this. Therefore, I suggest that the divine name which would have been understood by the earlier patriarchs is the Akkadian name El-lil or simply El ('Lord'). The fact that the latter name was recognised by the Israelites is demonstrated by several later references in the Bible, such as 2 Sam 22:32, *'Who is El but Yahweh?'* (Cross, 1973).

23.1 From Enlil to YHWH

It is widely believed by scholars that the Israelites came to know of the gods El and Baal from the peoples of Canaan, whose pantheon is in turn known from Ugarit (e.g. Cross, 1973; de Moor, 1980). However, the god El shares many attributes with the Akkadian god Ellil (= Sumerian Enlil), including his roles as the creator god and the head of the pantheon (de Moor, 1980). Therefore, I suggested above that Abram brought the knowledge of El with him directly from Mesopotamia, where he knew God as Ellil, 'The Lord, Breath [of God]'. Subsequently, when God renewed his covenant with Abram and gave him the new name 'Abraham', God promised him a son and revealed another facet of his character, El-Shaddai, 'The Lord who provides'.

We have already seen that the same cuneiform signs were used to write the names of the chief gods of the Mesopotamian pantheon, whether these names were being written in Sumerian or Akkadian. Therefore it is likely that Moses used the name YHWH to replace the divine name En-lil or El-lil. Appropriately, YHWH is translated as LORD in most English Bibles, which is also an accurate translation of El.

267

If we accept a modified version of Wiseman's theory, whereby the use of YHWH in Genesis replaces the older name of Ellil, we are still left with the mystery of why Genesis sometimes refers to God by this name, and sometimes as Elohim, a word that literally means 'gods' in the plural, but is used as a generic word for God.

In order to see where these different words for God are used in Genesis they are summarised in Table 23.1. In this table, names for the divine person are separated into three main types and then summed for narrative and dialogue (quoted speech) within different subsections of Genesis (chosen by the present author). Elohim, translated God, may be regarded as a generic noun, whereas YHWH, translated LORD is a proper noun or name of God. Three additional categories are noted on the right hand side of the table. For example, "God of..." has been separated from other usages of God (Elohim) because it is felt that the possessive expression necessarily excludes the proper noun. In other words, to say "the LORD of Abraham" would be presumptuous, so that the use of Elohim is involuntary.

Table 23.1 Usage of divine names in Genesis

Narrative section		God	LORD God	LORD	God of 'X'#	'X' of God	El -
The origins of mankind							
The Creation	n	32	-	-	-	-	-
Ch 1	d	-	-	-	-	-	-
The Garden	n	-	20	-	-	-	-
Ch 2-3	d	4	-	-	-	-	-
Cain & Abel	n	-	-	10	-	-	-
Ch 4	d	1	-	1	-	-	-
The history of mankind							
Ch 5-36	n	50	-	71	-	7	1
	d	29	-	43	24	5	6
The Egyptian period							
Ch 37-50	n	1	-	10	1	-	-
	d	27	-	-	3	2	2

d = dialogue   n = narrative   # including my God, our God, your God

The data in Table 23.1 have been arranged into three major sections, comprising chapters 1 - 4, 5 - 36, and 37 - 50. The first major section can be divided into three subsections based on different divine names. Ch 1 always uses 'God'; Ch 2-3 uses 'LORD God', except in dialogue (where God is used); Ch 4 uses 'LORD', except in a small amount of dialogue (where the usage is mixed). Therefore, to summarise this first section of Genesis, it appears that the usage of divine name changes from 'God' in Ch 1 to 'LORD' in Ch 4, and the use of 'LORD God' in Ch 2-4 acts as a bridge between the sections on either side.

In the middle section (chapters 5 through 36), essentially beginning with the Flood Story, the use of the names 'LORD' and 'God' alternates frequently. However, the relative usage of each divine name is similar in narrative and dialogue. Thus, 'God' is used 50 times in narrative and 29 times in dialogue, whereas 'LORD' is used 71 times in narrative and 43 times in dialogue. Hence, we can see that the name 'God' is used 41% of the time in Narrative and 40% of the time in dialogue; an almost constant proportion.

The final section of Genesis, (chapters 37 through 50) is totally different in its use of divine names. 'LORD' occurs (10 times) exclusively in narrative, while 'God' (other than the possessive) occurs 27 times in dialogue and only once in narrative. This one usage (46:2) occurs immediately after the possessive expression 'God of his father Isaac', and must be associated with it.

It is well known that the Joseph story has a linguistic character distinct from the first 36 chapters of Genesis. This is reflected in the mention of Egyptian names, customs and culture. However, the distinct pattern of divine names is evidence of a deeper and more fundamental difference in literary origin for the two major sections of Genesis. The simplest explanation for these differences is that Moses himself wrote the Joseph story using undigested oral or written material originating from within Egypt, whereas he transcribed the rest of Genesis from some form of Mesopotamian script (as proposed by Wiseman, 1936). This script was probably cuneiform Akkadian, which was the principal language of international communication during the time that the Israelites were in Egypt (the 'Amarna age').

Since Joseph also had a prominent place in the court of Pharaoh, it is likely that he learned to read Akkadian, and would therefore have been perfectly placed to commit all of the Primaeval and Patriarchal accounts to writing. However, Joseph cannot have written his own story, which includes an account of his death. Therefore, this was probably written by Moses, as suggested above. The usage of divine names in the Joseph segment can then be understood on the grounds that Moses knew the name YHWH (LORD), and therefore always used it in narrative (except in the single case noted). In contrast, the characters in Genesis 37-50 did not know the name YHWH (as stated in Exodus 6:3). The word Elohim was therefore used in all dialogue in the Joseph section.

The usage of divine names in Genesis Ch 5 - 36 is more complex. This segment of text is argued to have been transcribed by Moses. Therefore, we must attempt to deduce the reasons why Moses used a given name in a given context. We could attribute the choice entirely to Moses, but in that case we should expect to see the same pattern as in the Joseph text. The opposite interpretation is that Moses used a set of Hebrew names to consistently replace a set of older divine names. A third possibility is some mixture between the two extremes. The best assumption is probably that of Wiseman, that Moses introduced the minimum possible changes during translation of older texts.

Therefore, I conclude that a re-shuffling of the divine names occurred during the 400 year sojourn in Egypt. The name El by which God had revealed himself to Abraham became so corrupted by polytheism that it became a generic name for any god. God responded to this confusion of his name with a new revelation by which he set himself apart from the corrupted revelation. Therefore, Moses used YHWH as a translation of the old name El (meaning LORD).

23.2 From Cosmic Triad to Trinity

If Enlil was translated YHWH (LORD), what was the original Mesopotamian word which is written in Hebrew as Elohim and translated as 'God' in English? This problem may be easier to solve than expected, since the Sumerian word 'dingir' and the Akkadian word 'ilu', are both represented in cuneiform by the star sign. This had originally been the Sumerian sign for An, the God of Heaven, but with time An became such a shadowy figure that his very name became a generic word for the gods.

Since the patriarchs from Adam to Abram lived in Mesopotamia, it seems unavoidable that they knew God by these Mesopotamian names. Therefore, if we want to get a clearer picture of the identity of these different aspects of God's character, it may help to look at the Mesopotamian literary works that most closely parallel the biblical text.

The Flood Story represents the closest parallel between Mesopotamian literature and the Bible, and is therefore important for the light that it sheds on the Mesopotamian names for God. The three Mesopotamian versions of the Flood Story are preserved in different degrees of completeness (section 20.1) but important sections are present in all three versions which allow their usage of divine names to be compared.

In the Sumerian Flood Story (Jacobsen, 1987) four gods are pre-eminent. These gods, listed in the order An, Enlil, Enki, and Ninhursaga, are involved in the creation of the Sumerian people (i.e. mankind). Two other gods are also mentioned. These are the mother goddess Nintur, usually regarded as another facet of the goddess Ninhursaga; and Inanna, 'Queen of Heaven". Both of these goddesses grieve for the destruction of the human race in the Flood but are unable to intervene. In contrast, the four gods An, Enlil, Enki and Ninhursaga are named again as the enforcers of the decision, apparently of the divine assembly, to cause the Flood. However, it was argued in section 14.2 that Ninhursaga was a relic of a widespread pre-Sumerian fertility cult centred on the Mother Goddess, and therefore not part of the revelation of the True God.

The details of the building of the Ark are missing from the Sumerian Flood story, but in the Atrahasis and Gilgamesh epics, Enki secretly devises a plan to save a representative of the human race by warning him about the Flood and instructing him to build a boat. In these Akkadian epics, the role of An (Anu) in bringing the Flood is downplayed slightly and the role of Enlil emphasised. However, at different points in the text they are each assigned the responsibility. For example, in Atrahasis (tablet 2, section 7) Enki disclaims all responsibility for the Flood, exclaiming *"That is Enlil's kind of work!"*, but later (tablet 3, section 4) Mami, midwife of the gods asks *"What was Anu's intention as decision maker, it was his command that the gods his sons obeyed"* (Dalley, 1991, p. 32).

The reason for this apportioning of blame for the Flood in Atrahaisis is that the writer cannot accept the idea that the same God could be both the architect of the Flood and at the same time the deliverer of Man, in the form of Noah. Therefore, he divides the character of the Supreme God into two parts. The omnipotent Gods in the form of Enlil and An are blamed for the flood, whereas the merciful aspect of God's character is attributed to Enki, god of wisdom.

Having made the above observations, based on Mesopotamian written records, we now turn to the Bible in order to see what evidence

Genesis can provide about the relationship between the Sumerian gods and the God of the Bible. Light is thrown on this question by three critical verses (Gen 1:26, 3:22 and Gen 11:7) where God speaks in the plural; *"Let us make man in our image"*; *"The man has now become like one of us"*; and *"Let us go down and confuse their language"*. There is every reason why a later monotheist editor of Genesis might have wanted to render these quotes in the singular, but presumably (and correctly) he was afraid to change the very word of God spoken.

This evidence that God revealed himself to mankind in the beginning as a 'divine family' is also consistent with the intimate relationship between Adam and God. If the New Testament revelation of God is in the form of the Trinity: Father, Spirit and Son, then we should expect that Adam, a real person who shared intimacy with God before the Fall, also knew God in at least as many facets as we do today. Thus we are presented with the possibility that more than one of the deities of the Mesopotamian pantheon might represent a facet of the character of the True God, albeit corrupted by the flawed transmission of the Mesopotamian myths.

In this connection, I suggest that the position of An as the heavenly father of the Mesopotamian pantheon is consistent with the role of the Heavenly Father of the Bible. Secondly, the image of Enlil as the Lord, Breath of God, is consistent with the role of the Holy Spirit who carries out the will of the Father on the Earth. Enki is the third member of the Sumerian cosmic triad but also the most enigmatic. As noted before, Enki holds the divine offices of civilisation and his name means 'Lord of the Earth', but on cylinder seals from the time of the Akkadian dynasty to the Old Babylonian period (Van Buren, 1933) Enki is shown as the god of springs, with two streams of water, probably representing the Tigris and Euphrates, which either emanate from his shoulders or from a vessel that he holds in one hand (Fig. 4.2; 23.1).

In Mesopotamian literature the streams of water are described in the opening section of the myth 'Disputation between Bird and Fish', where we read the following about the god Enki (Kramer and Maier, 1989, p. 87):

Life-giving waters that breed the fecund seed, he tied to his hands
Tigris and Euphrates he let fall from his side,
Poured into them the waters of all the lands.

Fig. 23.1 Impression of an Akkadian cylinder seal showing Enki as the god of living waters. Musee du Louvre.

This representation of Enki as the 'god of living waters' is reminiscent of Jesus' invitation in John 7:37-38:

> *"If a man is thirsty, let him come to me and drink. Whoever believes in me, as the scripture has said, streams of living water will flow from within him."*

In addition to being the source of the rivers, some of Enki's important roles in Sumerian myths are as the creator of man from the clay of the ground (the Myth of Enki and Ninmah), as the god who organises the Land of Sumer (Dispute between fish and bird), as the friend of man (the Flood story), and as the god of wisdom (in the Akkadian Atrahasis Epic). In several of these roles Enki resembles Jesus, who, as well as being the Judge of the earth and the Saviour of mankind is also the personification of Wisdom (Edwards, 1999, p. 113; Braaten, 2001). Thus, Paul (1st Cor 1:22) speaks of Christ as the *'power of God and the wisdom of God'*.

Occasionally, an intimacy characteristic of the Trinity is seen between members of the Cosmic Triad, even in the corrupted Sumerian myths. Thus, in the myth 'Enki and the Organisation of the Earth' (Kramer and Maier, 1989, p. 39-40), Enki is described as 'beloved of An', and as 'a leading son of An' (but also the younger brother of Enlil). Similarly, the inscription of Lugal-zagesi speaks of An's relationship to Enlil as the 'Father who loves him'. These intimate pictures may be original.

Therefore, I conclude that some aspects of the Trinity are reflected in the so-called 'Cosmic Triad' of the Mesopotamian pantheon, An, Enlil and Enki. If these three names for God were used in the original Flood Story but replaced by two names in Genesis, this may explain how the apparently arbitrary use of the divine names in the Genesis account arose. The distinction between the three persons of God in the Flood Story may also throw some light on the process by which the Sumerians corrupted the Trinity into the beginnings of a pantheon of gods.

Does the link between the Trinity and the Cosmic triad mean that the polytheist nature of Mesopotamian religion was to some extent 'God's fault'? The answer is clearly no. Firstly, God does not answer to human criticism. Secondly, if the Trinity was revealed in ancient Mesopotamia, this revelation was a forerunner of the revelation of the Trinity through Jesus and explained by the apostles. Therefore, the concept of 'three Gods in one' should have been as accessible to the ancient world as it is to us. Instead, the corruption of the revelation must be blamed on the priesthood, who were entrusted with the knowledge of God but distorted it for their own benefit. Specific examples of the process of corruption are the 'Marriage' of An to Inanna and the development of a cult of chthonic gods (gods of the underworld) centred around Enki.

What we can see in the Bible is that God's revelation emphasised different aspects of his character at different times in human history. Thus, the evidence that we have examined suggests that the Cosmic Triad revealed to the Sumerians parallels the Trinity, whose identity was later revealed most clearly in the Great Commission given by Jesus before his ascension (Matthew 28:18):

"Go and make disciples of all nations, baptising them in the name of the Father and of the Son and of the Holy Spirit..."

On the other hand, the revelation under the Law, which was given to Moses, emphasises another aspect of God's character, which is the unity of the three divine persons. This was proclaimed in the First Commandment (Deut 6:4; Mark 12:29):

"Hear O Israel: The LORD our God, the LORD is one."

Although the sense of the Hebrew original is not completely clear, the quote by Jesus, translated into the Greek by Mark, makes it clear that the intent of the original was a clear statement of the unity of God. However, just as the revelation of the Trinity was corrupted by the Sumerian priesthood into polytheism, we can see that the revelation of the One God was also corrupted by the Israelite priesthood, leading them to reject and crucify Jesus. Therefore, the challenge for the Church is to hold on to both the unity of the Godhead and the importance of each person of the Godhead at the same time.

Having thus attempted to trace God's revealed character back to the earliest times, we will now examine the creation story itself.

CHAPTER 24

THE STORIES OF CREATION

Genesis chapter 1 is a masterful account of the creation of the Heavens and the Earth, at the same time very simple and yet also very carefully crafted. The obvious aspect that strikes the reader is the very clear day by day structure, emphasised particularly by the phrase *'there was evening and there was morning'*. At a slightly deeper level is a repetition of two sets of three days, followed by the seventh day as an epilogue. In the first set of three days God separates the different realms of the Cosmos, while in the second set of three days God populates these realms. The most subtle level of structure, barely visible in translation from the Hebrew, is a chiasmus with a turning point on Day 4 (Beauchamp, 1969, p. 94; Wenham, 1987, p. 7). It is characteristic of Genesis that it has a structure characterised both by repetition and by chiasmus at the same time. Such features are also well seen in the 'Ancestor Epics' of Abram, Jacob and Joseph (e.g. Garrett, 1991).

24.1 Chiastic structure

The chiastic structure of Genesis 1 is highlighted in Table 24.1 by placing the English words in the same order as the Hebrew. In addition to this carefully constructed pattern, Wenham (1987, p. 6) argued that there is further word-play in the Hebrew by the grouping of words in multiples of seven. For example, verse 1 contains seven Hebrew words. Of course, the verse division is modern, but it corresponds in this instance to the sense of the original Hebrew. Other words in the creation story that are repeated in multiples of seven are *God* (35 times); *Earth* (21 times); *Heaven* (21 times); *It was so* (7 times); *It was good* (7 times); *And God made* (7 times) and acts of divine naming (7 times). This evidence suggests that the creation story of Genesis Ch 1 was composed in its present form as a single unit. However, it could contain older Sumerian material, as was argued for the Babel story (section 9.1). This question will be examined below.

Table 24.1. The chiastic structure of Genesis Ch 1

~~~~~~

verse   pivotal phrases and words (underlined)

~~~~~~

1:1   In the beginning, he created
         God
         the heavens and the earth.

1:14a   to divide the day from the night
1:14b   for signs, for fixed times, for days and years
1:15   to give light on the earth
1:16a   to rule the day | God made the
1:16b   to rule the night | two lights
1:17   to give light on the earth
1:18a   to rule the day and the night
1:18b   to divide the light from the darkness

2:1   Thus the heavens and the earth were completed...
2:2   By the seventh day God had completed the work...
2:3   he rested from all the work of creating that he had done.

~~~~~~

24.2 Days of separation and population

The repetitive structure of Genesis 1, forming two triads, is shown in Table 24.2. Each of these triads addresses one aspect of the primordial state of the Earth. Its formlessness is changed into order by creative acts of separation between different realms of the cosmos. Its emptiness is then changed into abundance by creative acts of population in each of the realms (e.g. Ridderbos, 1957, p. 29; Kidner, 1967, p. 46).

Table 24.2. The repetitive structure of Genesis Ch 1

~~~~~~

Acts of separation	Acts of population
Light and darkness v 3-5	Heavenly lights v 14-19
Water above and below the sky v 6-8	Fish in the water and birds in the sky v 20-23
Land environment and the sea v 9-13	Land animals and mankind v 24-31

~~~~~~

The first three days describe the divine acts of separation. Firstly, light is separated from darkness. This occurs without the need for light-bearing bodies, which will not appear until day 4, a concept that prefigures the description of the New Jerusalem, God's holy city, which forms part of the New Heavens and the New Earth in the Book of Revelation. Thus in Rev 21:23, we read:

The city does not need the sun or the moon to shine on it, for the glory of God gives it light, and the Lamb is its lamp.

This description in Revelation is a metaphysical description that is not supposed to be a scientific explanation of the origin of light. In the same way, the creation of light in Genesis 1:3 cannot correspond to the Big Bang because Genesis 1:2 describes a pre-existent earth, 'formless and empty' but covered in water, over which the Spirit of God was hovering.

On the second day, God separates the waters below the heavens from the waters above the heavens, allowing the sky in between to form a vault. The earth below the sky remains covered in water and the waters above the sky will be the source of rain. This is not the picture of creation that you would expect to see in, say, Vermont, but it is how the world might have looked 8000 years ago from a sand-bank in the Persian Gulf.

The third day is characterised by a double creative act. Firstly God separates the dry land from the sea; then he completes the terrestrial environment by providing plants. These are not conceived of as objects populating the land so much as an intrinsic part of the environment that is produced 'by the land'. Hence, the three realms of the cosmos: heavens, seas and land are now ready for population.

On the fourth day, the heavens are populated by the sun, moon, and stars. The location of these bodies *in* the expanse of the heavens or sky has already been discussed (section 1.3). The sun and moon are not even named here, but are simply called the greater and the lesser lights. This is often assumed to be a polemic against the worship of these bodies in Mesopotamia. However, it is also possible that the absence of names indicates a very archaic source. The creation of the sun on day four, after the land plants on day three, again shows that this is not intended to be a scientific account. Creationists attempt to get around this 'problem' by arguing that these bodies were in existence before the fourth day but were not visible before then from the earth's surface. There is absolutely no evidence to support such an interpretation.

278

On the fifth day, God populates the waters and the sky with fish and birds. This is followed on the sixth day by the population of the land with animals. Echoing the third day of separation, this third day of population has two creative acts. After the making of the animals, God reaches the pinnacle of creation when he makes humankind, both male and female, in his own image. This emphasis on mankind as the pinnacle of creation is supported by the description of six aspects of the creation as 'good'. All of these aspects of the creation: Light, the land, plants suitable for food, the sun and moon, the fish and birds, and finally the animals, are created for the benefit of mankind, and therefore described as 'good'. In contrast, no such comment attends the creation of the sky in Gen 1:5, or the creation of mankind himself in Gen 1:27. Hence, we can see that the description of the creation as 'good' does not imply the absence of death at this point, but simply its fittingness as the environment to be inhabited by mankind (Sailhamer, 1996, p. 118).

24.3 Days of revelation

The account of creation in Genesis 1 seems to say that God created the Heavens and the Earth in six days, whereas scientific evidence suggests that the Earth took billions of years to reach its present state. This disagreement has pitted Science against the Bible for over 200 years, and in response there have been numerous attempts to solve the enigma. Four of the main approaches can be summarised as follows:

1. The day-age model
2. The re-creation model
3. The apparent age model
4. The days of revelation model

Each of these models has secondary variants which sometimes have features in common and sometimes differ, but the essentials of the four models are examined below, along with their strengths and weaknesses.

The day-age model suggests that the six days of Genesis 1 were actually long geological ages, based on the biblical affirmation 'A thousand years in your sight are like a day that has just gone by' (Psalm 90:4). This model has a long history which cannot be elaborated upon here (e.g. see Young, 1982). Some advantages of the model are as follows:

1. Since the first 3 days apparently took place before the creation of the sun and moon, it was argued that they could not be 24-hour days as we now know them.

2. Since the Sabbath rest of God is spoken of as continuing to the present day (Hebrews 4:4), the seventh day is evidently of long duration, so the others should be also.

3. The plants that were created on day 3 were in fact 'produced' from the ground, implying a period of growth that is more than one day.

However, in the opinion of the present author, the order of creation in Genesis 1 is not consistent with geological history, as was argued above (section 24.2). Furthermore, the phrase 'evening and morning' seems to be used specifically to emphasise the 24 hour nature of the days.

The re-creation model attempts to overcome these problems, and also the existence of a 'formless' Earth before the creation of light, by suggesting that the six days of creation were essentially 'fine-tuning' of a universe already in existence to make it suitable for mankind's occupation (Young, 1982, p. 52; Sailhamer, 1996, p. 42). This model was proposed long ago, for example by Buckland (1837), a prominent 19th Century geologist. It overcomes some of the objection to model 1 by placing the aeons of geological time in the period before the creation described in Genesis. However, since Buckland's time, human fossils have been dated to ages of around 100,000 years (e.g. McDermott *et al.*, 1993), placing the origins of the human species itself back into geological time. Therefore, this model can no longer be harmonised with geological evidence.

The apparent age model attempts to overcome the problems of geological evidence by suggesting that creation occurred in six literal days, a few thousand years ago, but that the universe was created with a built-in apparent age of billions of years, as implied by scientific evidence. This is essentially a metaphysical model. It is not testable by science since it argues that scientific evidence of the earth's age was 'manufactured' by God as part of the creative process. This model can reconcile a literal reading of Genesis 1 with geological evidence, but it has a fatal flaw: it cannot explain the Flood. Actually, none of the three models outlined above can satisfy the Creationist interpretation of the Flood as a global catastrophe. All of the above models attempts to interpret Genesis 1 in a literal or pseudo-literal manner, but if the Flood is also interpreted in a literal manner as a global catastrophe then this destroys the attempts at harmonisation with Geology, since geological evidence is not consistent with a global Flood (section 3.4).

The fourth model above does not attempt to see Genesis 1 as a literal account of creation. It interprets the *days* of creation as literal days, but suggests that God was not actually creating the universe in six days but revealing this creation to man in six days. One version of this theory suggests that the creation was revealed in a series of visions over a period of six to seven days. This model was recently supported by Garrett (1991), who drew comparisons between the seven-day structure of Genesis Ch 1 and that of the Book of Revelation, where a series of visions is comprised of six similar parts, followed by a seventh that is distinct. On the basis of this comparison, and the uniqueness of Genesis 1 in relation to Mesopotamian creation stories, Garrett suggested that Genesis 1 was a direct revelation to Moses in a series of visions lasting seven days.

This model solves the conflict between Genesis 1 and the scientific evidence for the age of the universe. It also explains parallels between Genesis 1 and the Ten Commandments given to Moses at Mount Sinai: Just as God gave ten commands to Moses, there are ten words of divine speech 'God said' in Genesis 1. However, there are several pieces of evidence that suggest that the material in Genesis 1 has a Mesopotamian source that predates Moses.

The first piece of evidence is the phrase in Genesis 1:26, in which God is spoken of in the plural as *'Let us make man in our image'*. This expression is not in accord with the strictly monotheistic law of Moses and its inclusion strongly suggests an older source that was preserved intact, despite the later condemnation of polytheism.

The second piece of evidence is the watery origin proposed for the Earth in Genesis 1:2. This view of creation is found in both Mesopotamian and Egyptian cosmology, but would have been totally alien to Moses in the bone-dry desert of Sinai. If Moses had received such a vision at Sinai, it would have appeared to validate the Egyptian story of creation, in which dry land appeared out of a watery waste identified with the god Nun (Brandon, 1963, p. 18). Such a validation would have been incomprehensible to the man who had shortly earlier pronounced the LORD's judgement on all the gods of Egypt (Ex 12:12).

The third piece of evidence is the application of Sabbath principles in the Bible and in history before the revelation to Moses at Sinai. For example, an emphasis on seven day time periods in the biblical and Mesopotamian Flood Stories suggests a seven day week, and this is supported by a reference to a 'bridal week' which lasts seven days in the story of Jacob (Gen 29:27). Furthermore, in the Fourth Commandment (Exodus 20:11), God speaks of the six days of creation as a past event, which would hardly be meaningful if Moses had received this vision at the same time as the ten commandments.

A final piece of evidence is the expression used to describe the passage of days in Genesis 1: *'there was evening and there was morning'*. This expression places its emphasis on the passing of nights as a means of counting out the days, which Gardner (2001) attributes to the use of a lunar calendar, as practised by the Babylonians (Langdon, 1935).

To avoid these problems with the 'Revelation to Moses' theory, Wiseman (1948, p. 128) suggested that the six days of creation were days of divine revelation to Adam, a model supported by Ramm (1954, p. 229). Wiseman argued that the revelation to Adam was analogous to the revelation of the Ten commandments to Moses, when God spoke to Moses *'face to face'* (Exodus 33:11). However, any such interpretation of the days of Genesis 1 must also satisfy the reference to these days in the Fourth Commandment (Exodus 20:11):

> *For in six days the LORD made the heavens and the earth, the sea, and all that is in them, but he rested on the seventh day.*

Wiseman suggested that the revelation to Adam in six days was accompanied by the recording of the revelation on a set of clay tablets and argued that the Fourth Commandment is referring to the making of a set of *tablets* called 'The Heavens and the Earth' in six days, not to the making of the *Universe* in six days. However, this seems to be rather a contrived explanation. Instead, I suggest that we should simply understand the word *'made'* in a figurative sense. The hang-up about whether the universe was created in six days is a modern phenomenon, because the ancients were less worried about the mechanics of creation. If God figuratively *'made'* or *'created'* the Heavens and the Earth in six days before Adam's eyes, it would not have worried ancient authors to speak of the event as if it had really happened in that time: the important fact was simply that God revealed his creation to a man in six literal days and then gave the man a day of rest on the seventh day (Wiseman, 1948/1977, p. 129; Van Till, 1986, p. 90).

24.4 The second creation story

It has long been recognised that Genesis Ch 2 represents a second creation story. Typically, the two stories have been attributed to very different cultural contexts or historical periods. However, the two stories share a similar 'primitive' viewpoint. A prime example of this is the concept of things not yet having names: the Sun and Moon are not named in Genesis 1, while the animals are not yet named at the start of Genesis Ch 2.

Much discussion has occurred about the differences or 'contradictions' between the two creation accounts, but these contradictions arise because readers have been totally focussed on the *order* in which things were created (e.g. days 1 to 6). In reality, the differences between the two creation stories can be attributed to a difference in viewpoint. Genesis 1 is presented from a cosmic perspective, where God's creative acts separate the different realms of the universe, referred to collectively in ancient literature as 'The Heavens and the Earth'. On the other hand, Genesis 2 is set on a local scale, describing how God prepared the 'Land' for Man's habitation. A major focus is on the sources of life-giving water which supply fertility to the ground. For example, Gen 2:5-6:

> *The LORD God had not sent rain on the earth (or land) and there was no man to work the ground, but streams came up from the earth (or land) and watered the whole surface of the ground.*

This description applies perfectly to the climate of Southern Mesopotamia, where rain is very rare but water is supplied by rivers that rise hundreds of miles away. This local viewpoint is continued when Genesis 2:7 describes the creation of man:

> *The LORD God formed man from the dust of the ground and breathed into his nostrils the breath of life.*

The first half of this verse is a pun. In Sumerian, *adam* means pasture (e.g. Hallo, 1970, p. 58) and the word passed with the same meaning into Akkadian and then Hebrew, where adamah means 'ground'. The fact that the pun is present in the Sumerian suggests that the story may go right back to the dawn of human understanding.

A comparison between biblical and Sumerian cosmologies shows that the distinctive styles of the two Genesis creation stories mirror two different cosmogonic traditions found in Sumerian literature. These distinct Sumerian traditions were most clearly identified by Van Dijk (1964), and have been reviewed more recently by Clifford (1994, p. 15).

Van Dijk identified a 'cosmic' motif, originating from the city of Nippur, which emphasised the duality between the Heaven (An) and the

Earth (Ki). The union between these entities supposedly gave rise to Enlil, the Lord Breath, who then separated Heaven and Earth. This union between Heaven and Earth, giving rise to the god Enlil, can be regarded as a corruption of the story found in Genesis, based on human deification of the Earth into the Mother Earth, who can then be united sexually with the Heavenly Father. However, the role of the Lord Breath (=Spirit) in separating the different spheres of the cosmos is a more accurate reflection of the story found in Genesis Ch 1, as seen in the account from the Barton Cylinder (section 13.2).

Van Dijk also identified a 'chthonic' motif, originating from the city of Eridu, which emphasised the role of Enki in bringing forth life by inundating the Earth with the subterranean waters of the Apsu via the two great rivers of Mesopotamia. This focus on the rivers of Mesopotamia is seen in Genesis Ch 2, and the creation of man from clay by Enki is also reminiscent of Genesis Ch 2.

Based on the identification of the Cosmic Triad of the Mesopotamian pantheon with the biblical Trinity (section 23.2), it is possible that the two separate cosmogonic traditions of Nippur and Eridu might be genuine, albeit significantly corrupted, reflections of Divine Revelation, which share a common origin with the biblical creation stories in Genesis Ch 1 and 2.

24.5 The first Great Commission

After God had created mankind, he blessed them and gave them the first Great Commission (Gen 1:28):

"Be fruitful and increase in number; fill the earth and subdue it..."

This command was repeated after the Flood (Gen 9:1), when God blessed Noah and gave him a similar commission:

"Be fruitful and increase in number and fill the earth."

Doubtless the physical increase of the human population was one aspect of this commission, but I suggest that a deeper spiritual commission was involved. I suggest this was a commission to spread the *knowledge* of the LORD God over the whole earth, so that the earth might be *filled* with the knowledge of God. However, instead of spreading enlightenment, those who had received the revelation of God filled the earth with violence and corruption, provoking God to send the Flood.

After the Flood, God repeated the commission, but again the recipients of God's revelation (the Sumerians) did not take the knowledge of God to the whole earth but built a religious institution- a city with a tower that reaches to the heavens. So God caused the Sumerians to be scattered amongst the Semitic speaking peoples of the Middle East, and indeed the Semitic peoples did learn about the existence of the Holy and True God from the Sumerians. However, the Semitic peoples placed an idol (Marduk) in God's place so that God chose Abram to take his revelation to a new place and become the Father of a People (the Israelites) whose job it was to take the knowledge of God to the peoples of the whole world. But the Israelites also failed in this task, so finally Jesus was sent to declare the second Great Commission to his disciples, who would establish the Church (Matthew 28:19):

"Go and make disciples of all nations, baptising them in the name of the Father and of the Son and of the Holy Spirit, and teaching them to obey everything I have commanded you."

The ultimate destiny of the Church is to become the 'Bride of Christ' in a true 'Sacred Marriage' with the Son of God (Rev 21:9). However, as an agent in world history, the Church is in permanent tension between spiritual and institutional forces. When the latter gain ascendancy, the transcendence of God over human institutions is emphasised, but the immanence of God as a numinous spirit is diminished. However, when the Church experiences the phenomenon known as 'Revival', the immanence of God in personal experience is rediscovered as the tangible presence of the Holy God. When this is experienced, it can help us to understand what the man (Adam) may have experienced before the 'Fall'.

CHAPTER 25

RETURN TO EDEN

The stories of the Garden of Eden and the Fall of Man are some of the most mysterious in the whole Bible. As we have seen with other parts of Genesis, their interpretation is often polarised between those who understand them as literal history and those who regard them as a retrospective invention by an author living hundreds or thousands of years later. The interpretation that I will follow is rather different, looking at these dramatic and mysterious stories as an expression of the spiritual experiences of Adam in pictorial language.

Firstly it is important to re-affirm that Adam was a real person who received God's first personal revelation and who passed his experiences onto his descendants[9]. The only way that God could be discovered 'gradually' by mankind would be if God was an invention of mankind, as many historians tacitly assume. On the other hand, if God exists and has revealed himself to mankind then he must have revealed himself to one person first. According to his descendants, that person was simply 'the man', who we refer to as 'Adam'.

25.1 Spiritual experience in the Garden

In order to understand Adam's story, it is necessary to try to imagine what it would have been like when God spoke to Adam before his Fall. It is said of Moses that he spoke to God *'face to face, as a man speaks with his friend'* (Exodus 33:11) despite the fact that this was after the Fall of Man. Through history, God has given some people, as a gift, the experience of 'rediscovering' some of this intimacy with him. Most people have never experienced this intimacy, and indeed, most don't believe it even exists. However, we can only understand the story of the Garden of Eden and the Fall if we have some understanding of Adam's spiritual state before the Fall. In an attempt to capture a glimpse of this state, I will quote some descriptions of vivid spiritual experiences through history.

The apostle Paul, around 50 AD, usually presumed to be speaking about himself in 2 Cor 12:2:

> *'I know a man in Christ who 14 years ago was caught up to the third heaven.... He heard inexpressible things, things that man is not permitted to tell.'*

The wife of Jonathan Edwards, leader of the 'Great Awakening' of 1742 (Chevreau, 1994, p. 76):

> *'I cannot find language to express how certain this appeared- my safety, and happiness, and eternal enjoyment of God's immutable love, seemed as durable and unchangeable as God himself... The presence of God was so near, and so real, that I seemed scarcely conscious of anything else.'*

Evan Roberts, at the beginning of the 'Welsh Revival' of 1904 (Jones, 1995, p. 16):

> *'At nine o'clock I was awakened out of my sleep and found myself with unspeakable joy and awe, in the very presence of Almighty God. For the space of four hours I was privileged to speak with Him as a man speaks with his friend. I saw things in a different light. I knew God was going to work in the land.'*

A vision experienced by Rick Joyner in 1995 (Joyner, 1996, p. 41):

> *'... As we worshipped, a golden glow began to emanate from the Lord. Then there was silver around the gold. The colors, the richness of which I have never seen with my natural eyes, enveloped us all. With this glory I entered a realm of emotion that I had never experienced before. The more intensely we worshipped, the more glory we beheld. If this was heaven, it was much, much better than I had ever dreamed.'*

These experiences have always been temporary: it is not possible to live in the natural world and in a state of permanent spiritual ecstasy at the same time. However, for Adam, this was a permanent experience before the Fall. This is why Paul recognises Jesus as a second Adam. They are the only two men who had unbroken intimacy with God, but in both cases this intimacy was eventually broken: in Adam's case by the Fall and in Jesus' case when he represented Adam by dying on the cross (as the 'Second Adam'). When this occurred, Jesus cried out, rhetorically, *"My God, my God why have you forsaken me?"* This experience of broken intimacy must have been so hurtful to Adam that he could only describe it in mysterious language. In other words, the story of the Garden of Eden and the Fall of Man only make sense when we see these stories as containing many symbolic features.

25.2 The symbolism of the garden

The creation of man is described in symbolic form in Gen 2:7, and is reminiscent of the Mesopotamian accounts of the creation of man from clay, like the work of a potter:

> *The LORD God formed man from the dust of the ground and breathed into his nostrils the breath of life, and man became a living being.*

However, similar words are used in Gen 2:7 to describe the creation of man as a 'living being' and in Gen 2:19 to describe animals as 'living creatures'. This implies that this breathing of life into man is a general description of his animation (Brandon, 1963, p. 124), a sense supported by Ecclesiastes 3:19. However, man differs from the animals in having a spiritual nature. This spiritual nature is not explicitly described in Genesis Ch 2, but we can deduce that it is made up of two parts, spiritual capacity and a spiritual empowering.

The spiritual capacity of mankind is demonstrated by the story about the creation of Woman (Gen 2:21). When Adam looked on the natural creation, he did not see any spiritual beings on his own level. In order to provide Adam with a suitable helper, God gives Adam a dream, in which he symbolically takes part of man's body and forms woman. Now the woman is spiritually part of man, and has the same spiritual capacity for relationship with God.

The attribution of woman to Adam's rib might be explained by the cuneiform sign for rib, which is the same as life (Kramer, 1956, p. 144). Hence, this can be viewed as a word play that was lost on translation into Hebrew (and English). It is important to note here that the concept of 'Mother Eve' coined by anthropologists has no spiritual basis but is simply a case of borrowing a biblical expression as a slogan to describe a certain model for the evolution of the human species.

The spiritual empowering of mankind is demonstrated by God's invitation to Adam and Eve to eat from the fruit of the Tree of Life. However, to understand the significance of its fruit, we must examine the symbolism of the trees in the garden (Gen 2:9):

*The LORD God made all kinds of trees grow out of the ground--
trees that were pleasing to the eye and good for food. In the middle of the garden were the tree of life and the tree of the
knowledge of good and evil.*

The supernatural function of the two trees in the middle of the Garden
of Eden suggests that they are symbolic rather than natural. Therefore,
eating the fruit of the Tree of Life is not a physical thing, but means tast-
ing (experiencing) life-giving dependence on God. The fact that
mankind must be separated from the Tree of Life after the Fall shows
that mankind is not inherently immortal, but must eat the fruit of the
Tree of Life to remain immortal (Munday, 1992). In other words, the
Tree of Life represents rejuvenation through communion with God
(Rev 22:2). It is this relationship that gave Adam a 'temporarily immortal' body. So before Adam received the fruit of the Tree of Life, we can
infer that he was a mortal being, like the animals, and after the Fall,
Adam returned to this mortal state.

We can see from this understanding of the Tree of Life that immortality for Adam was not something that could exist independently of
God, but was a product of relationship with God. Hence, the revelation
of God to Adam was part of the process by which he becomes spiritually empowered. As a human he had the capacity to relate to God, but
that capacity was only fulfilled when God revealed himself to the Man,
thus making available the fruit of the Tree of Life.

The quest to recover the mythical 'plant of immortality' from the
Garden of Eden is a central theme of the Akkadian Gilgamesh Epic.
This quest was obviously doomed from the start because Gilgamesh
was seeking a kind of 'secular immortality' apart from God, which does
not exist. However, echoes of the Genesis account of the Tree of Life
can be seen in two of the stories that make up the Epic. The first story,
based on the Sumerian myth 'Gilgamesh, Humbaba and the Land of the
Erin-trees' describes a journey to the 'Land of the Living' where a grove
of mysterious trees is protected by a monster (Hansman, 1976). This
story probably represents a faint echo of the account in Genesis 3:24,
which states that after the man was banished from the garden for his disobedience, the Tree of Life was guarded by Cherubim to prevent
mankind from freely partaking of the Tree of Life. In later Babylonian
and Assyrian art a stylised Tree of Life is often shown between two
winged beings which are reminiscent of biblical Cherubim (Fig. 25.1).

Fig. 25.1 Sacred tree guarded by two winged beings. Carved relief from the walls of the palace at Nimrud. British Museum.

A second echo of Genesis Ch 3 is seen in the 11th book of the epic, where Gilgamesh is told by the Flood Hero of a 'plant of rejuvenation' which grows at the bottom of the sea. He dives and recovers the plant, but on the journey home the plant is eaten by a snake while Gilgamesh bathes in a refreshing pool of water. Thus, in the epic, the loss of eternal life is caused by a moment's carelessness on the part of Gilgamesh, an echo of the sin of Adam and Eve in the Garden of Eden. Again, as in Genesis, a snake is involved in the loss of immortality, but in the Gilgamesh Epic the snake gains immortality instead of man: in ancient Mesopotamia the ability of the snake to shed its skin was regarded as a sign of rejuvenation.

The quest for the Tree of Life was a popular subject for artistic representation. For example, an Akkadian cylinder sealing (Fig. 25.2) appears to show Gilgamesh and Enkidu holding two goats. Between the goats, the Tree of Life is shown growing on a miniature mountain. The goats rest their front hoofs on the tree in a manner very similar to two models found in the Royal Tombs of Ur by Leonard Woolley (Fig. 25.3). Woolley (1954) likened these models to the biblical story of the sacrificial 'Ram in the thicket' (Gen 22:13). However, the beasts in these models are clearly goats rather than rams, and the prevalence of the Tree of Life - goat motif on cylinder seals suggests strongly that the tree here is also representing the Tree of Life.

The importance of sacred trees in the Sumerian temple is supported by literary references. For example, the Sumerian lamentation known as the 'Curse of Akkad' describes the cutting down of 'sacred trees' in the

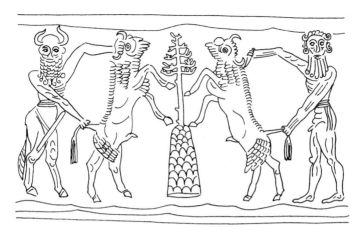

Fig. 25.2 Akkadian cylinder seal impression possibly showing the quest of Gilgamesh and Enkidu for the Tree of Life. British Museum.

temple courts as part of the desecration of Enlil's temple which provoked the cursing of Akkad (section 15.2). This suggests that the upper platform of the ziggurat, where the house of the god was located, may have been designed as a garden in an attempt to re-create the original 'Garden in Eden'. In a spiritual sense the worshippers probably hoped that the god would emerge from his temple 'in the cool of the day' to converse with his people, just as the LORD God had talked with Adam in the cool of the day (Gen 3:8).

The two trees in the Garden of Eden represent alternative choices for mankind. Therefore, in contrast to the Tree of Life, which represents immortality in communion with God, the tree of the knowledge of good and evil, at its most fundamental level, simply represents independence from God, or self-sufficiency apart from God. Thus, in Gen 2:17, God commanded Adam:

> *"You must not eat from the tree of the knowledge of good and evil, for when you eat of it you will surely die."*

Spiritually, Adam certainly died the moment he tasted the fruit of independence from God because this broke the channel of communication between God and Man. Furthermore, in the spiritual realm there is no 'grey area' for disobedience, and no chance of 'turning back the clock' after rebellion. In this way, Man followed in the 'footsteps' of Satan (the devil), who had first desired to be equal with God. Also, in this sense, the

291

serpent (Satan) was telling the truth when he said to Eve that if she ate the fruit her eyes would be opened and she would be like God, knowing good and evil. However, men and women were not created to be *like* God, knowing good and evil, but for dependence *on* God, knowing only good.

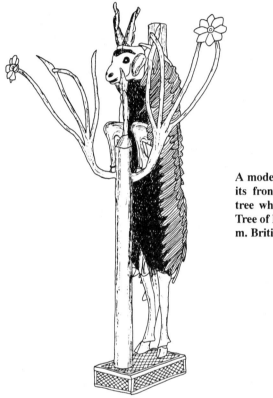

Fig. 25.3
A model of a goat resting its front hoofs in a gold tree which represents the Tree of Life. Height ca. 0.5 m. British Museum.

Outside the garden is outside intimacy with God, but also outside intimacy with the devil. Men must call on the Name of the LORD if they want to communicate with God (Gen 4:26b), but they must also call on the name of the devil if they want to communicate with the devil. Since the Bible is not interested in sorcery (except to condemn it) then we should not expect to see frequent reference to the devil. Only rarely in the Bible do we see the universe from the point of view of 'spiritual reality' where both God and the devil are clearly visible. Examples of this are in the Book of Job (Ch 2), and in the story of King Jehoshaphat and the deceiving spirit (1st Kings 22:19).

When Adam asserted his independence from God, there was, in the short term, no second chance; but in the long term, God had already decided to offer mankind a way back to intimacy with him, because man was deceived by the serpent. However, this second chance was only possible because God's son Jesus tasted spiritual death in Man's place. He thus became the true 'Divine Advocate' to reintroduce mankind to God the Father. Jesus also demonstrated the perfect dependence on God which was the intended destiny of mankind (John 5:19):

"I tell you the truth, the Son can do nothing by himself; he can do only what he sees his Father doing, because whatever the Father does, the Son also does."

According to Paul (Romans 15:12) all humans have inherited from Adam the independence from God that Adam chose. Therefore, in order to receive a second chance at the gift of spiritual life, we have to choose to give up again the independence that we have inherited. Because the Second Adam (Jesus) died to recover eternal life for humanity, the voluntary laying down of our independence will restore us to our spiritual life in God.

Throughout history, many visionaries have seen the restoration of spiritual relationship with God as the ascent up a cosmic mountain or ziggurat to a paradisaical garden where God lives in communion with man. Perhaps the earliest record of such visions is the dream of Jacob the Patriarch at Bethel (Gen 28:12). As he was fleeing from his brother Esau to seek his relatives in northern Mesopotamia, Jacob rested for the night near the city of Luz and had a dream as he slept with his head on a stone pillow:

He had a dream in which he saw a stairway resting on the earth, with its top reaching to heaven, and the angels of God were ascending and descending on it. There above it stood the LORD, and he said: "I am the LORD, the God of your father Abraham and the God of Isaac..."

This vision describes perfectly the Great Stairway of a Mesopotamian ziggurat, such as Jacob's mother Rebekah must have described to him from her childhood memories of Haran. We can now gain a vivid impression of the dream from the view up the restored central stairway of the great ziggurat of Ur (Fig. 25.4). The temple priests would ascend and descend on this stairway, just as the angels were seen to do in Jacob's dream, and at the summit of the stairs would be the house that was the very dwelling place of the god. After the dream, Jacob exclaimed *"How awesome is this place! This is none other than the house of God; this is the gate of heaven."* In saying this he was thinking in quite concrete terms of the reality of being in the actual presence of God.

Fig. 25.4 View up the restored central stairway of the great ziggurat of Ur.

The medieval poet, Dante Alighieri, had a similar vision of the restoration of spiritual communication as the climbing of a 'Mountain of Purgatory'. He describes it in the middle book (Purgatorio) of his epic work *'The Divine Comedy'*, completed in 1321. After ascending many levels of the mountain of Purgatory, which again seems to be reminiscent of a Sumerian ziggurat, Dante found himself at the summit of the mountain entering a divine forest which was a recreation of the

294

Garden of Eden. The cosmic mountain is envisaged in an illustration from a 15th Century edition of the Divine Comedy (Fig. 25.5). For a verse translation by Laurence Binyon, see Milano (1976).

Fig. 25.5 Dante presents his vision of the mountain of Purgatory with the Garden of Eden at its summit. Simplified from an illustrated 15th century edition of the Divine Comedy.

A vision similar to Dante's was described by Rick Joyner (1996) under the title *'The Final Quest'*. In this vision, Rick Joyner saw a 'Holy Mountain', also with many terraces. As a soldier in God's army, Joyner saw himself ascending this mountain at the same time as he fought in a great battle against the powers of darkness, including demons, vultures and serpents. It seems fitting to end this book by quoting from part of the vision in the middle of this battle which describes how he reached the top of the cosmic mountain (Joyner, 1996, p. 34-35):

> *Since there seemed to be little that we could do now against the enemy we decided to just try to climb as far as we could until we found something that would work against the serpents.*

We passed levels of truth very fast. On most of them we did not even bother to look around if there was not a weapon apparent that would work on the serpents...

Almost without warning we came to a level that opened up into a garden. It was the most beautiful place I had ever seen. Over the entrance to this garden was written "The Father's Unconditional Love." This entrance was so glorious and inviting that we could not resist entering. As soon as I entered I saw a tree that I knew was the Tree of Life. It was in the middle of this garden, and it was still guarded by angels of awesome power and authority... They seemed friendly, as if they had been expecting us... One of the angels called out, "Those who make it to this level, who know the Father's love, can eat."

I did not know how hungry I was. When I tasted the fruit, it was better than anything I had ever tasted, but it was, also, somehow familiar. It brought memories of sunshine, rain, beautiful fields, the sun setting over the ocean, but even more than that, of the people I loved. With every bite I loved everything and everyone more. Then my enemies started coming to mind, and I loved them, too. The feeling was soon greater than anything I had ever experienced... Then I heard the voice of the Lord, saying, "This is now your daily bread. It shall never be withheld from you. You may eat as much and as often as you like. There is no end to my love...

~~~~~|~~~~~

REFERENCES

For references with two quoted dates, the first represents the earliest edition (sometimes in a foreign language). The later date represents the edition consulted by the present author and is the one for which page numbers are given. In most cases the former date is the one cited in the text.

Library of Congress call numbers are given for books where possible, after each reference.

Aksu, A. E., Hiscott, R. N. and Yasar, D. (1999). Oscillating Quaternary water levels of the Marmara Sea and vigorous outflow into the Aegean Sea from the Marmara Sea--Black Sea drainage corridor. *Marine Geology* **153**, 275-302.

Aksu, A.E., and six others (2002). Persistent Holocene outflow from the Black Sea to the Eastern Mediterranean contradicts Noah's Flood hypothesis. *GSA Today* **12(5)**, 4-9.

Albright, W. F. (1940/1967). *From the Stone Age to Christianity; Monotheism and the Historical Process.* Johns Hopkins Univ. Press, 432 p. (BL 221 .A47)

Alster, B. (1976). On the earliest Sumerian literary tradition. *J. Cuneiform Studies* **28**, 109-126.

Alt, A. (1966). The God of the Fathers. Translation in: Wilson, R. A. *Essays on Old Testament History and Religion.* Blackwell, pp. 3-77. (BL 1188 .A433)

Amiet, P. (1966). Il y a 5000 ans, les Elamites inventaient l'ecriture. *Archaeologia* **12**, 16-23.

Astrom, P. (1987), Ed. *High, Middle or Low? Acts of an International Colloquium on Absolute Chronology.* Part 1, Paul Astroms Forlag. (GN 778.22 M415)

Bailey, L. R. (1989). *Noah: The Person and the Story in History and Tradition.* Univ. S. Carolina Press, 244 p. (BS 580 .N6 B35)

Bailey, L. R. (1993). *Genesis, Creation and Creationism.* Paulist Press, 259 p. (BS 651 .B235)

BAR Editorial staff (2000). Abraham's Ur: Is the Pope going to the wrong place? *Biblical Archaeology Review*, Jan/Feb 2000, 16-19.

Bard, E., Hamelin, B., Arnold, M., Montaggioni, L., Cabioch, G., Faure, G. and Rougerie, F. (1996). Deglacial sea-level record from Tahiti corals and the timing of global meltwater discharge. *Nature* **382**, 241-244.

Baring, A. and Cashford, J. (1991). *The Myth of the Goddess: Evolution of an Image*. Viking Arkana, 779 p. (BL 325 .M6 B36)

Bar-Matthews, M., Ayalon, A. and Kaufman, A. (1997). Late quaternary paleo-climate in the Eastern Mediterranean region from stable isotope analysis of speleothems at Soreq Cave, Israel. *Quaternary Research* **47**, 155-168.

Bar-Matthews, M., Ayalon, A. and Kaufman, A. (2000). Timing and hydrological conditions of Sapropel events in the Eastern Mediterranean, as evident from speleothems, Soreq Cave, Israel. *Chem. Geol.* **169**, 145-156.

Beauchamp, P. (1969) *Creation et Separation: Etude exegetique du chapitre premier de la Genese*. Aubier-Montaigne, Editions du Cerf, Delachaux et Niestle, Desclee de Brouwer. 491 p.

Bermant, C. and Weitzman, M. (1979). *Ebla, an Archaeological Enigma*. Weidenfeld and Nicolson, 244 p. (DS 99 .E24 B47)

Biggs, R. D. (1966). The Abu Salabikh tablets. *J. Cuneiform Studies* **20**, 73-88.

Biggs, R. D. (1974). *Inscriptions from Tell Abu Salabikh*. Chicago: Oriental Institute Publications **99**, 122 p. (PJ 4054 .A2 B5)

Bimson, J. J. (1978/81). *Re-dating the Exodus and the Conquest*. Almond Press, 288 p. (BS 1245.2 .B55).

Blenkinsopp, J. (1985). The Documentary Hypothesis in trouble. *Bible Review* **1(4)**, 22-32.

Bloesch, D. G. (1978). *Essentials of Evangelical Theology*, vol. 1. Harper and Row, 265 p. (BR 1640 .A25 B57)

Bloesch, D. G. (1994). *Holy Scripture: Revelation, Inspiration & Interpretation*. Inter Varsity Press, 381 p.(BS 511.2 B57)

Bottero, J. (1987/1995), translated by Bahrani & Van De Mieroop (1992). *Mesopotamia: Writing, Reasoning, and the Gods*. Univ. Chicago Press, 311 p. (DS 69.5 .B6813)

Braaten, L. J. (2001). The voice of Wisdom: a creation context for the emergence of Trinitarian language. *Wesleyan Theological J.* **36**, 31-56.

Brandon, S. G. F. (1963). *Creation Legends of the Ancient Near East*. Hodder and Stoughton, 241 p.

Bruins, H. J. and van der Plicht, J. (1996). The Exodus enigma. *Nature* **382**, 213-214.

Buccellati, G. (1966). *The Amorites of the Ur III Period*. Institutio Orientale di Napoli, 379 p. (DS 72.5 .B83)

Buccellati, G. (1993). Through a tablet darkly. A reconstruction of Old Akkadian monuments described in Old Babylonian copies. In: Cohen, M. E., Snell, D. C. and Weisberg, D. B. (Eds), *The Tablet and the Scroll: Near Eastern Studies in Honor of William W. Hallo*. CDL Press, pp. 58-71.

Buckland, W. (1837). *Geology and Mineralogy Considered with Reference to Natural Theology*. Carey, Lea and Blanchard. (BL 175 .B7)

Burney, C. (1977). *From Village to Empire/The Ancient Near East.* Phaidon/Univ. Cornell Press, 224 p. (DS 56 .B88)

Butzer, K. W. (1995). Environmental change in the Near East and human impact on the land. In: Sasson, J. M. (Ed.) *Civilizations of the Ancient Near East,* Simon & Schuster Macmillan, vol. 1, pp.123-151. (DS 57 .C55)

Byrne, J. M. (1997). *Religion and the Enlightenment From Descartes to Kant.* John Knox Press, 253 p. (BR 470 .B97)

Campbell, S. (1992). The Halaf period in Iraq: old sites and new. *Biblical Archaeologist* Dec 92, 182-187.

Caquot, A. and Sznycer, M. (1980). *Ugaritic Religion.* E. J. Brill. 28 p. (BL 1670 .C36).

Cassuto, U. (1961/1964). *A Commentary on the Book of Genesis 1-11.* Translated: Abrahams, I. Magnes. (BS 1235.3 .C37)

Charpin, D. (1980) *Archives familiales et propriete privee en Babylonie ancienne: etude des documents de 'Tell Sifr'.* Droz. (DS 71 .C46)

Chevreau, G. (1994). *Catch the Fire: The Toronto Blessing.* Marshall Pickering, 228 p. (BX 8785 .Z7 T6744)

Clifford, R. J. (1972). *The Cosmic Mountain in Canaan and the Old Testament.* Harvard Univ. Press, 221 p. (BL 447 .C57)

Clifford, R. J. (1994). *Creation Accounts in the Ancient Near East and in the Bible.* Catholic Biblical Quarterly Monograph Series, no. **26**, 217 p. (BL 325 .C7 C55)

Collingwood, R. G. (1967). *The Idea of History.* Oxford Univ. Press, 339 p. (D 16.8 .C592)

Cooper, J. S. (1983). *The Curse of Agade.* Johns Hopkins Univ. Press, 292 p. (PJ 4065 .C54)

Cornfeld, G. (Ed., 1961). *Adam to Daniel: An Illustrated Guide to the Old Testament and its Background.* McMillan, 559 p. (BS 621 .C642)

Cornwall, P. B. (1952). Two letters from Dilmun. *J. Cuneiform Studies* **6**, 137-145

Cross, F. M. (1973). *Canaanite Myth and Hebrew Epic.* Harvard Univ. Press, 376 p. (BS 1171.2 .C76)

Dalley, S. (1989/1991). *Myths from Mesopotamia: Creation, The Flood, Gilgamesh, and Others.* Oxford Univ. Press, 337 p. (BL 1650 .M98)

Dalley, S. (1998). The influence of Mesopotamia upon Israel and the Bible. In: Dalley, S. (Ed.) *The Legacy of Mesopotamia.* Oxford Univ. Press, pp. 57-83. (DS 56 .L44)

Deimel, A. (1923). Schultexte aus Fara. *Die Inschriften von Fara 2.* J. C. Hinrichs. (PJ 3223 .D4)

de Moor, J. C. (1980). El the creator. In: Rendsberg, G. *et al., The Bible World: Essays in Honor of Cyrus H. Gordon.* Ktav Pub. House, pp. 171-187. (PJ 3002 .Z5 G65)

299

Dickin, A. P. (1995/1997). *Radiogenic Isotope Geology.* Cambridge Univ. Press, 490 p. (QE 501.4 .N9 D53)

Driver, S. R. (1904/1948) *The Book of Genesis.* Methuen, 420 p. (BS 1235 .D7)

Edwards, R. L., Taylor, F. W. and Wasserburg, G. J. (1988). Dating earthquakes with high-precision thorium230 ages of very young corals. *Earth Planet. Sci. Lett.* **90**, 371-381.

Finegan, J. (1979). *Archaeological History of the Ancient Middle East.* Westview Press, 456 p. (DS 62.2 .F55)

Finkelstein, J. J. (1963). The antediluvian kings: A University of California Tablet. *J. Cuneiform Studies* 17, 39-51.

Finkelstein, J. J. (1972). *Late Old Babylonian Documents and Letters, Yale Oriental Series* 13, Yale Univ. Press, 534 p. (PJ 3711 .Y3 F5)

Flanders, H. J., Crapps, R. W. and Smith, D. A. (1963/1988). *People of the Covenant: An Introduction to the Old Testament.* 498 p. (BS 1197 .F47)

Frankfort, H. (1933). Gods and myths on Sargonid seals. *Iraq* 1, 2-30.

Frankfort, H., Frankfort, H. A., Wilson, J. A., Jacobsen, T. and Irwin, W. A. (1946). *The Intellectual Adventure of Ancient Man: An Essay on Speculative Thought in the Ancient Near East.* Univ. Chicago Press, 401 p. (BL 96 .F8)

Frayne, D. R. (1993). *Sargon and Gutian Periods.* In: *The Royal Inscriptions of Mesopotamia; Early Periods.* Vol. 2. Univ. Toronto Press. (PJ 3815 .F734)

Frumkin, A. (1997). The Holocene history of Dead Sea levels. In: Niemi, T. M., Ben-Avraham, Z. and Gat, J. R. (Eds.), *The Dead Sea: The Lake and Its Setting.* Oxford Univ. Press, pp. 237-248. (GB 1759 .D4 .D43)

Frumkin, A. and Elitzur, Y. (2001). Rise and fall of the Dead Sea. *Biblical Archaeolology Rev.* **27** (6), 43-50.

Frumkin, A., Magaritz, M., Carmi, I. and Zak, I. (1991). The Holocene climatic record of the salt caves of Mount Sedom, Israel. *The Holocene* 1, 191-200.

Gardner, B. K. (2001). *The Genesis Calendar: the Synchronistic Tradition in Genesis 1-11.* United Press of America, 374 p. (BS 1235.2 .G33)

Garrett, D. (1991). *Rethinking Genesis: The Sources and Authorship of the First Book of the Pentateuch.* Baker Book House, 273 p. (BS 1235.5 .G32)

Gibson, M. (1972). The archaeological uses of cuneiform documents: patterns of occupation at the city of Kish. *Iraq* 34, 113-123.

Gibson, M. (1992). Patterns of occupation at Nippur. In: deJong Ellis, M. (Ed.), *Nippur at the Centennial.* University Museum, Philadelphia, pp. 33-54. (DS 70.5 .N5 R46)

Goff, B. L. and Buchanan, B. (1956). A tablet of the Uruk period in the Goucher College Collection. *J. Near Eastern Studies* **15**, 231-235.

Gordon, C. H. (1958). Abraham and the merchants of Ura. *J. Near Eastern Studies* **17**, 28-31.

300

Gordon, C. H. (1987). Critical review of: Kramer, S. N. *In the World of Sumer: An Autobiography. J. Cuneiform Studies* **39**, 247-250.

Gragg, G. B. (1969). The Kesh Temple Hymn. In: Sjoberg, A. W., Bergmann, S. J. and Gragg, G. B. *Texts from Cuneiform Sources III.* J. J. Augustin Pub., 202 p. (PJ 4061 .C6)

Green, M. W. (1977). A note on an archaic period geographical list from Warka. *J. Near Eastern Studies* **36**, 293-294.

Green, M. W. and Nissen, H. J. (1987). Zeichenliste der archaischen texte aus Uruk, *Archaische Texte aus Uruk Band 2.* Gebr. Mann Verlag,

Haldar, A. (1971). *Who were the Amorites?* E. J. Brill, 93 p. (DS 72.5 .H35)

Hall, H. R., Wolley, C. L., Gadd, C. J. and Keith, A. (1927). *Ur Excavations*, vol. 1. British Museum. (DS 70.5 .U7 J6)

Hallo, W. W. (1958). Review of: Sollberger, E., Corpus des inscriptions 'royales' presargoniques de Lagash. *J. Near Eastern Studies* **17**, 210.

Hallo, W. W. (1963). Beginning and end of the Sumerian King List in the Nippur recension. *J. Cuneiform Studies* **17**, 52-57.

Hallo, W. W. (1970). Antediluvian cities. *J. Cuneiform Studies* **23**, 57-67.

Hallo, W. W. and Simpson, W. K. (1971/1998). *The Ancient Near East: A History.* Harcourt Brace College Pub., 324 p. (DS 62.2 .H3)

Hamilton, V. P. (1990). *The Book of Genesis, Chapters 1 - 17. (The New International Commentary on the Old Testament).* W. B. Eerdmans, 522 p. (BS 1235.3 .H32)

Hamlin, E. J. (1954). The meaning of "mountains and hills" in Isa. 41:14-16. *J. Near East Studies* **13**, 185-190.

Hansman, J. (1976). Gilgamesh, Humbaba and the land of the Erin-trees. *Iraq* **38**, 23-35.

Hasel, G. F. (1974). The polemic nature of the Genesis cosmology. *Evangelical Quarterly* **46**, 81-102.

Hassan, F. A. and Robinson, S. W. (1987). High-precision radiocarbon chronometry of ancient Egypt, and comparisons with Nubia, Palestine and Mesopotamia. *Antiquity* **61**, 119-135.

Hawkins, J. D. (1979). The origin and dissemination of writing in western Asia. In: Moorey, P. R. S. (Ed.), *The Origins of Civilization. (Wolfson College Lectures, 1978).* Oxford Univ. Press, pp. 128-165.

Hendel, R. S. (1987). When the Sons of God cavorted with the daughters of men. *Bible Review* **3**(2), 8-13, 37.

Heinrich, E, and Seidl, U. (1982). Grundrisszeichnungen aus dem alten Orient. *Mitteilungen der Deutschen Orient-Gesellschaft* **98**, 24-45.

Hoffner, H. A. (1990). *Hittite Myths.* Scholars Press, 92 p. (BL 2370 .H5 H57)

Howard-Carter, T. (1981). The tangible evidence for the earliest Dilmun. *J. Cuneiform Studies* **33**, 210-223.

Hughen, K. A., Overpeck, J. T., Lehman, S. J., Kashgarian, M., Southon, J., Peterson, L. C., Alley, R. and Sigman, D. M. (1998). Deglacial changes in ocean circulation from an extended radiocarbon calibration. *Nature* **391**, 65-68.

Hurowitz, V. A. (1997). Reading a votive inscription. Simbar-Shipak and the Ellilification of Marduk. *Revue d'Assyriologie* **91**, 39-47.

Hutton, J. (1795/1972). *The Theory of the Earth*. Creech. Reprinted by Stechert-Hafner. (QE 501 .H88)

Jacobsen, T. (1939/1966). The Sumerian King List. *Assyriological Studies* **11**, Univ. Chicago Press, 216 p. (PJ 3125 .C5)

Jacobsen, T. (1939b). The assumed conflict between the Sumerians and Semites in early Mesopotamian history. *J. American Oriental Soc.* 59, 485-495. Reprinted (1970) in: Moran, W. L. (Ed.), *Toward the Image of Tammuz and Other Essays on Mesopotamian History and Culture*. Harvard Univ. Press, pp. 187-197. (DS 69.6 .J23)

Jacobsen, T. (1946). Sumerian mythology: a review article. *J. Near Eastern Studies* **5**, 128-152. Reprinted (1970) in: Moran, W. L. (Ed.), *Toward the Image of Tammuz and Other Essays on Mesopotamian History and Culture*. Harvard Univ. Press, pp. 104-131. (DS 69.6 .J23)

Jacobsen, T. (1961). Formative tendencies in Sumerian religion. In: Wright, G. E. (Ed.), *The Bible and the Ancient Near East: Essays in Honour of William Foxwell Albright*,., pp. 267-278. Reprinted (1970) in: Moran, W. L. (Ed.), *Toward the Image of Tammuz and Other Essays on Mesopotamian History and Culture*. Harvard Univ. Press, pp. 1-15. (DS 69.6 .J23)

Jacobsen, T. (1963). Ancient Mesopotamian religion: the central concerns. *PAPS* **107**, 473-484. Reprinted (1970) in: Moran, W. L. (Ed.), *Toward the Image of Tammuz and Other Essays on Mesopotamian History and Culture*. Harvard Univ. Press, pp. 39-47. (DS 69.6 .J23)

Jacobsen, T. (1963b). Babylonia and Assyria (religion). Encyclopaedia Britannica vol. 2, 972-978. Reprinted (1970) in: Moran, W. L. (Ed.), *Toward the Image of Tammuz and Other Essays on Mesopotamian History and Culture*. Harvard Univ. Press, pp. 16-38. (DS 69.6 .J23)

Jacobsen, T. (1967). Some Sumerian city-names. *J. Cuneiform Studies* **21**, 100-103.

Jacobsen, T. (1976). *The Treasures of Darkness: A History of Mesopotamian Religion*. Yale Univ. Press, 273p. (BL 2350 .I7 J3)

Jacobsen, T. (1981). The Eridu Genesis. *J. Biblical Literature* **100**, 513-529. Reprinted (1994) in: *Sources for Biblical and Theological Study*, vol. 4 (Eds: Hess, R. S. and Tsumura, D. T.), pp. 129-142.

Jacobsen, T. (1987). *The Harps That Once...* Yale Univ. Press, 498 p. (PJ 4083 .H37)

Jacobsen, T. (1994). The historian and the Sumerian gods. *J. American. Oriental Soc.* **114**, 145-153.

Jastrow, M. (1915). *The civilization of Babylonia and Assyria*. J. B. Lippincott, 515 p. (DS 71 .J3)

Jawad, A. J. (1974). The Eridu material and its implications. *Sumer*, **30**, 11-~40.

Johnson, M. D. (1969/1988). *The Purpose of the Biblical Genealogies*. Cambridge Univ. Press, 310 p. (BS 569 .J6)

Jones, B. P. (1995). *An Instrument of revival: The complete Life of Evan Roberts*. Bridge Publishing. 279 p.

Jones, T. B. (1969) *The Sumerian Problem*. Wiley. 142 p. (DS 72 .J6)

Joyner, R. (1996). *The Final Quest*. Whitaker House Pub. 158 p. (BS 649 .A68 J68)

Kantor, H. J. (1952). Further evidence for Early Mesopotamian relations with Egypt. *J. Near Eastern Studies* **11**, 239-~250.

Kavoukjian, M. (1987). *Armenia, Subartu and Sumer: The Indo-European Homeland and Ancient Mesopotamia*. Trans. Ouzounian, N. Bibliotheque national du Quebec, Montreal, 243 p. (DS 165 .K3913)

Kidner, D. (1967). *Genesis: An Introduction and Commentry*. The Tyndale Press, 224 p. (BS 1235.3 .K47)

Kikawada, I. M. and Quinn, A. (1985). *Before Abraham Was: A Provocative Challenge to the Documentary Hypothesis*. Abingdon, 144 p. (BS 1235.2 K48)

King, L. W. (1902/1976). *Enuma Elish: The Seven Tablets of Creation*, Vols. 1 and 2. AMS Press (Reprint of original edition by Luzac and Co.), 274 p. (PJ 3771 .E5)

Kinnier Wilson, J. V. (1979). *The Rebel Lands: An Investigation into the Origins of Early Mesopotamian Mythology*. Cambridge Univ. Press, 150 p. (BL 1615 .K56)

Kitagawa, H. and van der Plicht, J. (1998). Atmospheric radiocarbon calibration to 45,000 yr B. P.: Late glacial fluctuations and cosmogenic isotope production. *Science* **279**, 1187-1190.

Kitchen, K. A. (1995). The Patriarchal age: myth or history? *Biblical Archaeology Review* **21** (2) 48-60.

Kramer, S. N. (1944/1972). *Sumerian Mythology: A Study of Spiritual and Literary Achievement in the Third Millennium B. C.* Univ. Pennsylvania Press, 130 p. (299.352 K89)

Kramer, S. N. (1948). Review of: Frankfort, H. *et al.* (1946), The Intellectual Adventure of Ancient Man. *J. Cuneiform Studies* **2**, 39-70.

Kramer, S. N. (1956/1981). *History Begins at Sumer*. Univ. Pennsylvania Press, 388 p. (DS 72 .K7)

Kramer, S. N. (1963/1970). *The Sumerians: Their History, Culture, and Character.* Univ. Chicago Press, 355 p. (DS 72 .K73)

Kramer, S. N. (1968). The Babel of tongues: a Sumerian version. *J. American Oriental Soc.* **88** (Speiser volume), 108-111.

Kramer, S. N. (1979). *From the Poetry of Sumer.* Univ. California Press, 104 p. (PJ 4045 .K7)

Kramer, S. N. and Maier, J. (1989). *Myths of Enki, The Crafty God.* Oxford Univ. Press. 272 p. (BL 1616 .E54 M97)

Kuniholm, P. E., Kromer, B., Manning, S. W., Newton, M., Latini, C. and Bruce, M. J. (1996). Anatolian tree rings and the absolute chronology of the eastern Mediterranean, 2220-718 BC. *Nature* **381**, 780-783.

Kupper, J.-R. (1961). *L'iconographie du dieu Amurru. Academie Royale de Belgique, Memoires* **55**, 94 p.

Lamberg-Karlovsky, C. C. (1982). Dilmun: gateway to immortality. *J. Near Eastern Studies* **41**, 45-50.

Lambert, W. G. (1965). A new look at the Babylonian background of Genesis. *J. Theological Studies* **16**, 287-300.

Lambert, W. G. (1973). A new fragment from a list of antediluvian kings and Marduk's chariot. In: Beck, M. A. *et al.* (Eds), *Symbolae Biblicae et Mesopotamicae: Francisco Mario Theodoro de Liagre Bohl, Dedicatae*, E. J. Brill, pp. 271-280. (DS 56 .S9)

Lambert, W. G. (1980). The theology of death. In: Alster, B. (Ed.), *Death in Mesopotamia. Copenhagen Studies in Assyriology*, vol **8**. Akademisk Forlag, pp. 53-66. (DS 57 .R46)

Lambert, W. G. (1986). Ninurta mythology in the Babylonian Epic of Creation. In: Hecker, K. and Sommerfeld, W. (Eds), *Keilschriftliche Literaturen. Ausgewahlte Vortrage der XXXII. Recontre Assyriologique Internationale.* Berliner Beitrage zum Vorderen Orient **6**, pp. 55-60.

Lambert, W. G. (1992). Nippur in ancient ideology. In: deJong Ellis, M. (Ed.), *Nippur at the Centennial.* University Museum, Philadelphia, pp. 119-126. (DS 70.5 .N5 R46)

Lambert, W. G. and Millard, A. R. (1969). *Atrahasis. The Babylonian Story of the Flood.* Oxford Univ. Press. 198 p. (PJ 3771 .A8)

Landmann, G., Reimer, A. and Kempe, S. (1996a). Climatically induced lake level changes at Lake Van, Turkey, during the Pleistocene/Holocene transition. *Global Biogeochem. Cycles* **10**, 797-808.

Landmann, G., Reimer, A., Lemcke, G. And Kempe, S. (1996b). Dating Late Glacial climate changes in the 14,570 yr long continuous varve record of Lake Van, Turkey. *Palaeogeog. Palaeoclim. Paleoecol.* **122**, 107-118.

Langdon, S. (1935/1980). *Babylonian Menologies and the Semitic Calendars.* Oxford Univ. Press (British Academy Series), Kraus Reprint, 169 p. (CE 33 .L28)

Larsson, G. (1983). The chronology of the Pentateuch: a comparison of the MT and LXX. *J. Biblical Literature* **102/3**, 401-409.

Laurin, R. B. (1978). The tower of Babel revisited. In: Tuttle, G. A. (Ed.), *Biblical and Near Eastern Studies: Essays in Honor of William Sanford LaSor.* W. B. Erdmans, pp. 142-145. (BS 540 .B4457)

Layard, A. H. (1849). *Nineveh and its Remains with an Account of a Visit to the Chaldean Christian of Kurdistan, and the Yezidis, or Devil Worshippers, and an Inquiry into the Manners and Arts of the Ancient Assyrians.* (DS 70 .L42)

Libby, W. F. (1952). *Radiocarbon Dating.* Univ. Chicago Press. 124 p. (QC 798 .D3 L69)

Lloyd, S. (1947/1980). *Foundations in the Dust.* Thames and Hudson, 216 p. (DS 70 .L48)

Lloyd, S. (1978/1984). *The Archaeology of Mesopotamia: From the Old Stone Age to the Persian Conquest.* Thames and Hutton, 251 p. (DS 69.5 .L58)

Lowe, A. (1986). Bronze age burial mounds on Bahrain. *Iraq* **48**, 73-84.

Magnusson, M. (1977). *Archaeology of the Bible.* Simon and Schuster. 239 p. (BS 621 .M33)

Majidzadeh, Y. (1976). The land of Aratta. *J. Near Eastern Studies* **35**, 105-113.

Malamat, A. (1968). King lists of the Old Babylonian Period and Biblical genealogies. *J. American Oriental Soc.* **88** (Speiser volume), 163-173.

Mallowan, M. E. L. (1964). Noah's flood reconsidered. *Iraq* **26**, 62-81.

Mallowan, M. E. L. (and Cruikshank Rose, J. 1933), Excavations at Tell Arpachiyah. *Iraq* **2**, 1-178.

Manning, S. W., Kromer, B., Kuniholm, P. E. and Newton, M. W. (2001). Anatolian tree rings and a new chronology for the East Mediterranean Bronze-Iron Ages. *Science* **294**, 2532-2535.

Matthews, R. J. (1993). *Cities, Seals and Writing: Archaic Seal Impressions from Jamdet Nasr and Ur.* Gebr. Mann Verlag. 73 p. (DS 70.5 .J35 M3)

Matthiae, P. (1977/1980). Holme, C., Translator. *Ebla: An Empire Rediscovered.* Hodder and Stoughton, 237 p. (DS 99 .E23 M3713)

McDermott, F., Grun, R., Stringer, C. D. and Hawkesworth, C. J. (1993). Mass-spectrometric U-series dates for Israeli Neanderthal/early modern hominid sites. *Nature* **363**, 252-255.

McEvenue, S. (1990). *Interpreting the Pentateuch.* Liturgical Press, 193 p. (BS 1225.2 .M34)

Meek, T. J. (1955). The Code of Hammurabi. In: Pritchard, J. B. (Ed.), *Ancient Near Eastern Texts Relating to the Old Testament.* Princeton Univ. Press, pp. 164-177. (BS 1180 .P83).

Michalowski, P. (1989). *The Lamentation over the Destruction of Sumer and Ur.* Eisenbrauns (Pub.) 219 p. (PJ 4065 .L3)

Milano, P. (1976). *The Portable Dante.* Viking press, 662 p. (PQ 4315 .A3 B5)

Millard, A. R. (1967). A new Babylonian Genesis story. *Tyndale Bulletin* **18**, 11-12.

Mitchell, T. C. (1988). *Biblical Archaeology: Documents from the British Museum.* Cambridge Univ. Press, 112 p. (BS 621 .M56)

Molony, F. A. (1936). The Noachian Deluge and its probable connection with Lake Van. *J. Trans. Victoria Institute* 67, pp. 44-52. Cited by Whitcomb and Morris (1961), p. 58.

Moore, A. M. T., Hillman, G. C. and Legge, A. J. (2000). *Village on the Euphrates: From Foraging to Farming at Abu Hureyra.* Oxford Univ. Press, 585 p. (GN 776.32 .S95 M66)

Moorey, P. R. S. (1976). The Late Prehistoric administrative building at Jamdat Nasr. *Iraq* **38**, 95-106.

Moorey, P. R. S. (1978). *Kish Excavations 1923-1933.* Oxford Univ. Press. 213 p. (DS 70.5 .K5 O84)

Munday, J. C. (1992). Creature mortality: from Creation or the Fall? *J. Evangelical Theological Soc.* **35**, 51-68.

Nissen, H. J. (1983/1988).*The Early History of the Ancient Near East (9000 - 2000 B.C.).* Translated: Lutzeier, E. and Northcott, K. J. Univ. Chicago Press, 215 p. (DS 62.2 .N5713)

Nissen, H. J., Damerow, P. and Englund, R. K. (1993). *Archaic Bookkeeping.* Univ. Chicago Press. 169 p. (PJ 4075 .N5713)

Noldecke, A. (1936). *Uruk Vorbericht* 7.

Nutzel, W. (1978). To which depths are "prehistorical civilizations" to be found beneath the present alluvial plains of Mesopotamia. *Sumer* **34**, 17-26.

Olson, W. S. (1967). Has science dated the biblical Flood? *Zygon* **2**, 272-278.

Oppenheim, A. L. (1964/1977). *Ancient Mesopotamia: Portrait of a Dead Civilization.* Univ. Chicago Press, 445 p. (DS 69.5 .O6)

Oppert, J. (1869). Cited in Jones, T. B. (1969).

Otto, R. (1923/1958), Harvey, J. W., Translator. *The Idea of the Holy.* Oxford Univ. Press, 232 p. (BL 48 .O82)

Parpola, A. (1985). The Sky-Garment: A study of Harappan religion and its relation to the Mesopotamian and later Indian religions. *Studia Orientalia* **57**, 216 p. (DS 1 .S785)

Parpola, A. (1994). *Deciphering the Indus Script.* Cambridge Univ. Press, 374 p. (PK 119.5 .P37)

Pettinato, G. (1979/1981). Translated. *The Archives of Ebla.* Doubleday and Co., 347 p. (DS 99 .E25 P47313)

Pettinato, G. (1986/1991), Richardson, C. F., Translator. *Ebla, a New Look at History.* Johns Hopkins Univ. Press, 290 p. (DS 99 .E25 P47213)

Poebel, A. (1914). *Historical and Grammatical Texts.* Publications of the Babylonian Section, vol. 4 & 5, Univ. Museum, Philadelphia. (PJ 3711 .P5)

Pollock, S. (1999). *Ancient Mesopotamia: The Eden that Never Was.* Cambridge Univ. Press, 259 p.

Postgate, J. N. (1992/1994). *Early Mesopotamia: Society and Economy at the Dawn of History.* Routledge, 367 p. (DS 69.5 .P64)

Pritchard, J. B. (1954). *Ancient Near Eastern Texts Relating to the Old Testament.* Princeton Univ. Press, 544 p. (BS 1180 .P83)

Radday, Y. T. (1972). Chiasm in Tora. *Linguistica Biblica* **19**, 12-23.

Ramm, B. L. (1954/1962). *The Christian View of Science and Scripture.* Wm. B. Eerdmans Pub. Co., 368 p. (BS 650 .R28)

Rasheed, F. (1972). Sumerian literature: its character and development. *Sumer* **28**, 9-15.

Rawlinson, H. C. and Norris, E. (1861). *A Selection from the Historical Inscriptions of Chaldaea, Assyria, & Babylonia.* British Museum. (PJ 3711 .B7 A32)

Reade, J. (2001). Assyrian king-lists, the royal tombs of Ur, and Indus origins. *J. Near Eastern Studies* **60**, 1-29.

Reimer, S. (1996). The tower of Babel: an achaeologically informed reinterpretation. *Direction* **25**, 64-72.

Ridderbos, N. H. (1957). *Is there a conflict between Genesis 1 and Natural Science?* Wm. B. Eerdmans Pub. Co., 88 p. (BS 651 .R532)

Roaf, M. (1990). *Cultural Atlas of Mesopotamia and the Ancient Near East.* Facts on File, 238 p. (DS 69.5 .R63)

Roberts, J. J. M. (1972) *The Earliest Semitic Pantheon: a Study of the Semitic Deities Attested in Mesopotamia Before Ur III.* John Hopkins Univ. Press, 174 p. (BL 1600 .R6)

Rose, L. E. (1994). The astronomical evidence for dating the end of the Middle Kingdom of ancient Egypt to the early second millennium: a reassessment. *J. Near Eastern Studies* **53**, 237-261.

Roux, G. (1992/2001) Did the Sumerians emerge from the sea? In: *Everyday Life in Ancient Mesopotamia.* Bottero, J. (Ed.), Nevill, A. (Trans.), Edinburgh Univ. Press, pp. 3-23. (DS 69.5 .B6713)

Rowton, M. B. (1960). The date of the Sumerian King List. *J. Near Eastern Studies* **19**, 156-162.

Ryan, W. B. F. and Pitman, W. C. (1998). *Noah's Flood: The New Scientific Discoveries About the Event That Changed History.* Simon and Schuster, 317 p. (BS 658 .R93)

Saggs, H. W. F. (1978). *The Encounter with the Divine in Mesopotamia and Israel.* Univ. London, Athalone Press, 243 p. (BS 1192.6 .S23).

Saggs, H. W. F. (1995/2000). *Peoples of the Past: Babylonians.* British Museum/Univ. Okalahoma Press, 192 p. (DS 71 .S24)

Sailhamer, J. (1996). *Genesis Unbound: A Provocative New Look at the Creation Account.* Multnomah Books, 257 p.

Salman, I. (1972). Foreword. *Sumer* **28**, a-~j.

Sandars N. K. (1971). *Poems of Heaven and Hell from Ancient Mesopotamia.* Penguin, 183 p. (PJ 3953 .S3)

Sarna, N. H. (1966/1970). *Understanding Genesis.* Schocken Books, 267 p. (BS 1235.3 .S33)

Sarnthein, M. (1972). Sediments and history of the postglacial transgression in the Persian Gulf and northwest Gulf of Oman. *Marine Geol.* **12**, 245-266.

Sauer, J. A. (1996). The river runs dry. *Biblical Archaeology Rev.* **22(4)**, 52-57, 64.

Schmandt-Besserat, D. (1992). *Before Writing.* Univ. Texas Press. (CJ 4867 .S36)

Schmidt, H. (1943). *Tell Halaf.* Walter de Gruyter & Co.

Seely, P. H. (1991). The firmament and the water above. Part I: The meaning of *raqia* in Gen 1:6-8. *Westminster Theological J.* **53**, 227-240.

Seely, P. H. (1992). The firmament and the water above. Part II: The meaning of 'the water above the firmament' in Gen 1:6-8. *Westminster Theological J.* **54**, 31-46.

Seely, P. H. (1997). The geographical meaning of "earth" and "seas" in Genesis 1:10. *Westminster Theological J.* **59**, 231-255.

Seely, P. H. (2001). The date of the Tower of Babel and some theological implications. *Westminster Theological J.* **63**, 15-38.

Senner, W. M. (1989). Theories and myths on the origins of writing: a historical overview. In: Senner, W. M. (Ed.): *The Origins of Writing.* Univ. Oklahoma Press, pp. 1-41. (P 211 .O75)

Sjoberg, A. W. and Bergmann, S. J. and Gragg, G. B. (1969). *The Collection of the Sumerian Temple Hymns and the Kesh Temple Hymn: Texts from Cuneiform Sources III.* J. J. Augustin Pub., 202 p. (PJ 4061 .C6)

Smith, M. D. (2000). Of Jesus and Quirinius. *Catholic Biblical Quart.* **62**, 278-293.

Smith, M. S. (1994) *The Ugaritic Baal Cycle, vol. 1. Supp. to Vetus Testamentum* **55**, 446 p. (BS 410 .V452)

Sollberger, E. (1962). The Tummal Inscription. *J. Cuneiform Studies* **16**, 40-47.

Speiser, E. A. (1963). The wife-sister motif in the patriarchal narratives. In: *Biblical and Other Studies* (Ed. Altmann, A.), Harvard Univ. Press, pp. 15-28. (296 .A468 B)

Speiser, E. A. (1964). *Genesis: Introduction, Translation and Notes.* Doubleday, 378 p. (BS 192.2 .A1)

Steiglitz, R. R. (1987). Ebla and the gods of Canaan. In: *Eblaitica (Essays on the Ebla Archives and Eblaite Language)* vol. 2, Eds. Gordon, C. H. and Rendsburg, G. A. Eisenbrauns, pp. 79-89. (DS 99 .E25 E35)

Sumner, W. (1973). The location of Anshan. *Revue d'Assyriologie* **67**, 57-62.

Teeple, H. M. (1978). *The Noah's Ark Nonsense.* Religion and Ethics Institute

Inc. 156 p. (BS 658 .T44)

Thiele, E. R. (1967). *A Chronology of the Hebrew Kings.* Zondervan. 93 p. (BS 637 .T48)

Uchupi, E., Swift, S. A. and Ross, D. A. (1996). Gas venting and late Quaternary sedimentation in the Persian (Arabian) Gulf. *Marine Geol.* **129**, 237-269.

Van Buren, E. D. (1933). *The Flowing Vase and the God with Streams.* Hans Schoetz. 149 p. (N 5370 .V3)

Van Buren, E. D. (1944). The Sacred Marriage in early times in Mesopotamia. *Orientalia* **13**, 1-72.

Van der Toorn, K. (1996). *Family Religion in Babylonia, Syria and Israel.* E. J. Brill, 491 p. (BL 1625 .F35 T66)

Van Dijk, J. (1964-65). Le motif cosmique dans la pensee Sumerienne. *Acta Orientalia* **28**, 1-59.

Vanstiphout, H. L. J. (1992). Repetition and Structure in the Aratta cycle: their relevance for the orality debate. In: Vogelzang, M. E. and Vanstiphout, H. L. J. (Eds), *Mesopotamian Epic Literature: Oral or Aural?* Edwin Mellen Press, 320 p. (PJ 4047 .M47)

Van Till, H. J. (1986). *The Fourth Day: What the Bible and the Heavens Are telling Us about the Creation.* Wm. B. Eerdmans Pub. Co., 283 p. (BT 695 .V36)

Vawter, B. (1977). *On Genesis: a New Reading.* Doubleday, 501 p. (BS 1235.3 .V38)

Wellhausen, J. (1883/1973). *Prolegomena to the History of Ancient Israel.* Reimer. Reprinted by Meridian Books. 552 p. (DS 121 .W48)

Wenham, G. J. (1978). The coherence of the flood narrative. *Vetus Testamentum* **28**, 336-348.

Wenham, G. J. (1980). The religion of the patriarchs. In: *Essays on the Patriarchal Narratives.* Ed. Millard, A. R. and Wiseman, D. J., Inter Varsity Press, 223 p. (BS 573 .E87)

Wenham, G. J. (1987). *Word Bible Commentary Volume 1: Genesis 1 - 15.* Word Books, 352 p. (BS 491.2 W67)

Whitcomb, J. C. and Morris, H. M. (1961/1970). *The Genesis Flood: The Biblical Record and Its Scientific Implications.* Presbyterian & Reformed Publishing Co., 518 p. (BS 658 .W5)

Wilson, E. J. (1994). "Holiness" and "Purity" in Mesopotamia. *Alter Orient und Altes Testament*, Band 237, Verlag Butzon & Bercker Kevelaer, 121 p. (BL 1615 .W56)

Wilson, E. J. (1996). The Cylinders of Gudea. *Alter Orient und Altes Testament*, Band 244, Verlag Butzon & Bercker Kevelaer, 276 p. (PJ 4070 .W55)

Wilson, I. (1985). *The Exodus Enigma.* Weidenfeld and Nicolson, 207 p. (BS 680 .E9 W55)

Wilson, R. R. (1977). *Genealogy and History in the Biblical World.* Yale Univ. Press, 222 p. (BS 569 .W54)

Wiseman, P. J. (1936/1977). *New discoveries in Babylonia about Genesis.* In: Wiseman, D. J. (Ed.), *Clues to Creation in Genesis,* Marshall, Morgan and Scott, 232 p. (BS 1235.2 .W5)

Wiseman, P. J. (1948/1977). *Creation Revealed in Six Days.* In: Wiseman, D. J. (Ed.), *Clues to Creation in Genesis,* Marshall, Morgan and Scott, 232 p. (BS 1235.2 .W5)

Woolley, C. L. (1936). *Abraham: Recent Discoveries and Hebrew Origins.* Faber and Faber Ltd. 299 p. (BS 580 .A3 W6)

Woolley, C. L. (1939). *Ur Excavations* vol. 5. (DS 70.5 .U7 J6)

Woolley, C. L. (1954/1963). *Excavations at Ur.* Ernest Benn Ltd. 256 p. (DS 70.5 .U7 W578)

Young, D. A. (1982). *Christianity and the Age of the Earth.* Zondervan, 188 p. (BS 657 .Y67)

NOTES

[1] The date referred to here is for the first edition. The edition actually consulted was a later one, as indicated in the bibliography.

[2] All biblical quotes are from the New International Version (NIV) unless otherwise stated.

[3] In this book the patriarch will generally be referred to as Abram before the covenant of circumcision and Abraham after the giving of the covenant, following the biblical example.

[4] The reader is reminded that a millennium gets its name from the thousands of years at its upper end, so the Third Millennium is the period from *3000* to 2000 BC.

[5] Slashes indicate the divisions between successive columns (reading from right to left). The superscript (^{ki}) indicates a place, and the asterisk prefix (star sign) indicates divinity. Hence this shows that the king was deified.

[6] The precise spelling of Kish is Kiš, which signifies a sound somewhere between Kis and Kish. However, in this book, all such spellings are simplified to the 'sh' sound.

[7] The Sumerian Flood Story may also have been read in this orientation, but was shown in the traditional orientation in Fig. 6.1 for the sake of convention.

[8] However, the three-ring totem on some early cylinder seals might also represent the Cosmic Triad.

[9] Adam was the first person to know God, but not the first human being.

INDEX

313

Alluvial soil, 76
Alster,B., 130, 152, 156, 159
Alt,A., 8
Altar, 81, 195-196, 217, 223
al 'Ubaid (Tell), 60-61, 73
    See also: Ubaid
Alulim, 72, 262
Amarna (el), 203, 206
    age, 269
    letters, 117, 225
Amar-sin, 181
Amau-shum-galanna, 138, 140
Amiet,P., 120
Ammi-saduqa, 69, 109, 181, 247
Amorite
    dynasties, 65, 189
    immigrants, 64, 209, 231-232
    invaders, 188, 214, 232
    wall, 232
Amorites, 64-65, 119, 225, 231-234
Amram, 201
Amun-emhet, 207-208
Amurru, 199, 231-234
    see also Amorites
Amut-pi-El, 212
An (god of heaven), 67, 69-70, 85, 113, 133-135, 139-140, 148-151, 153, 157-158, 165-166, 168, 172-174, 176, 190, 217, 220, 243, 270-271, 273-274, 283, see also Anu
Anachronism, 110
Analytical error, 30
Anath, 225-226
Anatolia, 53, see also Turkey
Ancestor epic, 276
Ancient cities: see by name
Angel (of the LORD), 222
Angels, 293-294, 296
An-Martu, 232, 234
Anna, 190
Annual growth ring, 31-32
Anshan, 101-102
Anshar, 195
Antediluvian, 74, 256, 257
Anthropomorphism (of gods), 170
Antioch (Pisidian), 202
Antum, 135

Anu, 85, 133, 174, 190-197, 217, 231, 271, see also An
Anu-banini, 141
Anunna gods, 134, 152, 192
Anunnaki, 69, 108, 134, 139, 151, 158, 193, 243-244
Anu ziggurat, 85, 89, 113
Anzu, 239-240
Apostasy, 198-199
Apsu, 108, 147, 161, 163-164, 194-195, 239, 284
Arabian desert, 18-19, 21-22, 44-45
Arabic, 116
Aram, Aramaic, 115-116
Ararat, 48-51, 100, 103
Aratta, 49, 100-103
Archetype, 118
Ark, 40-41, 49, 51, 70, 92, 100, 103, 252-253, 271
Armanum, 228
Armenia, 48-49, 102, 230
Arpachiyah (Tell), 60, 120
Arphaxad, 115, 118, 259
Arrow (bow), 240
Ashmoleum Museum, 80, 255
Ashnan, 69, 243-244
Ashur, 65, 115
Ashur-banipal, 69-70, 256
Ashtoroth, 178
Asiatics, 208-209
Assyria, 47-48, 194
Assyrian
    civilisation, 51
    empire, 199, 206-207
    people, 115
    kings, 117
    plain, 51
    script: see cuneiform
Assyriologists, 124
Athens, 112-113
Astral triad, 172, 195
Astrom,P., 109
Astronomical records, 109-110
Atrahasis (extra wise), 69-70, 191, 236-237, 264
Atrahasis Epic, 67, 69-70, 132, 142, 161, 190-192, 235-239, 242-243, 247, 263-264, 271, 273
Avaris, 203, 208

316

321

329